THE NEW DECORATING BOOK

Better Homes and Gardens® Books
Des Moines, Iowa

Better Homes and Gardens® Books
An imprint of Meredith® Books

The New Decorating Book
Editor: Denise L. Caringer
Contributing Editors: Sharon L. Novotne O'Keefe, Heather J. Paper
Contributing Writers: Candace Ord Manroe, Rhoda J. Murphy,
    Sharon Overton, Patricia Pollock
Contributing Design Director and Photo Editor: Jerry J. Rank
Copy Chief: Angela K. Renkoski
Contributing Copy Editors: Debra Blume, Mary Helen Schiltz
Contributing Proofreaders: Sheila Mauck, Mary Pas
Electronic Production Coordinator: Paula Forest
Editorial and Art Assistants: Susan McBroom, Jennifer Norris
Production Director: Douglas Johnston
Production Manager: Pam Kvitne
Prepress Coordinator: Marjorie J. Schenkelberg

Meredith® Books
Editor in Chief: James D. Blume
Design Director: Matt Strelecki
Managing Editor: Christopher Cavanaugh
Director, New Product Development: Ray Wolf
Vice President, General Manager: Jamie L. Martin

Better Homes and Gardens® Magazine
Editor in Chief: Jean LemMon
Executive Interior Design Editor: Sandra S. Soria

Meredith Publishing Group
President, Publishing Group: Christopher Little
Vice President and Publishing Director: John P. Loughlin

Meredith Corporation
Chairman of the Board: Jack D. Rehm
Chief Executive Officer: William T. Kerr
Chairman of the Executive Committee: E. T. Meredith III

All of us at Better Homes and Gardens® Books are dedicated to providing
you with information and ideas you need to enhance your home.
We welcome your comments and suggestions about this book on decorating.
Write to us at: Better Homes and Gardens® Books, Shelter Editorial
Department, LN112, 1716 Locust St., Des Moines, IA 50309–3023.

It's Your Home

Growing up in suburban St. Louis, I had my feet (and psyche) firmly planted in our beloved farmhouse with its fields, orchards, and shade trees.

I adored the place and the peace and privacy of its setting. But what I didn't understand until later was the extent to which my sense of home as an adult was being shaped by the sounds and images of those early years. I cozied my first apartment in the city with familiar elements: an old wicker chair, overflowing bookshelves, an Oriental rug, and, of course, a cat. Today in the home I share with my husband, Ron (and four cats), it's no surprise that I gravitate to our second floor with its low knee walls and vaulted ceilings—happy reminders of my snug childhood bedroom.

Even some room arrangements hint at the past. A friendly cloverleaf of Adirondack chairs in our year-round porch recalls a similar grouping from our backyard in the 1950s. And when I sit at my bay window desk today and look out into the woods, I feel the same contentment that I knew as a child when I sat in another windowed nook overlooking a different stand of trees.

Whatever their style, the most inviting rooms always start inside someone's heart. Decorating, you see, isn't really about decorating at all; it's about creating a home that nurtures and relaxes you by reflecting who you are and what you love. Think for a moment about the things that have shaped your vision of what a home should be. Maybe it's a bedroom hideaway lovingly recalled from your childhood, a screened porch where you rocked away an afternoon at a vacation lodge, your grandmother's dining room where the family gathered every Thanksgiving—or a room you may only have visited in your daydreams. By conjuring up images of such favorite places, real or imagined, you can cut through the sometimes confusing array of decorating choices, avoid being swayed by mere fads, and, instead, develop truly personal settings that will always please your eye and speak to your soul.

As you thumb through these pages, we'll give you the decorating help and inspiration—but you have to bring the dreams. After all, it's *your* home.

Denise L. Caringer
Editor, *The New Decorating Book*

THE NEW DECORATING BOOK

CONTENTS

BECAUSE IT'S YOUR HOME, it naturally reflects your personality, interests, and outlook on life. But it takes a strong vision of your own decorating style to pull all those elements together. Are you formal, casual, slick, or something in between? Tour this chapter's homes and take our fun "What's Your Decorating Attitude?" quiz to find out.

STYLE

RUSTIC & REFINED

ORGET STALE STYLE LABELS. IF YOU'RE A PERSON OF MANY DIMENSIONS LIKE HOME-OWNER HERMINE MARIAUX, USE AND DISPLAY WHAT YOU LOVE IN YOUR OWN UNIQUE WAY.

On one hand, Hermine Mariaux lives a casual, plop-your-feet-up-anywhere lifestyle and can't resist time-scarred primitives and folk art. But on the other hand, she's ever the sophisticate who insists on a crisp edge of slick, contemporary styling in her living spaces. Then again, she's a bit of the traditionalist, who appreciates the finely polished lines of classic furnishings. Can she have it all? With a mastery of eclectic styling, absolutely. And so can you.

CONTEMPORARY CONTEXT

The recipe for Hermine's flavorful melting pot approach to decorating is simple: Blend different ingredients but allow each to retain its unique flavor. In other words, be eclectic but don't muddy the waters. How? Start with the backgrounds—the floors, windows,

and walls that are the bones of your home. Choose one look for them and stick with it. For Hermine, this is the place for the clean, contemporary stamp—white, white, and more white—to provide a simple backdrop and ample breathing room for each of her character-filled treasures. Windows and French doors are undressed except for their white wood frames. She even made her wood floors go pale with paint in an effort to purify the context. "Color backgrounds don't bring out the individual qualities, shapes, and colors of both objects and fabrics," says Hermine, a marketing maven and former magazine editor. She boils down her decorating formula into three rules: Edit the number of pieces, make sure they're large enough to fit your space, and keep them simple.

Starting with an airy contemporary shell, Hermine Mariaux's living room takes on rusticity with bold silhouettes of folk art. "The objects I bring home," she says, "have simplicity of form, a sense of humor, and that special patina that only comes with age."

ONE: *Always keeping comfort and function in mind, Hermine sets a pair of big, squashy sofas in crisp black and white ticking in front of the fireplace. She extends her living room seating with an artful vignette of wicker chairs beside a table displaying a barnyard of iron windmill weights.*

TWO: *Hermine's century-old farmhouse welcomes casual, eclectic styling that emphasizes rustic folk art, light, contemporary backdrops, and a piece or two of refined furniture.*

THREE: *In the dining room, modern art hangs near a traditional 18th-century, Regency-style table that's crowned by a rustic iron chandelier. The various styles mix congenially because Hermine keeps the background and the furniture forms simple.*

3

ONE: *A primitive Canadian worktable and a pair of footstools proudly wear their original chipped paint for the rustic look Hermine loves. Nothing she buys is for looks only, but she makes sure each piece is worthy of attention. The kitchen's antique table functions as a contemporary island for food preparation and buffet service.*

TWO: *A rope-turned tester bed satisfies Hermine's taste for tradition. The lines of the vintage bed bask in full glory thanks to a low-key palette of neutral tone-on-tone bed dressings and deep pillows. "If you have fewer things—but things that are oversize and have meaning to you—your rooms will be cleaner, bolder," she says.*

TRADITION FOR TODAY

IMAGINE A HOUSE RICH IN OLD-WORLD ICONS AND RESPECT FOR THE PAST THAT'S ALSO HOME TO THREE YOUNG CHILDREN WHO HAVE RIP-ROARING RUN OF THE PLACE. IMPOSSIBLE?

Not a bit, when tradition takes a pragmatic turn. After all, traditional style wouldn't have survived this long without offering flexibility for real-life family living. That is exactly what designer Alessandra Branca brings to her townhome in Chicago. A Rome native, she grew up on classical art and architecture. Her grandfather encouraged her, she says, "to be aware of the beauty around me and to pay attention to details."

UPDATING THE CLASSICS

For Alessandra, traditional style is a blend of periods. She begins by emphasizing the inherent character of her late-19th-century, three-story home, then adds more antiquity—especially elements recalling the classicism of her birthplace. A new Palladian door, for example, provides a regal bridge between dining and living rooms, with columns from an antebellum plantation and cabinet fronts with Roman numeral X motifs. No matter where your home is, you can import a taste of Europe. From the doorway's Chippendale brackets to Louis XVI dining chairs, many of the home's appointments are period pieces. Pet canary Paganini even sings arias from a gilded Regency rosewood birdcage. The home's palette also suggests the gently aged state of a venerable villa in Italy or a farmhouse in Provence—yellow walls with English chintz upholstery in the family room, toile on master bedroom walls. In the formal living room, Alessandra made the room's antiques livable for her young brood with comfortable seating and easy-care sisal carpet.

Alessandra Branca puts her own spin on old-world elegance in her formal living room, where 18th-century painted French chairs, gilded English sconces, and Roman paintings rub shoulders with more contemporary overstuffed seating and a sleek cocktail table.

ONE: *In the living room, crisp silk taffeta window treatments are trimmed and tied back for a stunning look. The fabric is repeated on the Louis XVI chairs.*

TWO: *Alessandra didn't allow herself to be daunted by her home's century-old architecture. Instead of restoring its interiors to their original glory, she used antiques from a mix of periods to create a truly personal—and anything but museumlike—family home.*

THREE: *A buttery Provence yellow coats walls in the family room where chintz upholstery creates an upbeat mood. "I have a great love and respect for classical architecture, but lifestyles change, and houses must be able to adapt," Alessandra says.*

ONE: *Regal with red painted walls and chinoiserie toile de Jouy upholstery and window treatments, the home's guest room invites curling up in cushioned seating. An elegant, double-duty piece, the upholstered daybed, piled with pillows, serves as a sofa by day, sleeper by night.*

TWO: *The major statement in the master bedroom is made with another scenic toile de Jouy fabric, the pattern of which is taken from 18th-century chinoiserie drawings. Furnishings are comfortably classic, and accents, such as the ornate wall mirror, are antiques. Italian strung draperies open like a theater curtain at the pull of a cord.*

2

CLEAN & SASSY

NO LONGER A MERE REPLAY OF GOLDEN OLDIES, TRADITIONAL STYLE HAS CLIMBED BACK TO THE TOP OF THE CHARTS WITH A FRESH—EVEN FUNKY—NEW BEAT.

When she was commissioned by a young Washington, D.C., couple to decorate their Maine beach house, Mary Douglas Drysdale says she knew she had stumbled onto "a fairy tale." "This is very much a house about hospitality, a place to be shared," she says. She shared the couple's vision of luxury without pretension, grandness with simplicity.

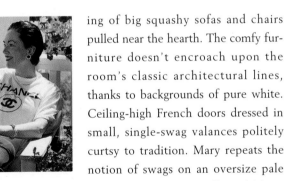

NEW TRADITIONALISM

Down what style path might that vision lead? "I see myself as a New Traditionalist," she says, "someone who embraces and respects the past but uses classical elements in a fresh way." Correct proportions and serious detailing are important, but too much formality is off-putting and stodgy. Spaces are designed to make people feel at ease. The family room of this beach house does just that, with its party-size gathering of big squashy sofas and chairs pulled near the hearth. The comfy furniture doesn't encroach upon the room's classic architectural lines, thanks to backgrounds of pure white. Ceiling-high French doors dressed in small, single-swag valances politely curtsy to tradition. Mary repeats the notion of swags on an oversize pale wood cocktail table with edges scalloped like a Matisse cutout. The living room's cocktail table is another invitation to put tongue in cheek, this time with an updated, overscaled interpretation of a classic butler's tray. In another twist on tradition, she defines architectural lines within spaces, then colors between those lines with furnishings clad in childlike colors and patterns. The home is filled with sauciness and comfort, yet it never loses touch with tradition.

Describing herself as a New Traditionalist, interior designer Mary Douglas Drysdale combines bold colors and classical elements in a beachfront home. As if ready for a swim, antique furnishings suit up in geometric mustard and raspberry fabrics.

2

3

ONE: Mary adds fresh touches to basic fabrics. Perfect for a beach house, the canvas slipcovers she designed for these dining room chairs include witty starfish appliqués on the back. The single motif on white is as dramatic as sculpture. The dining table is a renewed antique.

TWO: White paint allows traditional architecture to strut its stuff and provides a gallerylike backdrop for modern art and fabrics. Newly upholstered and accented with a star pillow, a century-old chair tweaks tradition without clichés.

THREE: Hospitality is the key to this shingle-style Maine home.

FOUR: Durable chenille and natural cotton, plus a sea grass rug, create casual childproof style.

4

2

3

ONE: Architecture takes a backseat to decorative play in all of the upstairs bedrooms. The exaggerated headboard in The Buffalo Plaid Room pokes fun at Queen Anne Revival styling; it's cut from plywood, covered in foam and muslin, then upholstered in crisp checks. Bordered by waves, the floor nods with wit to the home's location by the sea.

TWO: Mary plays jazz with a traditional classic, the Napoleonic bee motif. In The Bee Room, honey-hued walls host a friendly swarm of stenciled bees.

THREE: Overlooking the ocean, this guest room is dubbed The Green Room because even the pencil-post bed is painted the color of envy. Guests have fun choosing the space that fits their mood because all the guest rooms are supremely comfortable. Fabric accents in reds and yellows bring charm to the breezy space.

WHAT'S YOUR DECORATING

CASUAL

The best kind of decorating doesn't come from replicating a particular style but from reflecting your own unique way of looking at things. Conceived in the spirit of fun, this quiz, based on general decorating characteristics, is designed to help you learn more about your decorating attitude. Choose your answers honestly. If none of the answers is exactly you, select the one closest to your own taste. After you've finished, use the analysis on page 29 to find what your answers say about your decorating attitude.

1. On a game show, you win your choice of three all-expenses-paid trips. You select:

a. *Four days at a charming restored bed-and-breakfast nestled in the hills of Vermont*

b. *A tour of London, including a day at the Chelsea Flower Show*

c. *A skiing weekend in Aspen*

2. You have an opportunity to attend a dinner party escorted by a writer. You choose:

a. *The author of historical novels characterized by their settings in the palaces of Europe*

b. *A newspaper reporter famous for his political exposés*

c. *The editor of a well-known home magazine who is an expert in cooking, decorating, and gardening*

3. Your friends decide to get a special group rate by joining a leisure-activity club. You vote for:

a. *An ethnic restaurant-of-the-month club*

b. *Visits to local craftspeople and artisans*

c. *A local museum series of lectures about fine furniture, silver, and china of the 18th century*

4. You are planning a costume theme party around your favorite movie. You and your mate will dress as:

a. *Anna and Count Vronsky,* Anna Karenina

b. *Daisy Buchanan and Jay Gatsby,* The Great Gatsby

c. *Karen Blixen and Denys Finch-Hatton,* Out of Africa

5. You have a weekend with no commitments, so you decide to:

a. *Explore the countryside on your bike, then call your favorite friends over for dinner*

b. *Go to a hair salon, stroll through a museum, then read a book on historic British castles*

c. *Scurry through several new designer boutiques, purchase a butterfly chair for the entry, then see an old Greta Garbo movie*

6. After cleaning out your attic, you vow to:

a. *Remodel and turn the attic into a skylit loft*

b. *Trace the family heritage back to its European origins*

c. *Take time to put the wonderful old family pictures into an album—and to read those old love letters again next year*

7. After a hard day, you would love to come home to a room:

a. *With soft, comfortable seating, a fire in the fireplace, and lots of family pictures and personal mementos*

b. *With large areas of glass, a few pieces of classic furniture (both old and modern), and a collection of contemporary art and sculpture*

c. *With quiet elegance, venerable Queen Anne furniture, and mellow old Oriental rugs*

ATTITUDE?

ECLECTIC

8. If you could choose a special piece of art you like best, you would select:

a. *A period English landscape*

b. *An African mask*

c. *An American primitive painting*

9. For your windows, you would choose:

a. *Translucent pleated shades or no treatments*

b. *Mellow pine shutters with side curtains of natural muslin*

c. *Floral print fabric in a swag-and-jabot treatment*

10. To store your home electronics equipment, you would use:

a. *A wall system of high-gloss lacquer*

b. *An 18th-century-style armoire*

c. *Simple open shelves made from old, weathered wood*

11. You would prefer to sit and read in:

a. *A squashy armchair covered in soft, nubby fabric, where you can see geraniums blooming on a patio*

b. *An antique Chippendale wing chair covered in toile de Jouy, placed close to French doors that open onto a garden*

c. *A classic steel-and-leather Le Corbusier chaise, positioned to view the skyline at sunset*

12. To celebrate your latest big achievement, you would be likely to:

a. *Take a picnic of pâté, cold pasta salad, and white Zinfandel to the country*

b. *Pull out the best china and plan a candlelight dinner at home*

c. *Go to an exclusive four-star restaurant*

13. For a pet, you've always wanted:

a. *An Old English sheepdog*

b. *Saltwater fish in a tank*

c. *A Burmese cat*

14. When it's time to get away, you would hop on the first plane to:

a. *A restored house in Colonial Williamsburg*

b. *A rustic cabin nestled in the mountains*

c. *A resort outside Santa Fe*

15. Friends have given you tickets for events, but they're all the same night. You select:

a. *A folk music festival*

b. *A chamber orchestra concert*

c. *An art auction*

16. You would be most likely to attend:

a. *An exhibit of French Impressionist paintings*

b. *A sidewalk art fair*

c. *A retrospective of black and white photos*

17. Good friends are coming for a special dinner. You set the table with:

a. *Grandma's antique silver and old Wedgwood*

b. *Contemporary stainless flatware and pure white bone china*

c. *Unmatched old silver and a mix of handcrafted pottery*

18. A friend promises the present you're about to receive is "you." You expect:

a. *A book on Italian furniture design*

b. *An Irish mohair throw*

c. *A bottle of fine wine*

19. Your favorite wardrobe would include:

a. *Italian and Japanese designer fashions, and lots of linen and cashmere*

b. *Tweed suits, silk blouses, pumps, and a couple of smashing dinner dresses*

c. *Jeans, midcalf denim skirts, soft cotton shirts, and handmade silver jewelry*

20. Browsing at the bookstore, you're most likely to pick up books and magazines about:

a. *The latest furnishings and apparel designs*

b. *Country collectibles and down-home cooking*

c. *History and fine antiques*

21. You would be most likely to surround yourself in your home with these colors:

a. *Colors taken from nature*

b. *Deep jewel colors*

c. *Tone-on-tone neutrals*

22. You love your home, but admit you would move in a minute to this dream house:

a. *An old mansion with a carriage house and a formal rose garden*

b. *A rustic restored barn with a view of woods and a pond*

c. *An airy, open-plan, architect-designed house with walls of windows*

23. Your favorite accessories might include:

a. *One striking piece of Japanese pottery*

b. *Antique silver candlesticks*

c. *A collection of weathered antique game boards and Shaker boxes*

24. If you had your wish, you would love to step out of your back door into:

a. *Herb beds and a garden of cutting flowers*

b. *A pool for lap swimming*

c. *Gardens outlined with boxwood*

25. No one is surprised when one of your recent furnishings purchases is:

a. *A beautiful reproduction of a mahogany Chippendale highboy*

b. *A Hoosier pine cabinet*

c. *A glass-topped steel table*

26. It's your birthday, and your friends know the flowers that please you most are:

a. *An artful arrangement of lilies*

b. *A grouping of cacti*

c. *An unarranged bouquet of wildflowers*

27. You would use a curio cabinet to display:

a. *A collection of seashells*

b. *A grouping of Art Deco Bakelite table radios*

c. *A collection of old music boxes*

28. Your favorite kind of party is:

a. *A family brunch or barbecue*

b. *A sit-down dinner of several courses*

c. *A tasting party of any kind*

29. For your bedroom, you would choose:

a. *A pine canopy bed with lots of quilts*

b. *A metal four-poster dressed in a duvet of bold handpainted striped canvas*

c. *A vintage sleigh bed plumped with an array of crisp white eyelet-trimmed bed linens*

SLICK

FORMAL

30. When you think of the mood you want your home to convey, you lean toward:

a. High style and fashion, with each piece chosen for its design merits and used in clean, restrained settings

b. Comfort and a relaxed atmosphere underscored with a mix of natural, unselfconscious furnishings

c. Gracious, timeless surroundings created with classic furnishings of whatever age

SCORING THE QUIZ

The first step in analyzing your decorating attitude is easy. Simply circle "a," "b," "c," as you answered each question in the quiz, in the appropriate column. After you have circled all your answers, total each column's number of answers at the bottom.

COLUMN 1	COLUMN 2	COLUMN 3
1. a.	1. b.	1. c.
2. c.	2. a.	2. b.
3. b.	3. c.	3. a.
4. c.	4. a.	4. b.
5. a.	5. b.	5. c.
6. c.	6. b.	6. a.
7. a.	7. c.	7. b.
8. c.	8. a.	8. b.
9. b.	9. c.	9. a.
10. c.	10. b.	10. a.
11. a.	11. b.	11. c.
12. b.	12. c.	12. a.
13. a.	13. c.	13. b.
14. b.	14. a.	14. c.
15. a.	15. b.	15. c.
16. b.	16. a.	16. c.
17. c.	17. a.	17. b.
18. b.	18. c.	18. a.
19. c.	19. b.	19. a.
20. b.	20. c.	20. a.
21. a.	21. b.	21. c.
22. b.	22. a.	22. c.
23. c.	23. b.	23. a.
24. a.	24. c.	24. b.
25. b.	25. a.	25. c.
26. c.	26. a.	26. b.
27. b.	27. c.	27. a.
28. a.	28. b.	28. c.
29. a.	29. c.	29. b.
30. b.	30. c.	30. a.

Total _____   _____   _____

ANALYZING THE RESULTS

Don't worry. You passed. There are no wrong answers on this quiz. Now you can have fun using it to decide which of three main decorating attitudes best suits your tastes—casual, formal, slick, or an eclectic combination. No matter what style of decorating you prefer—romantic, country, 18th century, Art Deco, modern—it can fit into any one of these basic categories. For instance, graceful Chippendale chairs can be formal or slick, depending on your attitude and how you put your room together.

• *Casual.* If the majority of your answers were in Column 1, you have a casual decorating attitude. Relaxed comfort is the key for your furnishings. Do they feel good to sit on? To walk on? To be around? Chances are, you prefer unfussy furniture with carefree fabrics in earthy or neutral colors. Seating in your living room, for instance, is arranged in informal groupings for comfortable, relaxed conversation. Your accessories include favorite things, often offering a lighthearted bit of whimsy. Your home makes no demand but enjoyment.

• *Formal.* If most of your answers were in Column 2, you're most comfortable with a formal decorating scheme. Your home is likely to include a gracious melding of several styles from the past. In this broad-brush category, you may choose from such classic styles as period French, 18th-century Chippendale, or Queen Anne, as well as Oriental and even formal contemporary furnishings. Both antiques and quality reproductions can be combined in your rooms. Your furnishings are likely to be straightforward and clean, with graceful curves and flowing shapes arranged in symmetrical groupings. Colors are often rich and mellow, used with gentility and grace. Important in your decorating are the special accessories and mementos lovingly collected over time.

• *Slick.* If most of your answers were in Column 3, you long for a high-style, sophisticated look that is sleek, minimal, but not avant-garde. This attitude reflects an awareness of the world of design and an appreciation of elegant simplicity. A slick setting is usually carefully pruned so each element, be it contemporary or traditional, is chosen for its distinctive lines and for its integrity of form and function. Even color is often kept at a minimum, with hues drawn from the neutrals, especially black, white, and gray, often sparked with a touch of brilliant accent color, such as red. Your accessories are limited to a carefully chosen few that make a definite statement about your taste.

• *Eclectic combination.* If your answers fall almost equally into two or all three categories, it indicates that you enjoy eclectic surroundings that combine the best from a number of design periods and styles. You probably are quite aware of your personal style and may occasionally gently rebel against the rules. You will most likely find, however, that your answers lean, at least slightly, toward one of the categories above. The secret is to understand and consistently heed your main attitude toward furnishing your home so that you combine your disparate furnishings into a cohesive, harmonious whole.

Whether your attitude is casual, formal, slick, or eclectic, your fun challenge is to create a pleasing decorating scheme that draws on the best resource of all, your personality.

LIVING

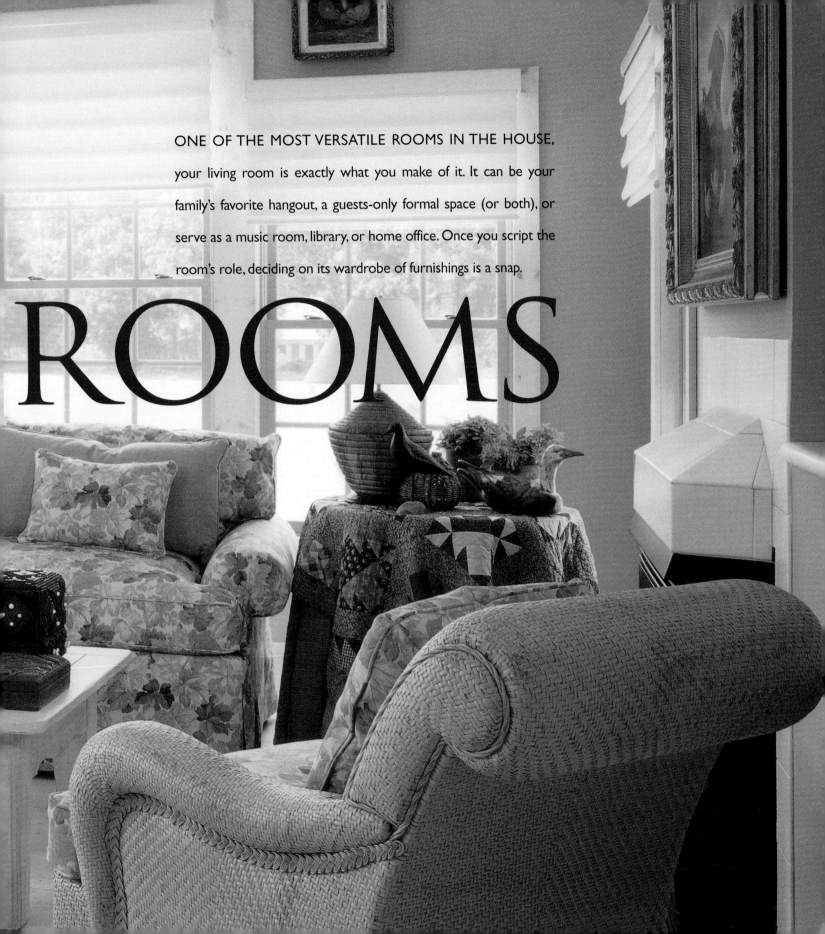

ONE OF THE MOST VERSATILE ROOMS IN THE HOUSE, your living room is exactly what you make of it. It can be your family's favorite hangout, a guests-only formal space (or both), or serve as a music room, library, or home office. Once you script the room's role, deciding on its wardrobe of furnishings is a snap.

ROOMS

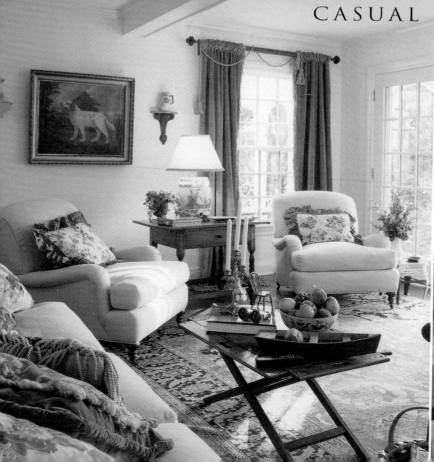

FORMAL SLICK

CASUAL ECLECTIC

WHAT'S YOUR ATTITUDE?

Suitability is one of the attributes of any well-designed room. You'll put yourself—and your guests—at ease if you tailor your furnishings choices to the way you really live. Look around your living room and ask yourself if the furnishings and the way in which they're arranged fit you. If, for example, you're the feet-up casual type, a room with white upholstery and no ottoman in sight is not suitable—it doesn't fit. On the other hand, if your living room is more for tea than television, more formal furnishings and arrangements may be in order.

ELEMENTS OF YOUR STYLE

Use the following design details to help you bring your living room in line with your decorating attitude. (Also read about formal and informal balance, texture, and pattern in the "Elements" chapter beginning on page 265.)

• *Fabricate your look.* Fabric weaves, finishes, and patterns can express different degrees of formality. Linen, for example, is a good choice for an eclectic room that combines slick and casual approaches; use it in natural hues in understated window treatments. To express a casual attitude—whether your style is contemporary or country—dress sofas and chairs in the same textural denims, plaids, and flannels you wear on weekends. Mix patterns for eclectic and casual styles. Matched fabrics fit a formal look, as do those that have a degree of sheen such as silk, damask, and glazed chintz. (For more on choosing the right fabric for your decorating attitude, see the "Fabrics" chapter, page 303.)

FOR MORE ABOUT HOW TO DEFINE YOUR DECORATING ATTITUDE, REFER TO OUR DECORATING QUIZ STARTING ON PAGE 26.

• *Frame a new view.* Window treatments are major players in reflecting your personal decorating attitude. Free-form curtains that are loosely draped express a casual, eclectic, or slick style. If you prefer a slicker, more minimal look, stick to trim, unadorned shades, blinds, or shutters. Turn to the standard repertoire of traditional draperies for a formal feel, with floor-to-ceiling panels topped by valances and elegant trims.

• *Furniture makes a statement.* Convey formality with antiques and reproductions that feature classic details: camelbacks on sofas, cabriole legs, ball-and-claw feet, shield- or lyre-shaped backs on chairs. Make a formal but modern statement with 20th-century classics such as Barcelona chairs. Oversize rolled-arm sofas with squashy cushions sum up casual style.

• *State a style with texture.* Rough textures such as berber carpet, sisal rugs, and twig furniture work in casual and eclectic rooms. Smooth textures—lacquer, glass, mirror, polished wood—can be slick and formal.

FORMAL: *Classic comfortable forms such as wingback chairs blend with traditionally trimmed draperies to exude formality in this living room.*

SLICK: *An unadorned background showcases shapely seating in graphic cabana stripes. Simple shutters control light and privacy.*

CASUAL: *Classic but slouchy seating gathers in an anything-but-formal arrangement to focus on a garden view.*

ECLECTIC: *Modern chairs, a replica pie safe, and Southwestern rugs used as throws mix it up and suit the homeowner's eclectic attitude.*

FORMAL ENTERTAINING

Elegant entertaining is all about gracious comfort and ease. Far from fussy, a formal living room can be one of the most welcoming spaces in your home—a place that makes you and your guests feel truly special and pampered. But, as with all rooms, there is no "one size fits all" plan on which you can rely. Instead, use these tips to identify your own needs:

• *How do you entertain?* If you usually invite a handful of friends or business associates in for cocktails and hors d'oeuvres, you may not need as much seating—and as many pull-around tables—as you will if your affairs tend to be dinner buffets for 50. Do you need smaller-scale furniture pieces in order to make room for a piano? If you hire the occasional harpist or chamber ensemble, create a flexible furniture grouping that includes lightweight open-arm chairs that can be rearranged to make room for musicians.

• *Arrange for conversation.* How many people you entertain makes a big difference in your design. For a crowd, divide and conquer. Instead of a single close-knit conversation grouping, scatter little groups around the room. Or, create one large grouping—two sofas facing off with a pair of chairs at either end—so guests can break off into groups themselves; this single grouping lends itself to four separate conversations at one time.

• *Cater to your guests.* Each sitting area should have tables nearby for beverages and snacks. If guests will be bringing hors d'oeuvre plates into the room, you'll need a cocktail table large enough for several guests to share. If guests will be standing and snacking, consider placing a sofa table against the sofa's back (if it isn't against the wall) and a hunt board on one wall as mini oases and to facilitate traffic flow.

• *Plan a movable feast.* As much as possible, build flexibility into your living room arrangement with furnishings that serve more than one purpose and are portable. Large upholstered ottomans, for example, work as movable seating or as tables.

Pretty without being prim, this living room combines formal seating with double-duty ottomans that can be seats or table space for appetizer plates. Each sitting area also has a table nearby. The symmetrical balance of the sofa wall and the dentil molding denote formality; dramatic pennant-cut valances and upholstery skirts add a playful, graphic touch.

PLAN FOR FLEXIBILITY

With smart planning, you can make your living room as versatile as the little black dress in your wardrobe—equally stylish for day and night events. With the right basics—classic furnishings (whether traditional or modern) and simple backdrops—you can easily shift from casual daytime living to dressier evening entertaining with a few subtle changes in accessories. For a stylish room with around-the-clock function:

• *Use dual-purpose furniture.* An ottoman that stashes the kids' toys, an armoire that holds a mini office (as shown on page 144 in "Home Offices"), and bookcases with enclosed compartments will help your busy daytime room clean up its act for an evening party.

• *Go basic with backgrounds.* Neutral, or at least subtle, backdrops entertain well day or night. White walls, ceilings, mantels, and window treatments pay no allegiance to a single style but are appropriate for all.

• *Keep it light.* Minimal window treatments, such as simple but elegant swags and jabots, shed the most light by day yet still look dressy for parties. At night, let a fire in the fireplace or a cluster of candles add radiance. Turn on the accent lights, too; a picture light over your favorite painting can dazzle a dark wall.

• *Introduce comfort.* Use overstuffed versions of traditional sitting pieces, such as rolled-arm sofas and wing chairs. For long wear and beauty, make your biggest decorating investment the sofa and cover it in an elegant but hard-wearing fabric, such as tapestry. Balance more-formal furniture with put-your-feet-up pieces, such as a pine cocktail table.

ONE: *The white backdrop and upholstered pieces are traditional classics, but accessories are equal parts formal and casual, so this living room is set for any occasion.*

TWO: *An old Welsh cupboard filled with collected dishware and mixed floral fabrics on sink-in seating peg this living room as an easy-going entertainer.*

CASUAL AMBIENCE

Maybe you've decided your attitude is casual, but you're struggling with the contemporary style you think must work with it. Relax. Traditional furniture and other design elements can be just as cozy and casual as you want them to be. All it takes is a few softening touches to lighten the mood.

• *Arrange furnishings casually.* Let sofas and chairs mill around informally instead of facing off formally by the fire. To send a relaxed message to family and guests, add ottomans and opt for a sturdy wood coffee table that won't mind if you put your feet up. Folk art or just-for-fun pieces and asymmetrically arranged artwork and collections also will scrub away a room's too-serious look.

• *Mix, don't match.* Loosen up an existing grouping of upholstered pieces with a mismatched wicker chair or wood rocker.

• *Take the formal edge off* a traditional living room by making space for a relaxing dining spot. Team a dining table with a bookcase or a wall of built-in shelves to give the dining area a snug library look.

• *Soften the edges with fabric.* Ruffled skirts soften traditional sofas, and fabric runners give dining tables a friendly feel.

• *Vary the wood finishes.* Pine and painted woods—even a single painted chair— bring informality to the living room.

ONE: Colonial cues abound in this open-plan living room, but, even with traditional furnishings, it refuses to take itself too seriously. A palette of simmering hues and bold patterns in the upholstery fabrics, informal displays of collectibles, and a mix of user-friendly painted and natural finishes on wood pieces relax the mood.

TWO: While true to classic design, this living room shuns formality by dressing its plump down-filled seating in roomy slipcovers. Instead of being centered on the bookcase, the sofa slides to one side but is balanced by the chunky round table in the corner. Art and objects are arranged casually for easy addition and subtraction at the collector's whim.

SMALL WONDERS

Believe it or not, it's no trick to transform a small, featureless living room into one that welcomes with comfort and architectural presence. Before you rearrange or remove furniture for your own small-room remake, rearrange your thinking and see the room's lack of square footage as a great start on an enviably intimate living space. The room shown here began as a plain Jane box. Today, however, it's an inviting place to entertain guests, catch up on the day's events with family, or hide out for a little solo R&R.

To transform your own less-than-grand living room, use these tips:
- *Add architectural character.* Line a blank wall with a grouping of ready-to-assemble bookcases or custom built-ins. Such storage will not only hold books and electronics but also will make the room seem larger by playing up its vertical and horizontal lines. Built around the room's front window, the shelving shown here gives the space its warm denlike ambience and creates a much-needed focal point.
- *Rearrange your space.* Break up your room's boxy shape by putting the sofa on a room-widening angle. Add an oversize ottoman instead of another chair to your conversation grouping. Here, the large round ottoman is easy to navigate around, and it serves as an extra sitting spot while adding a look of grand comfort.
- *Keep it simple.* Use light fabrics, wall finishes, and window treatments. Instead of full, gathered curtains, which can overpower a small space, the treatment here offers trim lines and a touch of color and pattern.
- *Stretch out.* If you have wall space, add additional tall or wide elements to carry the eye. In this room, a lofty but slim secretary reaches for the ceiling, while a rhythmic lineup of kindred tropical prints leads the eye across the wall behind the sofa.

ONE: *Flanking an existing window with shelves creates a striking focal point. A tall secretary provides storage and a desk without eating up too much of the small room's wall.*

TWO: *Angled even slightly like this, the sofa cuts across the boxy room and helps make room for a chair and ottoman. Light fabrics melt into the walls.*

SUBDIVIDE A LARGE ROOM

The beauty of a large room is its potential for variety. Broken into several intimate sitting and activity areas, it can invite you to relax and enjoy the garden view from a window seat, sit to write a letter at a corner desk, or visit with a few of your favorite friends by the fire. In fact, the only real mistake you can make in arranging a large living room is trying to turn it into a single, overly large conversation area.

• *Enjoy a window with a great view* by placing a chaise, two chairs, or a desk in front of it. Or, add a window seat, creating seating, storage, and architectural interest in one fell swoop.

• *Subdivide with furniture.* To subtly separate two sitting areas, let the pieces for seating turn their backs on one another. Provide some lightweight chairs that can pull around as needed. Use the room's narrow ends for tall case goods or a desk. A leftover corner can host a tea table and chairs.

• *Create unity.* Weave the space together with a large-print wall covering and window treatments. The same carpet or wood flooring will pull the room together; add area rugs to anchor separate groupings.

TWO: *At the narrow end of the living room, flowing draperies frame the window seat that stands in for the typical sofa. Armchairs clad in a neutral-hued plaid and a lightly scaled tray-style cocktail table round out the sitting spot. Patterned fabrics link this rambling space. Accent pillows on the seating pick up the plaids and floral motifs of the upholstery, walls, and windows. White half-curtains add privacy without darkening the room.*

ONE: *To make the most of an expansive living room, design comfort zones anchored with sink-in seating. These upholstered armchairs handle relaxed conversation for two by the fire, but they're within talking distance of the sofa, too.*

THREE: *The different sitting areas arranged in this large living room function independently, yet still look connected thanks to the large-print wall covering and window treatment that line the room's perimeter. When you create more than one conversation grouping, be sure to include small chairside tables or cocktail tables and scatter lamps to serve the activities intended for each location.*

Imagine the difference between plopping down on a sofa and staring at a blank wall versus looking at a fireplace, a beautifully carved armoire, or a colorful canvas, and you'll understand why every sitting spot needs a focal point. In the living room, perhaps a home's busiest place of multiple functions and furnishings, a focal point also gives the eye a starting point so it takes in the interior landscape with ease.

MAKE YOUR OWN FOCAL POINT

It's easy to find the focal point of a living room with a fireplace or a great bay window view. However, not all spaces have such wonders. But what architectural character and focus your home's builder may have left

FIND A FOCAL POINT

out, you can make up for with creativity.

• *Use color and scale.* Large-scale items, such as an armoire, bookshelves, or wall art, can become a focal point for a gathering of sitting pieces. Allow color to grab the eye, using brighter or bolder hues for your room's main feature. Focal points don't have to involve furniture; define a conversation area with a beautifully patterned rug or a large painting. A hunt board or sideboard typically found in the dining room can make a beautiful focus, too, if you pair it with a large wall-hung painting or oversize framed mirror.

• *Trim a window.* If you have a great window or view, flaunt it. Paint trim a different color from the walls or frame the window with colorful fabric to capture the eye but not obscure the view.

ONE: *The lofty height of this living room's antique armoire—especially when compared to the shorter seating and tables nearby—declares it a winning focal point. The furniture arrangement further underscores the armoire's importance because the conversation grouping is focused on the single starring piece.*

TWO: *Shutters framing floor-to-ceiling windows with a garden view weren't enough for this sitting area. To give the wall focal-point impact, the space between the opened shutters was treated boldly: A drawered chest anchors an eye-grabbing composition that includes a sculptural lamp, a casually propped print, and a bright red canvas.*

THREE: Bold color was just the beginning when this living room wall was chosen as the focal point. The deep green backdrop naturally draws the eye to that part of the room where the wood entertainment center with louvered doors is a magnet for seating. An artistic array of collectibles helps give the cabinet greater height and status.

FOUR: No window dressings are needed to embellish this dramatic window, the living room's unchallenged focal point. The white walls simply enhance the spectacular view, and, for balance, the window is flanked by a tall cupboard on one side and art on the other.

FAMILY

THE MORE WE SNUGGLE IN AT HOME, the more we ask of our family room. It's come a long way since '50s basements were converted to rec rooms. Just like this sunny, do-it-all space, the family room is today's media center, library, and dining and entertaining spot. It's where we relax together, stretch out, and connect. This chapter will help you design a family room that definitely works and plays in style—no matter what your square footage is.

ROOMS

Once reserved for immediate family members, family rooms have become the center of activity for almost every visitor, too. Casual and comfortable, these hardworking rooms have to fit many functions—and, of course, reflect your personal style. To fit all the decorating puzzle pieces, consider the four W's: Who's using the space? What's going on? Where are the activity areas? When is it used most?

• *Arrange seating around a focal point,* such as a view, a bookcase wall, or a fireplace. If a TV and fire-

START WITH FUNCTION

place compete for attention, group the two together by tucking TV gear into a shelf unit or closet next to or along a wall at a right angle to the fireplace. You can turn a seating group on the diagonal to face both a fireplace on one wall and a view or TV on a wall perpendicular to the fireplace. When two focal points lie on opposite walls, try breaking seating into two smaller groups, each with its own focus.

• *Direct traffic.* Let furniture pieces lead traffic around activity areas. In this room, the sofa floats in front of the fireplace, forcing traffic behind it.

• *Furnish wisely.* Choose one all-purpose table that handles homework, crafts, and casual meals. Corral clutter in armoires, wall units, and storage furniture. Select seating pieces in durable fabrics, such as tweeds and tapestries.

ONE: *Personalized for the homeowners' family, this intimate space is ready for any pastime. Oversize seating, a striking fireplace and window wall, and a mix of old and new accents exude comfort. Bands of horizontal trim anchor this two-story space at eye level.*

TWO: *Unglazed ceramic tiles wrap the focal-point fireplace in a palette of grays for cool contrast to the warmth of the fire and natural Douglas fir woodwork.*

THREE: *Weathered woods, such as this old chair, offer texture and vitality. Tables and chairs easily move and mix for varied functions.*

FOUR: *Every comfort is within reach of this plump slipcovered chair, softened with needlework pillows.*

WORK IN THE PERSONAL TOUCHES

ONE: *It's the mix of materials—wicker, natural and painted woods, vintage textiles, slick mirrors, and brass—that imbues this family space with rich visual texture. Only favorite family accents were invited.*

TWO: *A flexible table and a pair of chairs dress up for dining. Just inside the French-door entry, the table can host a dinner for two, work with the larger table for big parties, or simply display flower arrangements.*

THREE: *This room's easy mix of old chairs scoot where they're needed. Cloaked for meals, the painted round table is uncovered for family games and office work.*

- *Provide flexible lighting.* Include good general lighting for kids' playtime, task light for reading, and over-the-table lighting (a hanging pendant, recessed cans, or a strip of track), which can be brightened for homework and hobbies and dimmed for dining.

- *Make it personal.* This is the room where you display and enjoy the belongings that reflect your family at its happiest. Express yourself and paint a portrait of your loved ones with family treasures and just-for-fun finds. Items such as vacation souvenirs and children's artwork also make great conversation starters when guests arrive.

- *Group for impact.* Avoid dotting small objects around a room. Instead, gather small accessories together for high impact on a wall, shelf, or tabletop. When combining photos, art, and collectibles, have a unifying theme, whether it be color, materials, subject matter, or motifs. Finally, be sure to play the "odds": Three items are more interesting to the eye than four.

- *Walls for mementos.* Keep scale and height in mind when arranging things on walls. Large or vaulted spaces require larger objects or groupings. No matter what a room's height, artwork should always be hung at eye level—higher in hallways, lower in a sitting spot when you'll view the art while seated.

- *Preserve and protect.* It may be comforting to display Grandmother's spongeware for all to see, but make sure valuable and one-of-a-kind items are out of harm's way. Antique family photos may be damaged by sunlight, so have them copied and framed, then tuck the originals away.

UNIFY WITH COLOR

Today's most coveted floor-plan option—the open kitchen-dining-living area known as the great-room—can pose the trickiest decorating problems. How to pull these three areas together so that they blend without boring? On these next four pages, you'll see how you can use color and your own sense of style to unify such spaces.

• **Create flow with floors.** For the smoothest, most expansive flow of space, especially when rooms are not large, use the same flooring material and color throughout. If you do change flooring materials—between a kitchen and adjacent dining or living area, for instance—it's usually best to keep materials in the same color family to avoid jarring contrast. Use area rugs to define and anchor different groupings.

• **Let walls and windows carry your eye.** Treatments don't have to match, but they have to be color-related. In the room shown here, a predominantly white wall covering in the kitchen and dining area stops short of the living area walls, which are simply painted. But the green trellis design and floral border carry out and visually balance the color scheme set by the living area's dark-green seating and rug.

• **Repeat fabrics and accent colors** from one space to the next, varying the colors' intensity as desired. In the living room here, a larger dose of dark greens adds coziness; white predominates in the airy kitchen, which requires more brightness.

• **Key your colors to the room's natural light.** Add "sun" to a north-facing room (or one used mainly at night) with touches of yellow or red; cool off a sunny room with green or blue. If your room has both exposures, simply adopt a palette of cool and warm tones—a yellow and blue scheme, for instance. With a flexible color scheme like that, you can easily emphasize warm or cool colors where you need them.

ONE: *Color scheming is easy if you choose white plus one color. Here, white with green creates a country French mood—and a cool counterpoint to this home's desertlike setting. The mirrored armoire, with video gear inside, forms a sparkling focal point for overstuffed seating.*

TWO/THREE: *Wall coverings carry the green hue to the adjacent dining area and kitchen. Instead of repeating the floral pattern, the owner added drama with the following foolproof pattern-mixing techniques.*

• *Add geometrics. Valances of gingham on French doors complement the botanical print border. In the kitchen, an open trellis wall covering maintains the garden theme.*

• *Mix three scales. The small gingham, medium floral, and large-scale trellis work together without competing.*

USE STYLE

Pulling a large, multipurpose room together with a seamless flow of style can be easier said than done. For casual, family room ambience, an easy-going, eclectic mix of furnishings and accessories is more relaxing than a carefully matched set. But how can you make sure that your choices will work together?

• *Name that room.* Develop a clear vision of the look and mood you want your room to have, and if you can, make up your own name for it. Is it prairie pioneer? Modern seashore? English cottage? Midwestern lake house? Victorian farmhouse? Perhaps the label you choose will be something like, "Aunt Susan and Uncle Bill's living room in Vermont." With the room's style and attitude firmly in mind, you will continually gravitate toward furnishings that work together.

• *Pick a dominant fabric pattern* to foster the look you've chosen. A rugged plaid, for instance, can work well in a room inspired by the Scottish highlands or Rocky Mountains. Sweet miniflorals can lend a romantic cottage look. Awning stripes might be just the thing for a room that you've decided to call "a day at the beach."

ONE: *Plaid seating, a kindred rug, and handmade accessories cast a rustic country spell. Painted pieces—a blue wicker chair, decoy, and Southwestern carved snakes—add more variety to the mix.*

TWO: *A stone fireplace makes a natural focal point for seating. TV-video equipment hides in a closet clad to blend into the paneled walls.*

AS YOUR LINK

• *Use easy go-betweens.* To break up a dull, matched set of pieces, work in mixable naturals, such as wicker and mellow woods. Also look for (or create) painted wood or wicker chairs or tables to punch up your color scheme and add variety to your room's materials.

• *Let one texture dominate.* Decide on the degree of casualness you want. The more rugged the textures, the more casual the room's feeling. Once you decide on the main texture, add lesser amounts of other textures for a pleasing blend of smooth and rough surfaces.

TURN ANY ROOM INTO A GREAT-ROOM

Make a family room appear out of thin air? With a little ingenuity, you can transform an infrequently used space into one ready for action. Do you walk right past a standoffish formal dining room every day? Can you substitute a sofa bed for a standard one and take over an idle guest room?

CASUAL, TWO-IN-ONE SPACE

As you can see here, you don't have to give up your dining room or guest room to have a family room, nor do you need a lot of square footage to pull off this kind of practical room transformation.

• *Arrange for two functions.* Move the dining table to one side to make way for a sink-in love seat and an easy chair. Dining chairs can pull around for dining or conversation as needed.

• *Lighten up.* Make lighting less formal by swapping the typical chandelier or pendant lamp with a strip of track lighting that can illuminate the table while spotlighting artwork or by bouncing light off the walls for an indirect, general glow. Add lamps, too, for reading, hobbies, and homework.

Fun and functional, this 11×14-foot family room used to be a formal dining room. Now it's opened up to the kitchen and used every day. The seating mix hugs the wall on one side, and there's an old multipurpose farm table on the opposite side. When guests come to dine, the coffee table trunk moves out, so the table can be moved away from the wall. The armoire holds a TV.

• *Turn tables.* Versatile drop-leaf, gateleg, extendable, or flip-top tables are ideal for small spaces. A long but narrow harvest table can slide into a sliver of floor space.

• *Expand storage.* Move in a bookcase, a closed storage cabinet, or an antique armoire to stow the television, along with kids' games, dishes, and table linens. Draft other double-duty pieces, such as old chests or trunks, as coffee and end tables so you can fill them with games, work files, and guest linens if your sofa hides a bed inside.

This family room media center, tucked behind louvered bifold doors, is made from a closet organizer system the homeowners installed. They used the same versatile system to surround windows with handsome bookcases.

CREATING STORAGE

The more living you pack into one space, the more you have to display, disguise, organize, store, and hide. For almost every activity that goes on in the family room, there's a corresponding set of items and equipment that need to be neatly housed nearby. Convert every spare inch of space into storage to avoid irritating clutter.

BORROW SPACE FROM WALLS

A mere 12 to 24 inches of floor space along one wall yields an enormous amount of storage between the floor and ceiling. Build shelving and open or closed cabinets to accommodate various storage needs. As you see in the room at left, you can easily build a closet-style storage unit concealed behind standard louvered doors. Or, add a lineup of ready-made modular storage units. Whether you're building or buying storage, be sure to measure your TV and other electrical components, and plan with a tape measure in hand. Not all storage units are deep enough to hold today's most popular 27-inch TVs.

HOME THEATER TIPS

• *Set the scene* for watching movies, sports, or special presentations on your big-screen or projection television by installing window treatments that completely block sunlight and glare.

• *Ask the audio-video experts* which type of speakers best suit your family room. They also can advise you about the number of speakers you'll need and their placement.

• *Corral the wires* behind home theater systems by bundling them together. Flexible hollow tubes, which look like vacuum cleaner hoses, fit neatly around the bundles. Identify the connections on all pieces of equipment with a small hangtag on each wire before you bundle them up.

Living in the Information Age means the television—be it a mammoth home theater or 20-inch portable—is never far from view. But there are times when we wish it weren't so visually domineering, especially when friends are gathered for lively conversation or the family has converged to catch up on each other's news.

In these family rooms, creative storage and customized furniture pieces solved the "big eye" problem by corralling and camouflaging not only the television but also the rest of the requisite electronics gear.

TV HIDEAWAYS

ONE: *Even though this collector's taste in accessories leans toward American folk art and antiques, she loves an uncluttered look. She outfitted shelves in a storage wall with a simple roll-down shade to hide her large TV.*

TWO: *This family room gained an instant focal point and storage in the maple electronics armoire, which has matching, freestanding*

shelf units on each side for books and collections.

THREE/FOUR: *Left doorless to mimic the display wall opposite it, this room-divider cabinet holds needed audio/video essentials on one side and provides a kitchen work area and serving counter on the other.*

2

3

4

5

6

FIVE: *An angled cupboard tucked into a corner of this basement family room stores the television as well as books, games, and videos. Its doors are fashioned of tongued-and-grooved wood; the TV is set off by colorful spindles. A companion cupboard holds the tapes and the stereo equipment.*

SIX: *A well-designed media wall can solve storage problems in just a slice of precious floor space. Echoing this contemporary home's strong horizontal lines, a long, low grid of clean-lined storage gathers books, collectibles, the television, and the fireplace into one cohesive focal point.*

DINING

IS YOUR MEALTIME AN EPICUREAN FEAST

for two, fast food for four, or family style for a

crowd? No matter who's coming to dinner and

what's on the menu, you deserve a dining area

that reflects your personal style and your

lifestyle. In this chapter, we'll help you make the

most of large and small dining rooms, as well as

kitchen eating spots. We'll even help you find

room for dining in the most unlikely places.

WHAT'S YOUR ATTITUDE?

You know how awkward it feels to dress formally if you're a jeans-and-T-shirt kind of person: The high heels wobble or the tie pinches. The same holds true for dining area decorating. If you're the casual soup-and-salad type, even when entertaining, why sit down beneath a sparkling chandelier in a roomful of antiques?

BE YOURSELF

You've heard it before: To thine own self be true. (To test your decorating attitude, see the quiz beginning on page 26.) To devise a hard-working dining spot that caters to your true self, adopt this plan:

• *Find your comfort zone* and design for it. If you don't dress for dinner, why put yourself in an environment that demands more than you're willing to give? If a rugged farm table puts you at ease, it will work fine for your guests, too. In fact, guests will be more comfortable when you are. On the other hand, if the idea of dimming the lights and setting out the silver is what you love most, a more elegant atmosphere is in order.

• *Decide on an overall look.* Then design the walls, window treatments, and floor coverings to fit; be careful to work with your home's architectural style and features.

• *Choose furnishings creatively.* Whatever your style, look beyond the obvious dining "set." A built-in banquette (a long, usually upholstered bench) on one side of the table can help seat a crowd in style; a charming group of mismatched chairs, such as the pine and wicker chairs *above*, adds personality.

ONE: *This casual dining nook illustrates how to work with existing architecture. An antique bench and Swedish farm table balance and take advantage of the space below the high windows. Wicker adds a soft counterpoint to the blend of woods.*
TWO: *This formal dining room takes a refined yet fresh look at the past. The vintage feeling gets a contemporary spin with a glass-top table, star sconces, and window frames hung as wall art. Crystal garland drapes the shapely iron chandelier.*

2

ARE YOU CASUAL?

For some of us, relaxation means a good book. For others, it's a walk in the woods, listening to music, or dining with friends. You can take just as many paths on your way to achieving a casual dining space. There's no single relaxed look that's right for dining areas. But there's sure to be a casual style that's exactly right for you.

RELAX IN STYLE

Whether your dining room is farmhouse friendly or leans to cottage casual, use the following pointers as guides for creating an informal style.

• *Materials matter.* Not all woods, fabrics, and finishes are created equal. Some proclaim their pedigree and shout, "Hands off." Others invite use, which is essential for an informal mood. As a general rule, choose rough textures instead of smooth; wicker, rattan, pine, and iron are less formal than glossy wood veneers or sleek glass. The more weathered or distressed a piece of furniture or an accessory is, the more informal it feels. The same is true of fabrics; coarse weaves project the casual style. Stay away from shiny textiles. Silk, taffeta, damask, and even

chintz—unless they're washed—have a sheen that suggests formality. Factor easy care into your casual scheme.

• *Mix, don't match.* A mixture of furnishings will relax the room. Try a collection of similar-shaped, but one-of-a-kind, vintage chairs around the table. Even one oddball chair at the end of the table breaks up the uniformity that's a trait of formal style. Or, use a set of matching chairs with a table of different material—for example, wood chairs with a glass-top table or wicker chairs with a wood table.

• *Bring fabric to the table.* Cotton tablecloths, woven runners, and chair cushions with zippered covers for washability make any dining area more approachable. Dress down formal chairs with slipcovers in textured fabrics or canvas, and relax a formal table with a floor-length cotton skirt.

ONE: *Free-spirited, this dining area includes mismatched wicker chairs around a plain pine table. A wicker settee, flanked by wall-mounted lamps, invites settling back with a favorite magazine.*

TWO: *Ticking and a coordinated print make for homespun dining. Blue-and-white plates and fabric work together to make the narrow window appear wider.*

ARE YOU FORMAL?

When you can devote only one area of your easy-living home to formality, the dining room surely warrants consideration. Since you spend limited time there, it can be as formal as you like without intruding upon rooms where you kick back or curl up.

CIVILIZED TWIST

Formal dining doesn't have to be uncomfortable. It's just a different kind of leisure—a civilized, unhurried sharing of your best, from manners and conversation to foods and wines. It's a time to indulge the senses and appreciate life itself. The good news for contemporary design fans is that formal dining pieces don't have to be traditional only. The design principles for a formal look work equally well in contemporary and traditional spaces. Here are some of the ways to add formal grace to your dining room.

• *Use symmetrical balance.* Symmetrical arrangements—mirror images on either side of an imaginary center line—provide the most formal balance. Use symmetry for some of your most important table, wall, and furniture arrangements.

• *Have it your way.* Set your own degree of formality by sprinkling in a casual touch or two. For example, tie-on chair pads relax the dining room *above*.

• *Combine elegant finishes.* Dress up with gleaming mir-

rors, lacquered finishes, polished veneers, and crystal stemware and candlesticks.

• *Formal doesn't mean fussy.* Nothing makes a stronger formal statement than furniture with pure, classic lines, be it 18th-century antiques or contemporary classics. Team those with lustrous fabrics, especially silks. Raw silk and silk-linen blends are good choices for formal contemporary settings.

• *Match furnishings for effect.* Pick a dining suite, a pair of identical sconces, and matching frames for artwork.

ONE: *New French country chairs join an old French table in a traditional setting. Formal cues are the elegant wall and window treatments.*

TWO: *Matched furnishings and symmetry create classical formality. Showcasing sculptural chairs against white adds a slick touch.*

Dining rooms are among the easiest spaces to plan because most of them tell you what's needed by their shape and size. Determine the area's furniture configuration and traffic flow, then use common sense, a tape measure, and these tips. For more on planning dining space, turn to pages 254–255 in "Room Arranging" and to the room arranging kit beginning on page 258.

• *First choose your dining table* to conform to the area's shape. Long tables—formal banquet or casual farm tables—make efficient use of long, narrow dining spaces. A pint-size dining room may demand a small square table, perhaps teamed with a bench along one side to squeeze in

HOW TO PLAN

an extra diner. The table's shape affects the look of a room, too. For example, a round table softens the lines of a square room.

• *Keep room scale and balance in mind.* Maybe you can squeeze a large table into a tiny room or place a table for two in a cavernous space, but proportionally neither will look right. If you must use a large table in a smallish room, consider a glass-top one to consume less visual space. Evaluate vertical space, too; a room with a soaring ceiling may require high-back chairs. Finally, plan for a mix of high and low pieces, adding a tall hutch or a sideboard topped with a wall-hung painting for variety.

• *Situate the dining table* so traffic flows smoothly around it— usually near the room's center. (The exception? To turn a dining room into a multiuse space, push the table to one side to make room for lounge chairs or a sofa.) Plan at least 8 square feet for a table for four, plus about 36 inches so chairs can be pulled out.

A corner cupboard lifts the eyes in this dining room, and its shelves open above the tops of Windsor-style dining chairs to avoid a collision of busy lines. There's ample space to walk around the long, narrow dining table that fits the room shape.

• *Allow elbow room* for comfort. Place settings should be 20 to 24 inches wide and 15 inches deep. Reserve a 12-inch-wide strip down the table's middle for centerpieces and serving dishes.

Small
YET GRACIOUS

Unless you regularly (and formally) entertain large groups, a less-than-ample dining room may be all you need. In fact, as long as a small dining room comfortably accommodates a regular-size table, its lack of square footage actually can be a plus. The smaller the space, the more intimate. What better mood to set, both for family affairs and for small dinner parties.

DEFINE BY DESIGN

The design adage "when it's small, paint it white" doesn't necessarily apply to dining rooms. These spaces can benefit more from an opposite approach. Here's how:

• *Draw your eye to the table* by setting it atop a colorful area rug or centering the table in front of a window and adding a focal-point window treatment. Light the table with an overhead fixture on a dimmer.

• *Embellish the backdrop.* Paint walls a rich color or cover them with ele-

ONE: *Wrapped in a rich, earthy-hued paint, this small dining room conjures a more intimate mood for entertaining. Open-back chairs add comfort without mass, and a ceiling-high cupboard turns spare wall space into a focal point with colorful dishes displayed on shelves above closed storage.*

2

gantly patterned or textured wall covering. A contrasting wallpaper border at the ceiling line defines the room's perimeter and creates a feeling of intimacy, too. Don't be afraid of a bold paint color; a surprising cranberry red wall can add unexpected richness and warmth.

• *Think vertically.* When floor space is at a premium, make the most of height, both to delight the eye and to squeeze in maximum storage. Outfit the walls with floor-to-ceiling shelves. Or, work a towering hutch or Welsh cupboard into your plan. The tall lines of such pieces can add a look of grand height, but—unlike cupboards with doors—their open upper shelves won't block up space.

• *Go light on scale.* Two identical-sized groupings of dining tables and chairs may seem to be of different sizes if one is made with chunky woods or dark finishes and the other is lighter in scale. For a small room, consider chairs with reed-thin legs, fine graceful curves, and open backs.

• *Line a wall.* If your space is cramped, push the table against the wall. A rectangular table is better here than a round one.

TWO: *Several fool-the-eye tricks expand space in a small room. Metal gives the dining pieces their light scale; an angled grouping helps visually widen the space and lead traffic around the table to the door; and shutters widen the window.*

THREE: *The strong vertical lines on the coordinated wall coverings and curtains unify and add height to this small room. Airy wicker, open-back chairs, and a bare table allow the eye to travel smoothly through the space.*

3

FINDING SPACE

Today most of us dine all around the house. Tonight, it might be dinner for eight in the dining room. Tomorrow morning? Coffee and a bagel on the run in the kitchen. And on Sunday morning (if you're lucky), it might be a leisurely brunch in the master suite. All that variety demands creative space planning. Start with a good understanding of your special dining needs.

DOUBLE-DUTY DINING

• *Combine dining with an office or den.* As home building costs soar and square footage shrinks, a room reserved for formal dining is a luxury fewer can afford. A dining room can easily share its space with one of these rooms when the table doubles as a desk and a cupboard or hutch holds books as well as dishes. Push the table to one side and add a small love seat or easy chairs, and a mid-size dining room doubles as a den.

• *Squeeze a table into unexpected places.* Be creative. A half-round ("demilune") or drop-leaf table can accent a hallway—and make a great lunch-for-two spot. Or, set a modest rectangular dining table flush against a family or living room wall or directly behind a sofa. Even a slim sofa table can serve dinner when you just pull up a couple of chairs. To give B&B-style romance to a master bedroom, snug a slim dining table or sofa table against the foot of the bed, in front of a window, or replace a nightstand with a larger table that can double for cozy late-night snacks.

ONE: *Once a wasted, walk-by hall space, this spot serves breakfast for two thanks to the addition of a half-round table and space-saving armless chairs.*

TWO: *A big French farm table and new chandelier put a seldom-used hallway window seat to work as an irresistible dining spot. A garden view and comfortably upholstered seating pieces encourage family and friends to linger.*

GATHER
IN THE KITCHEN

It's no wonder that the eat-in kitchen tops the wish list of most home buyers and remodelers. A staple of older homes and a selling point of new ones, the farmhouse kitchen relaxes family and friends with its casual, back-door air—and speaks to the heart with its reminder of the past.

HARDWORKING STYLE

Give your kitchen's informal eating area special decorating attention.

• *Use easy-care fabric and finishes* so breakfast nooks and kitchen dining areas offer great looks without worry. Use hard-wearing stain- and water-resistant fabrics, and add chair pads with zippered covers for easy removal on laundry day. For wood tabletops, choose tough paint or polyurethane versus easy-to-stain oil finishes.

• *Repeat hues and fabrics* from other parts of the room. Painted chairs, new tie-on chair cushions, and table runners can echo the palette or pattern of the kitchen's tile, wallpaper, or window valance.

• *Explore using architectural furnishings.* Pull a table up to a window seat for dining. Built-in booths make efficient use of floor space and give the kitchen a distinctive look.

• *Keep traffic in mind.* Arrange dining pieces so they're out of the busy flow of traffic.

• *Light up.* Replace the switch for existing ceiling lights with a dimmer. If there are no over-the-table lights, wire in a hanging pendant or strip of track so diners aren't kept in the dark at night.

ONE: *White painted chairs tie the dark dining table, camouflaged with a blue and white floral cloth, to the white kitchen. Mismatched, the chairs bring an informal flavor to the kitchen and pick up the kitchen's blue accents in seat upholstery.*

TWO: *A booth makes good use of tight space. Here built-in benches join a new farm table. You can buy new booths, finished or unfinished, that look built in but simply slide into place.*

THREE: *The window seat along this sunny window wall becomes a comfortable dining spot when the long, skinny table is drawn close. The to-the-wall arrangement creates ample space for the busy back-door traffic lane.*

2

3

ONE: *This carved cupboard offers the best of both worlds. It has closed storage below for utilitarian pieces, but its upper doors are left open to show off picture-perfect china. Shirred fabric in the back adds color and softness as it unifies the display.*

TWO: *When floor space is tight, opt for wall-hung storage. This small shelf unit with crown molding and a painted wainscot back teams with an antique bench to bring vintage character to a new suburban dining area. Objects on display carry out the room's color palette.*

STYLISH STORAGE

THREE: *This dining spot makes the most of a built-in arched niche by turning it into a view for people at the table. This intriguing display looks tidy because it presents only a few treasured objects with ample scale.*

Dining rooms don't require as much storage as harder-working kitchens and baths, but some functional storage is desirable. Mealtimes and entertaining are easier when linens, good china and silverware, and serving and tabletop pieces are nearby.

STORAGE STYLES

Utilitarian storage is only one option. As one of the home's most important showplaces, the dining room benefits from open storage where you can put favorite possessions on proud display. Check our list of storage ideas:

• *Use freestanding storage pieces.* Purchase a hutch, buffet, sideboard, or other cupboard. A low sideboard is ideal if you have a large painting or mirror to cover the wall above it. If not, think tall when picking armoires, hutches, Welsh cupboards, and the like. For visual impact, leave upper cabinet doors open to show off a shelf display, then hide the rest behind closed doors below.

• *Hang it on the wall.* No dining space is too small for vertical storage or a small wall rack. Wall-mount shelves above table height. Or, encircle a room with a unifying display shelf. A plate rack no longer than 18 inches offers charm when lined with vintage dessert plates.

• *Build it in.* Built-in china cabinets or shelf-lined niches turn blank walls into handsome and functional dining room assets. To find space for built-ins, either borrow from an adjacent room or hallway or bring an existing wall out about a foot, create a well-designed storage unit, and drywall around it, as shown *left*. Or, make use of dead corner space with custom corner units or by building in new unfinished corner units. For formal symmetry, treat corners identically.

REFRESHER COURSE

Visually down-in-the-dumps dining rooms need more than new storage and inventive space planning. Thankfully, fresh paint and fabrics are guaranteed to lift any room's spirits. Paint is inexpensive, so redo until you get the mood right. And, with new upholstery, those old dining room chairs you thought about replacing can star again.

FABULOUS FACELIFTS

First decide how you want your family and friends to feel while dining; color can alter a person's mood. Then jump-start your room with mood-setting color and pattern, such as:

• *Colorful walls.* If you entertain often, go red. It stimulates lively conversation and appetites and can perk up a roomful of neutrals. In candlelight, red walls create a soft rosy glow that flatters complexions. A restful sage green paint soothes and invites lingering at the table, but the mood can turn cool or deteriorate into boredom without warm color contrasts or liberal use of crisp white for energy.

• *Slipcovers on the chairs.* Using these is an easy way to change not only the look of your chairs but also the look of the entire room. Select fabrics that work with the rest of the room; bold colors and busy patterns are best when window treatments and walls are pattern-free. For a conservative change, make or buy simple seat cushions that add color and texture without concealing the chair design. Or, drape miniskirt slipcovers over the backs and seats. For a bigger change, pop on floor-length slipcovers to give plain wood chairs an upholstered look.

ONE: *Old-world stucco walls of this new cottage-style dining room prove red isn't just for formal spaces. The vivid backdrop dramatically silhouettes the hutch, which is painted white like the wainscoting for contrast.*

TWO: *White paint and slipcovers in a checked fabric update turn-of-the-century walnut chairs in this free-spirited, yet formal, dining room. Miniskirts show off the chairs' carved legs, and the host and hostess chairs have fully covered backs.*

COMPANY'S COMING

What happens when it's your turn to host Thanksgiving dinner for the clan? Even if you finally have your dining room just the way you like it, there's no way your dining space will hold that many people. Now what?

ARRANGE FOR FLEXIBILITY

Don't panic. The beauty of our homes is that they're ours, meaning we can do what we want with them as our needs dictate. When the troops head to your home for a family feast, it's time to practice the fine art of furniture rearranging. Be flexible. Unless your furniture is nailed to the floor, there's no reason it can't be shifted around to accommodate a crowd. Follow this plan:

• *Relocate the dining table.* Let dining and living or family room pieces trade places for the occasion. Set the dining table by the fireplace to keep guests toasty. Then put in all the table's leaves and round up extra chairs or benches for the overflow crowd.

• *Create makeshift tables.* If you don't have a banquet-size table, make tables out of old doors and sawhorses or line up a row of card tables. Top them with fabric dressings, candlesticks, and individual centerpieces. Or, gather several smaller, more intimate tables in the room. They'll match when skirted with white sheets.

• *Bring back the kids' table.* When it's only family, separate the grown-ups and children. Let kids plop down on big pillows around a coffee table.

• *Dig out the TV trays.* They didn't die with the 1950s; they took to the closet waiting to be reborn. New versions in pine turn single chairs into dining spots for one—and hold extra serving bowls and platters when placed at tableside.

Moved from dining to living room, this temporary fireside dining spot makes any feast memorable. With all of the leaves in place, extra chairs or a bench are needed. Some of the chairs come from other rooms, so seating is casually mismatched. Candle lamps supplement the room's other lighting.

BED

ROOMS

MORE THAN A MERE SLEEPING SPOT, THE MODERN BEDROOM

is an all-hours retreat. Yes, you can still catch forty winks or more there,

but the bedroom is also the place to watch television, set up a home

office, and even share a quiet dinner. Comfort comes first, and there's no

end to the pampering amenities you can add. This chapter offers ideas to

help your bedroom live up to its potential. Here an antique bed dressed

up in a vintage quilt and plumped pillows sets a romantic mood.

FORMAL   CASUAL

ECLECTIC   SLICK

WHAT'S YOUR ATTITUDE?

Making your bedroom fit your personality isn't a matter of choosing and duplicating a particular style—18th century, Victorian, or Bauhaus modern, for example—but of putting things together to reflect your personal decorating attitude. How formal or casual are you? Do you like to surround yourself with cozy clutter or do you prefer to display only a few objects in more artistic, gallery-like fashion?

TAKE THIS PILLOW POP QUIZ

To visualize how different attitudes affect decorating choices, imagine for a moment a sofa topped with a pile of pillows—some matching and some not—and ask yourself how you'd edit and arrange them.

• *Formality and symmetry go together.* Would you pick out two matching toss pillows and place one at each end of the sofa? If so, you lean toward formality.

• *Casual calls for asymmetrical balance.* Would you be likely to place a large pillow at one end of the sofa and two or three smaller ones at the other? And would your fabric choices probably be pattern-free neutrals? If you answered yes, you're the casual type.

FORMAL: *Symmetrically placed tables and lamps, a classic toile wall covering, and an inviting but oh-so-tidily made bed suggest formality.*

CASUAL: *Forget symmetry. A relaxed arrangement, feel-good materials in neutral naturals, and a decidedly mussed look create casual ambience.*

ECLECTIC: *White accented with bold Matisse-inspired hues links this eclectic mix of modern and cottage furnishings and accessories.*

SLICK: *Slick styling works for traditional as well as modern furnishings. In this minimal setting, a classic tester bed can show off its fine lines.*

• *Slick means paring down.* Would you toss out all but one or two exquisitely shaped, handcrafted pillows, or perhaps eliminate the toss pillows entirely for a cleaner look? If so, you lean toward slick, minimal schemes.

• *Eclectic means mixing styles*—as long as they are equally formal or casual. Would you group pillows covered in mismatched but color-keyed fabrics—say, blue striped pillows with some in blue and white patchwork quilt fabrics? If you would, you're the eclectic type.

Don't be hemmed in by decorating attitude labels; few people fall exactly within the bounds of one category. Instead, relax and use this information as a guide not only in arranging such things as pillows but also in choosing and arranging major bedroom furnishings. By knowing your attitude and using the following tips, you can create a bedroom that comforts you and your eye.

• *If you prefer formality,* you simply won't feel at ease unless you center the bed along a wall or between two windows, then flank it with matched lamps and tables.

• *If you're more casual,* you may feel distinctly uncomfortable with such symmetry. Try moving the bed to one side of the room or place it on an angle in a corner. Then balance the off-center bed with a storage piece, reading chair and lamp, or bold artwork.

• *If you lean toward slick minimalism,* you won't relax unless you pare down. Start with a bold bed, then add a handful of well-designed accents. Provide plenty of closed storage to keep clutter to a minimum.

FOR MORE ABOUT HOW TO DEFINE YOUR DECORATING ATTITUDE, REFER TO OUR DECORATING QUIZ STARTING ON PAGE 26.

WHAT ARE YOUR ESSENTIALS?

The word "essentials" takes on a broader meaning when applied to your bedroom. Because the room serves as your own personal refuge, it's as important to include those special touches that make you feel truly at ease as it is to select a comfortable mattress. Before you can design your dreamy retreat, determine not only how you will use the room—for sleeping only or as a part-time den, for instance?— but also what kinds of furnishings and materials you deem essential. This is the time to indulge yourself: Do you really *need* those eyelet-trimmed bed linens or that fat eiderdown duvet? Maybe the answer is *yes*.

• ***List the basics***—sleeping, storage, and seating. What size bed fits your space—and the way you live? Do you need a king-size bed, or would you prefer a queen-size with room left over for a lounge chair and ottoman? How much storage do you require? If you have a large walk-in closet with built-in shelves and drawers, maybe you can forget the dresser and free up floor space for a writing table. What about nightstands? A small table may suffice, but if you take newspapers and stacks of books to bed with you, find room for a larger bedside table. And don't forget good lighting. Lamps with three-way switches let you dial the wattage up for reading or down for relaxing. Sculpt space with accent lights, too—a picture light above a painting, a strip light to highlight a shelf of collectibles. (For more help, see the chapters on "Lighting," page 366, and "Arranging," page 242.)

• ***Include the essential amenities.*** What will make you feel pampered? If you love music, add a sound system. Make space to display treasures, family pictures, and favorite books. Even a sleeping spot for a pet may be a priority in your private domain.

This cozy attic bedroom proves you don't need a large space for grand comfort—and practicality. By the window, an antique writing desk offers an inspiring view of the forested backyard. The comfy wing chair encourages idle moments. Space-saving built-ins handle all kinds of storage.

FLOOR PLAN POINTERS

Before creating the bedroom of your dreams, it's important to plan on paper. And, as you sketch out your space and pencil in furnishings on your floor plan, here are a few of the priorities you'll want to keep in mind.

• *Consider the size of the bed.* You can treat yourself to a larger bed if you don't need a lot of storage furniture—in a guest room or a bedroom that includes a large closet with many built-ins. Keep scale in mind, too; the bed's *apparent* size is more than a matter of its dimensions. A tall, scroll-like metal headboard, as shown *right*, will consume less visual space than a carved wood Victorian-style headboard of the same size and shape; dark woods and finishes will take up more space than light ones. Carefully match the height of bedside tables to the bed, making sure they are at least as high as the top of the mattress. Some standard nightstands may be too low for today's higher beds, such as replica Shaker four-posters.

• *Create easy access.* For day-to-day convenience, avoid placing the bed so close to the room's entry door that it forms a frustrating roadblock every time

ONE: *A charmingly curlicued headboard gives this bed focal-point impact, yet its open design keeps it from overpowering the modestly sized sleeping area. There's just enough space around the bed for bed making and for access to a walk-in closet. Had these lamps been set atop standard-height nightstands, their beams would have been too low for reading, but the light's just right when taller side tables are used.*

TWO: *A chest makes use of a sliver of between-windows space, and an upholstered chair and footstool turn a corner into a retreat.*

you go in or out. For convenient bedmaking, allow at least 2 feet on both sides of the bed. Don't forget that closets and dressers require floor space, too. Allow about 3 feet of dressing space in front of a closet (or more if your door swing demands it) and at least 36 to 40 inches in front of chests and dressers for drawer pullout space.

• *Stow in style.* Unless you have a separate dressing room packed with efficient built-ins, allow space for storage pieces. Don't limit yourself to the furniture pieces that are sold with your bed. Instead, consider supplementing a tall highboy, armoire, secretary, or dresser-mirror combination with a wall of new built-ins *(as shown on pages 96–97 and 102–103)* to make the best use of space and to add architectural interest.

MAKE A SMALL ROOM LIVE BIG

Square footage doesn't make a bedroom a well-designed, high-function retreat. It's how you put your square footage to work that does. If you have a small space, study the following ways to make it look and live bigger than its dimensions.

SCALE UP THE FURNISHINGS

Throw out the old decorating dictum that says a small space requires equally small furnishings. On the contrary, you'll use less of your precious floor space if you use fewer pieces of a slightly larger scale than if you use a larger number of small-scale pieces. That's not to say you can't use small-scale elements, but be sure to use them sparingly to reduce visual clutter.

• *Finesse the floor plan.* In a small room, stick with an arrangement that keeps the major pieces parallel or perpendicular to walls; a diagonally placed bed may take up too much floor space. Think vertically and opt for built-in storage or tall freestanding storage pieces; an armoire or chest-on-chest can stow twice as much gear as a dresser—without consuming any more floor space.

• *Keep things light.* Expand a small space with light colors, simple backdrops, mirrored walls or large inexpensive home-center mirrors. See-through furnishings—glass-top tables, gauzy curtains, and lightly scaled furniture with exposed legs—also provide airiness.

ONE: *This small sleep spot comes up big as a getaway. It makes room for put-your-feet-up comfort with a lightly scaled armchair and ottoman, both slipcovered in the fresh floral print fabric of the bedcover and window treatments.*
TWO: *Exuding all the charms of a country inn, this master bedroom teams a slim four-poster under a canopy of intricately crocheted netting with delicate pink and peach sponged walls to keep the look light and airy.*
THREE: *Even the smallest bedroom deserves to be treated to little luxuries. Conjuring the graceful past, this vintage vanity and accompanying slipcovered chair tuck into a corner. Mirrors expand the tight space, and an armless chair offers comfort without bulkiness.*

PULL TOGETHER A BED & BATH

Coordinate colors in a bed-bath suite, but plan for variety, too. (For more details, see pages 296–301 in the "Color" chapter and pages 52–55 in "Family Rooms.")

• *Pick a palette.* For interesting variety, emphasize one color in the bedroom and another in the bath. Here the palette consists of teal, yellow ocher, and white. A cool teal wall covering with a star motif wraps the sleeping area in serenity, while the same wallpaper motif in yellow ocher brings a higher-energy glow to the bath.

• *Unify with fabrics.* The shower curtain and window treatments are in a complementary fabric with the same motifs.

• *Stick to one mood.* This suite offers relaxed, acquired-over-time ambience thanks to a casual blend of revived secondhand finds. A salvaged tub, junk-store lamps, and an antique chest warm the bath; a reupholstered armchair and mismatched lampshades personalize the bedroom.

ONE: *Anchored by a stately pine four-poster, this master suite has a predominant teal and ocher color scheme that links design elements and spaces.* **TWO:** *A painted chest is the star of this unexpected bath grouping of artwork and mismatched secondhand lamps.* **THREE:** *The bath's Belle Epoque sink is one of several vintage finds that gives this master suite its aged character.*

Once making the bed was a simple affair. All you had to do was pop on the same old sheets and pull up the spread. Today, however, sheets come in many fibers and thread counts, and bedmaking itself means creating your own snuggle-in choice of elements. Here are some options for today:

MAKING THE BED

• *Replace a spread with a duvet*—a plain, usually down-filled comforter with a removable cover. It does the job of top sheet, blanket, and bed cover—all in one.

• *Add a feather bed.* Its cover should be

BEDDING BASICS

tightly woven to keep pointy quills in their place. For protection, you can slip the feather bed into its own removable, washable cover, then simply plop the whole thing over your existing mattress for four-star luxury every night.

• *Layer on prints and fun touches.* Dress your bed with a mix of prints, breaking up florals with snappy stripes, gingham checks, and colorful solids. Be playful with bed toppers, too; layer on a lace tablecloth or vintage throw.

BUYING LINENS

• *Save money.* Mix less expensive white and solid sheets with more costly prints, pillows with hand-stitched embroidery, and elegant comforters. Ready-made duvet covers can be pricey, but it's easy to make one by sewing two flat sheets together on three sides and adding buttons or snaps to close the end. (Use the same duvet-cover idea to stitch up a new cover for a dated, old comforter.)

• *Add comfort.* Cotton sheets soften with washing and let the body breathe; cotton-polyester blends wrinkle less but aren't as soft. Pima and Egyptian cottons are extra lustrous. Thread count, the number of threads per square inch, shows quality—180 to 200 is standard; 350 means luxury.

Create a mix-and-match bedding wardrobe. Reflecting the owner's personality, a downy duvet in country-style ticking teams with a lace skirt, breezy florals, and striped chambray.

ONE ROOM TWO WAYS WINTER...SUMMER

2

ONE: Use color and pattern to change the mood with the seasons. Here a beautiful floral fabric warms cold winter nights with images of a summer garden. The flowers crown the bed and slipcover the foot-of-bed bench. Stippled on the walls, a soft apple green paint provides a cool accent to the sunny shades in the floral fabrics, and a needlepoint rug adds warmth underfoot. Even windows layer on the warmth with floral drapery panels and softly scalloped valances.

TWO: When temperatures start to sizzle in summer, it's time to cool off with an airy scheme of summer whites. Winter's heavier bed linens and the floral canopy take the summer off, replaced with lacy linens and gauzy curtains for the bed and window. The bench also slips into a white summer frock. Underfoot, a cool whitewashed floor is revealed when winter's rug is whisked away.

CHANGE YOUR STYLE

ONE: This room made a great beginning for first-time homeowners. Starting with a classic four-poster and soft blue walls and linens, the couple created a casual but romantic getaway on a budget. A framed poster (on an easel) brings color to the corner behind the bed, and a piece of fabric is simply folded up and tacked above the window's miniblinds. White links antiques with secondhand pieces.

TWO: Growing more sophisticated over time, the owners opted for a slicker, more serene scheme. They painted the walls cream, then used a level and pencil to draw lines 15 inches apart for the wide taupe stripes. Kilim rugs and a new armoire add color and pattern. To turn an unfinished armoire into an instant antique, they stained it, painted on the green and gold, then did some sanding to remove some of the paint.

ONE: Turn a blank wall into a storage-filled focal point. Brand new built-in closets and window seats (with hinged lids for storage below) add storage—and style, too.

TWO: Tuck a chest in at the foot of the bed. Linens and sweaters can hide inside, and there's plenty of room on top for displaying collectibles and books.

1

2

TRICKS
WITH
STORAGE

THREE: A slice of wall space at the foot of the bed makes a great spot for built-in storage that's angled to lead traffic smoothly into and out of the room. To soften cabinetry lines, shelf edges are rounded and pilasters run from crown moldings to floor.

FOUR: Reassign a cocktail table to foot-of-bed duty as a mini library to keep stacked books handy and also inject color and texture into the space.

FIVE: Flank a bed with new bump-out closets to increase a room's storage space—and give the bed visual importance. To create a headboard and turn the closets and bed into one cohesive unit, add behind-the-bed shelving.

INSTANT HEADBOARDS

Ingenious ideas like these go straight to the head of a classy bed. Whether mounted on the bed frame or freestanding, all four of these headboard styles get high marks for their looks and clever use of unexpected materials. Perhaps you've never thought of shopping for a headboard at the lumberyard or garden center, but that's where these do-it-yourself toppers got their starts. Outdoor landscaping and fencing products turned these basic beds into one-of-a-kind charmers.

MAIL BONDING

Two ordinary mailbox posts frame this bed with ruggedly handsome character. Shorten unfinished posts to desired height. Use a 12-inch-wide piece of plywood as a spacer and stabilizer between the posts. Using wood glue and screws, fasten a ³⁄₄×1¹⁄₂-inch cleat to each end of the plywood; screw cleats to posts below mattress level. Drill holes in posts to match holes in bed rail. Attach the headboard with bolts and washers.

GARDEN DREAMS

Romance a bed with a lacy lattice arbor and climbing rose fabric backdrop. Shop garden and home supply stores for an arbor kit to fit your bed size, or be creative with readymade lattice panels. If the pieces come unpainted, add coats of primer and fresh white paint. After you assemble the arbor, cut a plywood shape to fit the arbor back and staple batting and a floral sheet over the plywood. Nail the floral fabric-covered back to the back of the arbor.

STOCKADE STAND-UP

Go ahead, fence yourself in. A section of unpainted stockade fencing snugly encloses the head of the bed. The light, natural pine—knots and all—forms a perfect rough-hewn backdrop for the natural, neutral linens and a vase of roadside weeds. Stockade fencing panels come in 8-foot sections at home improvement centers. You'll need bolts long enough to go through the panel and the bed rail and still fasten in place. Cut the panel to bed width; sand off rough spots as needed. Mark positions for bolts on the panel to match those on the bed rail. Drill holes for the bolts through the panel, then fasten the headboard to the bed rail with bolts and washers.

PICKET PERFECT

Designed with movable side wings so it can fit into a corner, this headboard of fence pickets cradles a bed arranged on the diagonal. To assemble your own, measure the bed's width to determine the width of the center section. Decide on the desired width for the sides—our side panels each contain four pickets—then purchase the fencing, four hinges, screws to attach the hinges, bolts, and washers. Cut the fencing into the appropriate widths. Prepare the center section, following instructions for the stockade-panel headboard. Hinge the sides to the center section at the fence crosspieces and bolt the headboard to the bed. For a rugged look, leave the fence pickets natural or stain them. To spark a little gothic romance, prime the pickets and then paint them white.

GUEST

ROOMS

EXTENDING THE WARMEST WELCOME TO overnight guests is the ultimate in hospitality. You want their home away from home to be as inviting as a country inn, even though their space may have a day job as a home office or family room. This guest room has a true getaway feeling with its half-round canopies on the twin beds and a homey mix of fabrics and vintage accessories.

CREATE COMFORT ANYWHERE

A guest's oasis—in homes not blessed with a spare room—usually begins with a sofa bed. Today, these furniture staples offer more comfort and beauty than their chunky predecessors. They've also given birth to a range of related, dual-function pieces: attractive and easy-to-open daybeds, sofa beds, futon sofas, and flip-open sofas and chairs.

The challenge comes when you try fitting guest room function, comfort, and privacy into a room your family uses every day. Always arrange the room knowing how much space the opened bed will occupy; can guests walk around it safely and easily? Decorate with day and night uses in mind. A cozy quilt might double as a daytime throw; a footstool can be used as a bedside table.

PRIVACY POINTERS

When carving sleeping space out of living space, add privacy for guests.

• *Beef up window coverings.* If you normally use sheers or simple cafe curtains, add opaque roller shades.

• *Make a folding screen* out of window shutters or antique doors. It can serve as a movable room divider or a cover-up for windows and French doors without window treatments.

• *Curtain a doorway.* Gather decorative fabric onto a temporary tension rod placed within a doorway. For extra-wide spaces, use a tension rod made for shower curtains.

ONE: *There's plenty of English ambience in this living room guest quarters, but beneath the quilt throw is a 10-year-old sofa bed still on duty.* **TWO:** *Whisk off the quilt, open the sofa bed, and pile on lacy pillows, and your guests will feel right at home.* **THREE:** *From the walls to accents, this two-way space is serene and elegant in a green and ivory palette.*

DEVOTED TO GUESTS

Reserve a room for visitors? Of course. If you have a spare room, here's how to turn it into a truly welcome guest oasis.

BEGIN WITH BASICS

Start by reviewing last year's guest list—your mother-in-law for the holidays, a couple of old friends on a weekend jaunt, your daughter's college roommate. When choosing a bed, pick one that fits the space and the needs of your most frequent guests. You can always rent a crib or rollaway bed for extra company or guests with children. For starters, buy one or two twin beds or a queen-size bed. Keep fresh, fluffy pillows on hand and offer guests a choice of synthetic or natural fillings. To guarantee sweet dreams, top the mattress with a featherbed, dress the bed in luxurious linens and a down-filled duvet, and pile on the pillows.

BE YOUR OWN GUEST

Before guests arrive, take the time to try out the room yourself. You'll learn plenty about the mattress comfort and the room's temperature, lighting, convenience, and privacy. Take a book and a cup of tea in with you and see how things work. For convenience and a homey feel, is there room for a nightstand, reading lamp, comfy chair and ottoman, a writing desk, mirror, alarm clock, radio, and, if possible, a television? Do window treatments offer adequate privacy? Clear space in the closet and storage drawers, and offer guests scented, padded hangers for their clothes. Set out spa amenities, such as shampoos, soaps, lotions, a hair dryer, thick towels, and a unisex terry robe.

ONE: *Flea market meets country auction in this collector's guest room with a robin's-egg blue backdrop. A 1950s bedspread covers the chair and pillow.*
TWO: *A small space with all the essentials in one cozy spot wraps guests in comfort. The furnishings share a floral theme enhanced by the trellis wallpaper, which "raises" the low ceiling with its vertical lines.*

LET HOME OFFICES WORK OVERTIME

When setting aside space for full-time guest quarters isn't an option, there are plenty of alternatives. A room used as a home office every day is ideal for plugging in a part-time sleeping area.

• *Introduce a wall bed.* The bed-in-the-wall idea is back and much improved over the original concept. Now many Murphy-style wall beds come in their own cabinets, which bolt securely to the studs in the wall. When the bed is lowered, a safety mechanism holds the bed's position securely anywhere along the way down. As with a sofa bed, check the amount of space the bed will consume when it's opened. Choose lightweight or roll-around tables and chairs that will easily move out of the bed's way when guests arrive.

• *Consider a daybed.* Perfect for an at-home worker's time-out spot, as well as for guests to sleep, today's space-saving daybeds come in all furniture styles, from country to traditional and contemporary. If you find an antique wood or metal daybed, sleigh bed, or trundle bed, check the frame closely to make sure new mattresses will fit properly.

MIX BUSINESS WITH PLEASURE

Blending a home office and a guest room means combining a work area with a relaxation zone. Put away projects and paperwork so guests can conveniently use the desktop. Also, choose a simple decorating scheme that suits both purposes. The following tips will help you treat your guests right.

• *Use color and pattern.* Since the space has a dual personality, use color with a strong hand and pattern with restraint. Bold use of color on the window wall, the floor, or one large piece of furniture directs the eye away from any clutter of tiny items, files, or supplies you have on office shelves. Busy miniprints are better in small amounts. Use them on clusters of accent pillows and in a wallpaper border or chair-rail treatment.

• *Close the office.* Before guests arrive, you'll want to be sure that guests won't be awakened by an incoming fax or incessant phone calls. Unplug the fax machine, the computer, and the business phone line, if possible. Swept-clean surfaces and table-tops allow guests to spread out their things and, perhaps, catch up on their own homework or the latest best-seller.

ONE: *Clever decorating rescued a disjointed, lackluster sleep-and-studio duo. Now this tiny suite features a cozy daybed with a hidden trundle bed. The scheme is united by Shaker furniture and a painted floor that picks up the old quilt's pattern.*

TWO: *Modular office and storage components make good use of this hardworking guest space. Storage hugs one side of the fold-down bed, here in the closed position.*
THREE: *When guests arrive, the sleek wall bed pulls down easily, and ample storage keeps the room clutter-free. A roll-around file cabinet also works as a nightstand.*

WELCOME THEM WITH AMENITIES

Feather your guests' nest with fabulous extras to make the room inviting and their stay memorable. You probably have many of these extras, and you can pick up some special treats at the grocery store.

SUITE PERFECTION

In the best bed-and-breakfast inns, the rooms are only the beginning. It's the details that make you feel pampered—the fresh flowers in a crystal vase, the scented stationery on the desk, the mints on the pillows. Here are some ideas for bringing that B&B ambience home:

• *Add a bed tray* for bedtime snacks and a leisurely breakfast. Put a crystal water carafe on the dresser.

• *Keep guests current* with the newspaper, maps, magazines, tourist information, and a couple of best-sellers.

Be sure a telephone book is handy.

• *Portable potables.* Offer bottled waters, easy-open juices, and a small coffeemaker plus mugs. Add an ice bucket and keep it filled.

• *Snacks on tap.* Fill a basket with fresh fruit, wrapped snack bars and candies, and bags of pretzels. If you have space, tuck a small bar refrigerator into a closet or cabinet.

• *For entertainment,* provide a television, radio, cassette or compact disc player, music tapes or CDs. Write out a list of local stations and provide a copy of a current local TV schedule.

• *Telephone and computer hookups* allow guests to phone home and catch up with the laptop they might have carted along.

ONE: *Ruffles, flourishes, and soft-hued fabrics make this retreat a guest favorite. A curtained four-poster bed and relaxed, natural-textured furnishings soothe the soul.*

TWO: *This breezy cottage-style bedroom combines neutral colors, porch wicker, and woods with luxurious vintage bed linens.*

Your home's spaces may be finite and limited, but your imagination isn't. Open your mind to unexpected guest sleeping spots.

SHOP FOR SPACE

Take a turn around your home, assessing each room, alcove, closet, and hallway for possibilities. The best candidates for dual purposes are rooms your family may use only occasionally. A home office, a library, a music room, or even a formal dining or living room could be refurbished to lead a double life with multitalented furniture. Unexpected solutions could be a finished attic with a futon sofa, a floor mattress tucked under the eaves, or a closet converted into a snug built-in bunk. Consider turning a four-season porch into an old-fashioned sleeping porch swathed in tropical netting. Or, if your home is a newer vintage, you might have a top-of-the-stairs loft space that would work well.

USING SPACE CREATIVELY

SAVVY STORAGE

Finding storage for guests' paraphernalia may be a challenge if you don't have a full-time guest room. Make use of what you have with these tips:

• *Clean out* a hall closet and add convenient skirt hangers for women.

• *Stow guests' clothes* on an over-the-door hanger or on a decorative Shaker-style peg rack mounted on the wall. Add a corner coat tree.

• *Corral bathroom clutter* on an extra tray table or in a big basket.

• *Stow suitcases* under a guest bed or on a fold-out campstool tucked into a corner or at the foot of the bed, or move them to a laundry room.

• *Provide bins, boxes, or baskets,* sized to fit under a lamp table, coffee table, or bed, for other belongings.

• *Use vertical spaces,* such as bookcases and armoires, for guest linens.

ONE: *In an unusual approach to privacy, romantic railcar-style berths are tucked into a wide hallway adjacent to a painted-to-match bath. It works for adult guests and visiting children, thanks to private lights and curtains.*

TWO: *Pretty in pastels, this kid's room can sleep a pint-size guest in a built-in window seat softened with a custom pad of high-density foam. When adding a window seat, include a hinged lid so you can store linens underneath.*

THREE: *Turn a den into a guest room— or a guest room into a den. This inviting sleigh bed doubles for sleeping and as a spot to lounge with a good book. New open-back shelves add bookish ambience and hold essentials.*

1

2

3

IN A CHILD'S REALM, NO DREAM IS too fantastic. A crumpled quilt can be a mountain range, a rug a jungle river, and a window seat a castle. In this charmer, a hand-painted meadow blooms across the walls, and accents come straight from the garden. Children's rooms need space for learning, exploring, and dreaming. And unlike the forever-young Peter Pan, the endearing rooms in this chapter will grow up with your child.

KIDS'

ROOMS

WHERE DO YOU BEGIN?

Among the most fun spaces to decorate, kids' rooms welcome gutsy colors, playful touches—and maybe a cartoon character or two—so easily. Plan to rework your child's room three times during the growing years: once for the baby-to-toddler transition, once for the early school years, and again for adolescence. As we show in this chapter, with careful planning and wise furniture choices, you can reduce the extent (and cost) of that inevitable redecorating.

When redecorating, let your child help choose colors but resist the temptation to overembellish. Little ones love to pretend, and they need some plain surfaces that give their imaginations room to roam. Children are hard on furniture, so opt for sturdiness over style. In major furniture pieces, avoid themes, and keep backgrounds fairly neutral. Cinderella and Winnie the Pooh may consume your child today, but tomorrow the Little Mermaid and Buzz Lightyear could step in. Satisfy a child's ever-changing passions with easy-to-change sheets and art.

NURSERY BASICS

If you're about to become new parents, planning and decorating the nursery truly brings home the exciting realization a baby is coming. For starters, you'll need:

- **A safe crib.** New cribs meet today's safety standards. Pre-1992 cribs should be in good repair, have slats no more than 2⅜ inches apart, and a drop side that, when lowered, is at least 9 inches above the mattress.
- **Rock-a-bye seating.** A rocking chair or glider with flat arms and an ottoman make feedings comfy. Add a nightlight or dimmer switch to soften the mood.
- **A double-duty changing table.** Look for one with a high top rail and open shelves for diapers now and stuffed animals and books later. Some styles double as dressers to adapt to a growing child's storage needs.

ONE: Passing up obvious baby themes, this lively nursery is perfect for a boy or a girl. It's almost ageless, decorated in bright hues, high-contrast accents, and artful wall borders that the parents-to-be hand-painted in acrylics.
TWO: Awning valances were stitched from a pattern, and custom roller shades were made by ironing fabric onto a fusible shade kit.

PICK A PALETTE

Think of the hours you'll spend in the baby's nursery, and you'll understand why nursery schemes should please you as well as your baby. Nursery decorating is your chance to have some fun—and comfort, too. Plan for adjustable lighting so you can opt for brighter light when changing the baby, and dimmer and more relaxed illumination when nursing. Try to work in a daybed or twin-size bed for yourself, too.

COLORS KIDS LOVE

Although it's true that infants are attracted to bright colors and high-contrast patterns, avoid going overboard. Infants get plenty of stimulation from virtually everything around them; they don't need more from the walls. White or pastel backdrops may be more soothing to a child (and to Mom and Dad), and you can add brighter colors and patterns with accessories.

When picking colors, consider the natural light first. Warm up cool, north-facing rooms (or those with few windows) with sunny hues, and cool down bright south- and west-facing spaces with greens, blues, or purples.

Keep an eye on the future when choosing the room's major design elements and make sure they're easy-care.

BRING IN PATTERN

• ***Dress up walls*** with scrubbable wall coverings in simple prints that aren't too babyish. On painted walls, use decorations you can peel off when your child outgrows them. Avoid a too-busy look; if walls have pattern, keep rugs neutral or a solid color.

• ***Add a motif*** to painted walls at crib height for your baby to see. A graphic wallpaper border, even on just one wall, provides definition and charm.

• ***Pick enduring, classic prints*** such as stripes, checks, and florals for draperies and upholstery. Do the room's accents—duvet covers, pillows, and valances—in playful, easy-to-change prints.

ONE/TWO: *Unsure of your color scheme? Build on a wall covering design. This wallpaper border, glued onto cut-to-fit wood cornices, sets the room's palette. The diamond-shaped fields in the border's background inspired the painted wall. Under one window, pastel wood steps work as a window seat and as a place to stow books—and bears.*

THREE: *Furnishings echo colors from the walls, one painted in a large harlequin pattern and the others clad in subtle mini-diamond wallpaper.*

ONE: Beneath an artist's mural of children at play, this colorful lamp is a clever do-it-yourself accent that's inexpensive to make. It's a round terra-cotta planter converted into a lamp base, then painted and topped with a self-adhesive shade wrapped in gingham. Colorful buttons are hot-glued along the shade fabric's seam. (Learn how easy it is to wire your own lamp on page 374 in the "Lighting" chapter.)

TWO: Adorned with a trompe l'oeil scene of ivy-covered lattice, linen roller shades provide sun control and a garden view. The medium for the yellow lattice is thinned wall paint, and textile paints were used for the greenery. The artist painted a matching pillow, adding the baby's name and birthdate.

add MAGIC WITH PAINT

Children's passions tend to be intense but fleeting, which makes paint an invaluable decorating tool—inexpensive, yet endlessly versatile. Because kids love anything, no matter how small, that makes their rooms look and feel special, use paint to put favorite colors on walls, floors, ceilings, shutters, shades, and furniture.

BRUSH ON PERSONALITY

Better a pretty but plain painted wall than a badly done mural. If you doubt your artistic skill, consider hiring a professional. If you don't mind spending the money, a professional decorative painter can make your child's room extraordinary with murals and special effects. Some decorative paint techniques, such as sponging, stamping, and stenciling, are so easy that even young kids can help. Or, try the following easy projects.

• *Experiment with masking tape* to create your own striped or checked designs. Or, for a fun dotted wall behind a bed or below a chair rail, stick 1-inch pieces of quality painter's masking tape on a white wall—8 to 12 inches apart or at whatever interval suits you. Leave masking tape tails for easy removal of the pieces. Roll on your child's favorite color, then peel off the tape.

• *Make the kids a huge blackboard.* You won't mind your children scribbling on the walls if you paint a wall section with blackboard paint and trim it with molding.

PAINT IT RIGHT

Paint fumes aren't healthy for little ones, so paint the nursery before the baby arrives. The pointers below will help ensure your painting success.

• *Acrylic paints dry faster* and have less odor than oil paints, and they're durable enough for furniture and floors. For example, paint a car racetrack on a floor or place settings on the top of a tea table. Protect with nonyellowing polyurethane.

• *Use gloss or semigloss paint* on walls because either makes a durable, easily cleaned finish.

• *Prepare floors for painting* by cleaning them thoroughly. On vinyl floors, wipe on a liquid deglosser or liquid sander. Cover the surface with a quality-bond primer before painting.

• *Get wood ready* by cleaning, sanding, and priming surfaces. Remove furniture hardware; consider adding colorful new pulls and knobs.

THREE: *What little girl wouldn't love the painted magical meadow above with bright plaid "wainscoting"? This sunny palette has plenty of hues to spin off in accents such as the painted shade and birdhouse.*

FOUR: *Refreshed with green paint, this old flea market shadow box with mirrored back holds a charming display of 1940s ceramics and toys.*

DO-IT-YOURSELF NURSERY

Nothing makes young children prouder than rooms decorated especially for them by Mom and Dad. Seize this chance to be creative. And fear not—even a novice can bring charm to a nursery or add whimsy to a child's room using these simple strategies.

TURN BORING TO BRIGHT

Carved out of a decidedly blah guest room, this nursery combines a high-contrast palette, bold colors, and cottagey white furnishings to buoy its mood. These parents simply installed beaded-board paneling with a hammer and finishing nails, marked off the tops of the walls with masking tape, and painted on the fat yellow stripes. Graphic patterns like this are timeless and work well for boys and girls. The parents avoided mixing patterns and opted for solid-color bedding and pillows. Then they selected accessories that would set the nursery theme. As the baby grows, redecorating will be as easy as substituting a bed for the crib and changing the accessories.

EARN YOUR STRIPES

The nursery walls' circus-tent stripes are easy to make, even for the novice. Pick up the following materials at the paint store: painter's masking tape, made specifically for decorative painting; a carpenter's level; measuring tape; latex wall paint; a pencil; and paintbrushes. Use the following step-by-step guide for this and other painted wall treatments.

• **Plan your design** on paper. If you're not an experienced painter, stick with stripes or simple geometric patterns.

• **Prime walls** with a premium-bond primer. When dry, cover walls with a white latex base coat and let dry thoroughly.

• **Measure and mark** the design on walls with a pencil, using the level to keep lines straight.

• **Carefully mask** along the outside edge of each pencil line with quality painter's masking tape. With your fingers, tightly seal the edge next to the pencil lines to keep paint from bleeding. Leave the other side of the tape free for easy removal.

• **Paint one color at a time** in places where different colors join. Work around the walls, masking off and painting one section at a time.

• **After the color's on,** gently remove the masking tape while the paint's still wet. Be careful not to smear fresh paint as you pull up the tape.

ONE: *Thanks to all the crisp white in this guest-room-turned-nursery, eye-catching colors sparkle as if through a prism. Old furniture blends with new under coats of fresh paint.*

TWO: *Using a sewing pattern, the owner had the crib outfitted with linens and bumper pads made from a bouquet of solid-color sheets.*

THREE: *For instant charm, walls are covered three-quarters of the way up with 4x8-foot sheets of beaded-board-style paneling. For more quick architecture, there's a high treasure shelf.*

FOUR: *Easy-on-the-budget enamel and acrylic paints transformed this mail-order mirror and Shaker-look dresser. The mirror frame is a patchwork of the room's hues painted on with the aid of masking tape.*

FIVE: *This spirited scheme started with a favorite kaleidoscope-colored quilt tossed over the rocker.*

ONE: Consider a vintage trundle bed when you need to make the most of space in a modern-day room for two. Here custom-made Roman shades, wall hangings, the wall border, flooring, and bedcovers carry out a patchwork theme.

TWO: Striking fabrics that don't show roughhouse dirt set off the white laminate bunk beds and storage in this boys' room.

Inexpensive framed posters carry out the linens' color scheme.

THREE: Sisters share this unusually sunny attic bedroom that's transformed into a flowery bower. Luxuriously layered linens and matching fluffy comforters dress the beds. Twin beds are a great separate-but-equal solution for shared space and also work well for one because there's always room for a friend.

ROOM FOR TWO

Children often want to share a room with a sibling. It works best if the children are as close in age as possible and of the same sex. Don't put a toddler with a child more than a year or two older because you'll spend your days picking up Lego pieces, marbles, or other tiny toys that could find their way into the little one's mouth. Even if you have twins, carve out a separate area in the room for each child. Give them a common playing and sleeping area, if they wish, but use furniture, a screen, a bookcase, or even a hanging curtain to divide the room into separate territories. At the very least, give the youngsters something that locks for stowing treasures—a box or chest, closet, or drawer of their own.

DOUBLE-UP STYLE

In designing shared space, let each child pick colors or patterns to identify individual areas and possessions. It's a self-esteem booster. When buying beds, follow these guidelines:

• *For two sleepers,* choose twin, trundle, or bunk beds. To avoid the inevitable disagreements over who gets to sleep in the coveted top bunk, set up a monthly or weekly schedule and let the children switch off; children younger than 6 years are too young to sleep on top.

• *Check safety features* on metal beds. The American Society of Testing Materials makes the following recommendations. Top and bottom bunk bed posts should fasten securely together or have a 1¼-inch lift for separation. A wedge—a rigid block used for testing—should not be able to slide down between the mattress and the foundation. Side rails should be bolted on or difficult to remove. Guard rails should be difficult to remove or require a fastening device for release.

• *Look at ladders* to make sure they're sturdy. Steps should be 10 inches wide and have a 12-inch vertical space between each step.

CHOOSE FURNISHINGS THAT WILL ENDURE

Buying new furniture and redecorating every year aren't options for most families, so children's furniture should be sturdy, functional, and flexible enough to grow with the child. Antique pieces work as well as new unpainted furniture. With paint and pretty cushions, that old daybed in the attic can become a delightful sleeper.

DESIGN TOGETHER

If your daughter wants a purple room, offer a compromise; paint one wall purple, the rest white, and maybe the ceiling a pale lavender. Once they're preschool age, give kids several choices in wall coverings, paints, and fabrics. Parents should retain veto power over the final selections.

PRESCHOOL PARADISE

For this age, buy furniture you can wipe clean—laminates, plastics, and painted surfaces are ideal. Balloon and tailored Roman shades, valances, cafe curtains, and shutters are better than full-length draperies. Cord pulls on miniblinds are dangerous for young children, so cut them short or clip them up high with a clothespin or blind clip. Low-pile carpeting, woven rugs, and wood floors let puzzles lie flat and toy trains run smoothly.

TEEN TERRITORY

Eager to establish their own identities, teens want to personalize their rooms, so give them space. If you paint walls instead of using expensive wall covering, you won't cringe when they tack up posters. Dress up cork boards with crisscrossed ribbons or fabric coverings for displaying mementos. For entertaining friends, add floor seating with oversize pillows, and if there's room, scoot in a futon sofa or flip chair. Slipcovers make easy-care cover-ups.

ONE: *This room's young owner might delete a few stuffed animals when she reaches her teens, but the medley of country-fresh fabrics and classic furnishings will please her for years to come. A pair of French country prints and a wallpaper border combine to create a wainscoting effect. Drapery colors are picked up in the linens on the quaint wood bed, a new piece that fits right in with the secondhand painted chest at bedside and the corner rocking chair.*

TWO: *A painted sleigh bed, with storage to match, lends character to this boy's room, yet it will never date. The snappy striped bed linens are carefree because the comforter fabric has a stain-resistant finish. The oversize bulletin board behind the bed has plenty of space for displaying favorite posters and award-winning ribbons.*

THREE: *Reupholstered in crisp checked fabric, an old daybed becomes the star of this romantic room. Endearing accents and the hand-painted motifs on the chest and wall mural are tied to the garden and woods outside.*

MAKE THE MOST OF SPACE

It isn't the square footage itself but how you use the space that spells success in decorating kids' rooms. With double-duty furnishings, such as beds with drawers beneath them and wall storage units with pull-down desks, even the smallest spaces can play, study, sleep, and grow. Add some visual tricks, such as vertical shelf units to "raise" the ceiling, and small rooms can feel larger, too.

MAKE STORAGE ACCESSIBLE

Children of any age are more likely to put things away when they know where everything goes and can reach it.

• *Redo closets* because they're usually not designed for short folks. Lower rods for hanging clothes when kids are small; they always can be raised later. Or, buy custom-height rods. Consider do-it-yourself closet organizers with lots of pullout bins and cubbyholes for kid stuff. Add peg racks for everything from baseball caps to necklaces.

• *Add stow-away options* such as open shelves on the wall and bright-colored plastic stacking bins and baskets for sports equipment and doll accessories. For young children, copy the open storage units of nursery schools so toys and books are easy to see and reach. Buy dressers with shallow drawers to keep things from getting lost at the bottom; drawers should have stoppers so they can't be accidentally pulled all the way out.

• *Allow room for* crafts, homework, and the computer. Fit a triangular desk into a tight corner. Or, skirt an old table as a little girl's vanity today and uncover it later on for a big girl's computer station. Make sure there's enough task lighting by the bed and desk.

ONE: *Washed in soft neutral tones and set with nostalgic furnishings, this storybook bedroom effectively uses space under the roof. The angled ceiling holds the canopy.*
TWO: *New skylights and built-in shelves create a sleeping alcove under the pitched roof; shelves keep books and toys handy at bedside.*
THREE: *By building in a cozy bed next to the windows and adding storage below, this small bedroom lives bigger than it looks.*

HOME

EVERYONE WORKS, MANAGING busy families, home businesses, or both. But it's putting the "home" in home office that makes going to work a pleasure. Dressed in beachy textures and quilts, the homey headquarters here serves clients by day and family dinners by night. With similar ease, all of this chapter's home offices make stylish power plays with nary a metal file cabinet in sight.

OFFICES

WHAT'S YOUR WORK STYLE?
WARM AND HOMEY

The advantage of a home office is exactly that: It's at home. There's no commuting—and no dress code, either. If you like working in bare feet with classical music in the background, go ahead. Your home office should be as personal as your home (To check your decorating attitude, refer to the quiz on pages 26–29.) Your space doesn't have to feel like a conventional office; it just has to work like one. To pick the right space for your home office, make a list of how you plan to use it.

• *Is it strictly for business?* Is it a research library, hobby room, or multipurpose hobby and home management center? Can it be devoted to desk work or will it house occasional overnight guests?

• *Is privacy important?* Should it be within earshot of family activities? Will other family members use it? You'll need more privacy and, perhaps, a separate entrance if client meetings are on your agenda.

• *What will you store?* Do you need space for research materials, a computer, or craft items?

MAKE IT PERSONAL—AND FUNCTIONAL

It's your home, so relax and make your office as inspiring as this writer did. White walls, taupe carpet, and a new white desk create a gallerylike backdrop for a comforting array of nostalgia. The neutral palette indulges this collector's whims, accepting whatever she feels like displaying—flea market finds, kids' art, and family photos. To save space in a small office like this one, adapt the following ideas.

• *Arrange your work area in an efficient L or U shape* to keep essentials handy.

• *Use homey, multipurpose storage pieces,* such as stacked fabric-covered boxes, wicker baskets, old trunks, or lidded benches that can double as tables and seating, and tall antique cabinets that stow supplies and books in a sliver of vertical space.

ONE: *Beneath a sunny window, a favorite photo joins rustic and refined treasures on the top shelf of the wall-to-wall storage. For cohesiveness without clutter, the objects have white tones in common.*

TWO: *Down-home style meets high-tech efficiency in this work space that combines laminated modular units into an L-shaped computer station and desk. New floral cushions update old wicker seating.*

2

WHAT'S YOUR WORK STYLE? STREAMLINED

Just as it takes discipline to stick to your tasks and meet deadlines, it requires planning to design a home office that truly helps you succeed.

PLAN FOR PRIVACY

If your office works full time, locate it in a separate room—in a spare bedroom, a remodeled garage, a den, or a basement. If your office is out of the mainstream and has a door, you can leave paperwork and projects spread out and undisturbed by passing neatniks. You'll need a quiet spot for placing and receiving phone calls. If you'll be hosting client meetings, a space with its own entrance or one near an outside door offers the most professional environment.

ONE: Memories of her mother's garden inspired this interior designer to invite the outdoors into her office with verdant walls and carpet. Beautiful and practical, the antique screen hides bolts of fabric, and the deep-doored built-ins organize a library of product-sample books.

TWO: For meetings and projects, a generous glass-topped work surface is close to the natural light that filters through plantation shutters.

THREE: Mixing business with pleasure, cabinets stow office gear and display collectibles. A gilt mirror visually expands space.

ARRANGE FURNISHINGS CLEVERLY

In this home office in a converted bedroom, an interior designer customized storage to keep the tools of her trade organized and accessible. Cabinetry holds samples and catalogs. When work's over, it's easy to clear the decks and the clutter. Use the following tips to tailor built-ins or modular storage systems to your needs and space.

• *Use tall storage units* to make the most of space. For an expansive look, do not enclose all the shelves with doors. Highlight open shelves with low-cost plug-in strip lights made for shelves or with small halogen spotlights.

• *Consider an angled desk,* as shown here, to provide a more generous work area and to visually widen a narrow room with its long, diagonal line.

TUCK IN A WORK SPOT

Away from the bustle of the household, a comfortable bedroom workplace may be all you need for part-time homework, household bookkeeping, or leisurely correspondence. In this most private of settings, you can adopt your own comfy, robe-and-slippers dress code, and replace the white-noise hum of the corporate world with the chirping of birds just outside the window.

SLIDE A DESK INTO ALMOST ANY BEDROOM

• *Use a snippet of space.* Slide a simple writing table into a corner, beneath a window, or at the foot or side of the bed to give you a part-time office area.

• *Look beyond traditional desks* when shopping. A slim sofa table placed at the foot of the bed can make a wonderful writing spot, and an antique farm table in place of the usual nightstand can turn bedside space into a functional after-hours workplace. Depending on your storage needs, you can even claim a closet for desk space or add a wall of modular bookcases, including an efficient flip-down desk.

BEAUTIFY BEDROOM WORK SPOTS

• *Brighten a desk* with blooms in a tiny vase and a gathering of framed family photos.

• *Cover reference books,* such as the phone book and dictionary, with colorful fabrics or leftover wallpaper.

• *Use pretty containers for workaday items—* flea market bowls for stamps and wood or fabric-covered boxes for stationery.

ONE: *An old table and an armoire add efficiency to a small slice of guest room space. A nearby electrical outlet and telephone jack will accommodate a laptop computer.*

TWO: *Snuggled into a corner, this antique drop-lid desk has a strong work ethic; it moonlights as a family photo gallery.*

THREE: *In this countrified bedroom, the desk's job description includes bill-paying, correspondence, and serving as a nightstand. The blanket chest warmly stores paperwork.*

BUILT-IN STYLE

Not everyone wants an office that screams "Office"—especially if the home workplace is seen from a public living room or entry. Handsome built-ins can offer efficiency and architectural presence. Extending from wall to wall and from floor to ceiling, built-ins house everything from books and files to the computer and TV. By stowing office gear along one wall, built-ins also free up floor space for other uses—a work-and-dining table, as in the two offices shown here, a grouping of sectional seating, or an inviting lounge chair and floor lamp.

WIRING BUILT-INS

• *Plan enough phone lines* and grounded electrical outlets for computers and other office equipment you'll be using.

• *Illuminate shelves* with lights or under-counter halogen lights made for kitchens.

OFFICE BY DAY, DEN BY NIGHT

Home offices move gracefully from day-time to nighttime duties when you team built-ins with anything-but-corporate furnishings. In decidedly homey style, graceful round tables, instead of massive, hard-edged desks, can double as quiet spots for after-work cocktails or dinner for two. Flexible window treatments and lighting also bridge the gap between day and night. Shutters and miniblinds, perhaps softened with fabric curtains, modulate natural light to control glare on work surfaces and add beauty and privacy when the sun goes down. Finally, remember to supplement desk lamps with decorative accent lights and other general lighting, such as recessed can lights and track lights on dimmers.

ONE: *This wall does everything but the work itself. The desk, files, reference library, electronics, and refreshment bar are in one custom-built unit. The table doubles for client conferences as well as for entertainment.*
TWO: *An oasis of quiet and calm just off a busy kitchen, this streamlined study has a user-friendly storage wall, a mix of minimalist furnishings, and access to a deck for fresh-air work breaks. An Oriental rug defines the desk area, and plantation shutters adjust to fit lighting needs.*

2

MOVABLE STYLE

One way to be sure your office keeps pace with the changing business environment is to opt for flexible furnishings. You can rearrange freestanding desks, bookcases, and the like as needed, plus they're ideal if you move often or if yours is a part-time work space that may be here today and in the spare bedroom tomorrow. In response to the work-at-home trend, furniture manufacturers offer modulars in every style from country to traditional, so you can find a set to fit your home's decor. Also check into dining and bedroom pieces that are adaptable.

CRUNCH THE NUMBERS

Measure your planned office space before you shop for furnishings and equipment.

• *Standard desks* are 30 inches high; computer and typewriter stands are usually about 26 inches high. Look for pieces with adjustable work surfaces and legs.

ONE: *Perfect for the living room, today's new armoire offices are prewired for electronics. Open the office and unfold the drop-down work surface during the day, then close it all up when company comes.*

TWO: *Assemble-yourself modulars store a multitude of materials in a 10×10-foot office. A tall fabric-clad screen balances the visual weight of the black storage pieces.*

• *File cabinets* come with 15×29-inch letter-size drawers or legal-size drawers that are 3 inches wider. Hanging-file and specialized drawer inserts convert ordinary chests into officeware.

• *Computers fit* into ever-smaller spaces. One popular model has an $11\frac{1}{2} \times 12\frac{1}{2}$-inch keyboard and $9 \times 9\frac{1}{2}$-inch monitor. Always add an electrical surge protector.

• *Prebuilt shelves* allow you to customize vertically; open-shelf sizes begin at about 18×30 inches with depths starting at 12 or 13 inches.

• *Closet organizer systems* include freestanding units with wood finishes for storage.

• *Modular storage pieces* come in a range of dimensions, from stackable cubes to shelf units you customize with optional drop lids, shelves, doors, and drawers.

MAKING IT PERSONAL

Designing your home office is like writing a personal essay with color, furniture, and accents. Sure, you'll have the requisite machines—computer, fax, printer, and phone. But to temper that technology and make your space really user-friendly, add textures, art, sentimental collections, and even antique furniture. Because this is, after all, your home, you may find that the most personal touch of all is coziness. The nook-and-cranny offices shown here wrap their users in homey warmth.

• *Add a view.* It's soothing to look out over the backyard flower garden or the woods when you're pondering ideas or taking a break. If a window isn't close by, create your own view with a favorite painting or other wall art.

• *Bring in a vintage crew* of antiques or secondhand pieces to give your place a shot of character and comfort. A computer works just as well resting on a Queen Anne desk or English armoire shelf. Dress up that Arts and Crafts-style swivel chair with new fabric cushions. An old drop-leaf table is a handy way to extend work space.

• *Display your best-loved* art, photos, and collectibles on shelves, walls, and, if there's room, on the desktop. Accent seating and windows with colorful fabrics. Use Oriental and other rugs to warm and define your space; add a friendly lineup of plants to the sill.

• *Use color* to forge visual links. Choose hues for office walls and other design elements that fit with your home's palette. Walking into your office shouldn't jar the senses, so repeat or blend paints used throughout the interior.

ONE: *An old table and roomy wicker chair comprise this work area highlighted with library shelves and an inspiring view of rolling hills.*

TWO: *Pulled up to elegantly draped windows, an antique desk and chairs infuse this French-style bedroom with new focus and function. A footstool hides books beneath the desk.*

THREE: *In an out-of-the-way corner, this office warms up with wall art that adds a view where there isn't one. Instead of the conventional drawers, the built-in desk's stacked cubbyholes fill the storage bill and create openness.*

FOUR: *A salvaged slab of granite makes a sleek, durable surface for this workstation. There's a gap at the back for power cords.*

FIVE: *This wall organizer offers storage, a fail-safe filing system, and shelves for books and collectibles. Its two-toned color scheme fits the room's airy palette. Unseen from this vantage point, tiny letters of the alphabet label each of the small drawers: Check "S" for scissors.*

SPECIAL

RELAX
A FORMAL ENTRY

ONE: *Nothing fussy here. A fern-painted canvas floor cloth joins a tangle of weeds on the door and a family of rosemary topiaries in clay pots to welcome visitors in casual style.*

TWO: *By showcasing friendly prints and walking sticks, this entry gives a warm introduction to the family's interests and personal style. Casually arranged flowers underscore the informality.*

First impressions are formed in seconds. For the home with a formal entry, this means the opinion on how the entire home looks and feels hinges upon this opening. Unfair? Only if the entry doesn't reflect the style to follow. If the rest of your home is friendly and informal, why create a false impression by sticking to formal definitions? Creative attention to the floors, walls, and furnishings can take the starch out of an entry that's too stiff for your tastes and can be the first indication that your home is special.

WRITING THE PRELUDE

Here's how to turn a bland entry into a welcoming space that truly reflects your approach to life and style.

• *Introduce yourself.* If art, collections, or plants are part of your home's charm, say that early with paintings, wall-hung or table displays, or plant stands.

• *Add inventive lighting.* A crystal chandelier is the old standby for a formal entry, but if shimmery glamour doesn't fit your home, make a different statement. Focus spotlights or pinpoint lights on a favorite painting or tabletop grouping. Stack sconces on top of each other to dramatize a corner. Direct floor-based lights up on a plant to cast dappled shadows.

• *Give the entry definition.* Even if you have wall-to-wall carpeting, add an area rug reflecting your home's style: a kilim or rag rug for an informal or contemporary home, an Oriental or needlepoint rug for traditional style. For safety, secure the rug with a no-slip liner or double-sided tape.

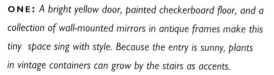

ONE: A bright yellow door, painted checkerboard floor, and a collection of wall-mounted mirrors in antique frames make this tiny space sing with style. Because the entry is sunny, plants in vintage containers can grow by the stairs as accents.

TWO: More than a looking glass, this shuttered mirror mimics a window and expands the small entry. An old bench, wall border, and pegboard display introduce a country collector's passions.

PERSONALIZE
A SMALL ENTRY

THREE: *Woody texture and rich green paint wrap this little greeting space in warmth. The graceful, elegant shapes of an artfully composed table, chair, and lamp heighten the style.*

FOUR: *Square footage is at a premium today, meaning many homes have no official entries. This gardenlike entry was created by putting a tall lattice screen right beside the front door.*

Don't let their pint size fool you: No rule says small entries must be plain vanilla spaces. With a few warming touches, even the smallest entry can make a big impact and set the mood for the whole house that follows. Transformed from a mere point of entry to a mini world all its own, this special space will provide the pleasure of discovery for you and your guests.

ART AND COLOR

A diminutive entry may not be able to hold much. But without cramming it full of objects, you can warm it with a few carefully chosen pieces that are either functional, decorative, or, preferably, both.

• ***Paint on panache.*** One of the easiest and least expensive options for changing the scene is paint. Turn a tiny entry floor into a just-right canvas for hand-painted artwork. For example, cover the whole floor with stenciled checkerboard for impact. Consider the front door as a design element and paint it in one bright hue. Saturate walls with rich color or paint just the portion beneath a chair rail or on a staircase. Most wall covering prints are too busy for dressing a small entry head to toe, so try only a wallpaper border at the ceiling, midwall, or floor line.

• ***Let walls add gusto.*** Vertical surfaces can visually enlarge space. Hang mirrors with different frames and intriguing textures; refinish flea market picture frames or paint them cottage white or folk art bright and add mirrors. A wall-hung shelf or pegboard can hold personal collectibles.

• ***Make an entrance.*** If your door opens right into your living room, create a mini wall with a floor screen, fabric panel, or even a tall bookcase placed perpendicular to the wall. Add comfort with a small table or chair that won't impinge on space.

SLOW THE PACE IN HALLWAYS

Anyone who thinks hallways should function as elevator music—in the background and hardly noticeable—is missing a major design opportunity. Even the smallest home has some kind of hallway to connect its rooms. And why not spend a little time and effort to turn those ho-hum passageways into places worth a second—or third—look?

MAKING CONNECTIONS

The most common solution remains one of the best: Decorate the walls of hallways in gallery fashion. Without taking up square footage, this makes passage a visual treat.

• *Start with art.* If you don't have a collection of art or prints, gather current or ancestral family photos for a wall-hung display; frame old sheet music, hobby or sports mementos, textiles, or other collectibles for wall art. For uniformity, keep framing treatments similar in style—no sleek contemporary frames of pickled wood beside ornate carved and gilded ones.

• *Make it work.* When the hallway offers ample elbow room, consider subtracting a foot or more from its width for floor-to-ceiling shelves, either built-in or freestanding. Add shelves at the short end where a hallway terminates. Take advantage of an extra-wide or jogged hallway by adding shelves or a seating piece. Turn a wide stairway landing into a mini retreat with a window seat and reading light. Since hallways are transition spaces between living areas, group two chairs and a small table for a conversation and afternoon tea spot.

• *Set up shop.* Dead-end hallways that are not through routes are prime spots for well-organized home offices and computer work stations. If there isn't a window, you can build in desk and storage space floor to ceiling. If you want to preserve light from the window, consider a variety of modular pieces that will allow you to customize and organize even the smallest spaces.

ONE: *A wide passageway was transformed into a library with the addition of sleek built-in bookcases that would be equally at home in the family or living rooms. Antique sconces illuminate the passageway, and the colorful volumes and nautical art reflect the home's seashore setting.*

TWO: *A plain and simple farmhouse entry hall opens wide in an oversize space that easily could have been wasted. Tucked between the entry and living room, the corner becomes a practical, handsome reading nook.*

CREATE AN ATTIC HIDEAWAY

Instead of adding a new room onto your home, look up. Transforming existing vertical space—specifically, an old-house attic or a new-house bonus room above a garage—into living space makes economic sense. The storybook charm of a treetop hideout and quirky ceiling slopes is romantic reason enough. With these tips, attics make idyllic playrooms, children's bedrooms, adult sitting rooms, or master suites.

• *Brighten with skylights.* Without tampering with your home's roofline, skylights increase natural light. Consider energy-saving glass, and control light with miniblinds or pleated shades.

• *Streamline furniture.* Just like a ship's cabin with stow-away built-ins, line walls with cabinetry instead of chests and bookcases. Tuck low-slung seating and shorter chests under the eaves, too.

• *Contour your space.* Visually shorten and square up the typical long, narrow attic with a fireplace or a simple built-in bookcase across one end. Widen the space with rugs and diagonal furniture groupings. Raise the ceiling with vertically striped wall coverings.

ONE: *It needn't take much to turn a dark attic into a bright treetop retreat. Here new operable roof windows admit light and air, and a clean-lined gas fireplace steps in to square up the tunnel-shaped space. Old collar ties look like beams when clad in cedar planks.*

TWO: *Under-the-eaves space is used efficiently with angled bedside shelves that follow the contour of the ceiling. As the ceiling height rises, taller furnishings—the bed, chests, mirror, and lights—edge out into the room. Instead of following the rule of using light colors in a small room, this sleep spot boasts dark blue walls that suggest the infinity of the night sky.*

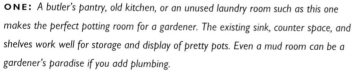

ONE: A butler's pantry, old kitchen, or an unused laundry room such as this one makes the perfect potting room for a gardener. The existing sink, counter space, and shelves work well for storage and display of pretty pots. Even a mud room can be a gardener's paradise if you add plumbing.

TWO: Think outside the box—or the house—when seeking hobby space. A backyard shed makes an ideal, if surprising, warm weather sewing center. A large worktable angles into the corner, an old clothes-drying rack holds hanging fabrics and pattern pieces, and chairs welcome guests.

FIND ROOM FOR HOBBIES

Short of adding on a room, how can you find space for hobbies? Few homes, except big-budget custom designs, have the square footage to dedicate one or more rooms to off-hours pleasures. Yet, hobbyists from gardeners to artists, stitchers to modelmakers want nothing more. Here's where a home's misfit places—a laundry, basement dead space, or even a big closet—can save the day.

DESIGN CRAFTY SPACES

Not every space will work for every hobby. Only you know the demands of your favorite pastime, so analyze your needs before designing your space.

• *Steal space.* Maybe you don't have a laundry or utility room waiting to do double duty. If not, look to a main room—even a living or family room—for a corner that can cater to your passion. In picking a space, consider: How messy is your activity? Will it be a maintenance nightmare on a polished wood floor? Will clutter quickly stow away, or do you need to conceal the hobby corner with a folding screen? Is quiet important? If creative writing is your avocation, find an out-of-the-way space with a door, even if that means refitting a guest room closet with a desk.

• *Choose hardworking furnishings* that will play along with your leisure pursuits. How important is storage? What kind do you need—deep drawers for bulky items, wide flat drawers for artwork? Whether it's open or closed storage depends on how much paraphernalia you want to keep out of sight. For workspace, will a portable folding table suffice or do you need to leave projects spread out? Will you need special task lighting for sewing and tying fishing flies or the natural light from windows for oil painting?

THREE: *When a built-in closet was customized, this family room turned into a spot for sewing and gift wrapping. The machine area gets plenty of light from windows and under-shelf task lighting, and doors close off the clutter when company comes.*

FOUR: *This laundry room does double duty and serves the gardening enthusiast, too. Hard surface flooring, laminate countertops, and a sink make it a no-fuss space for potting and watering plants.*

T

he corner beneath the eaves, the tiny top-of-the-stairs wall space or landing, or that odd good-for-nothing cranny may be just the space you've been looking for. Small in size, these little leftovers can add up to big home improvements when you put them to work one by one. To do your own space exploration, tour your home as if for the first time. Look for blank walls, dead-end nooks, or little junk rooms or pantries with doors that are always closed, then recast them for storage, sitting, or displaying your favorite things.

USE LEFTOVER SPACES

ONE: *Corners, especially ones with low-flying angled ceilings, make especially snug getaways. This one adds a chair and ottoman for reading and keeps the mood light with mushroom walls and upholstery. Hurricane lamp sconces don't intrude but brighten the space.*

TWO: *A high-traffic mud room gets a visual lift with a bright area rug and shelves that weave it into the home's fresh country style. Brackets fancy up the shelves, and there's a painted table for arranging garden flowers.*

4

5

THREE: This antique Hoosier cabinet makes practical use of a sliver of space between wall and window. Top to bottom, it's an efficiency expert's dream with open and closed storage for dishware and linens. Its counter pulls out just under the windowsill, making space for serving refreshments and buffets.

FOUR: The owner of this home turned top-of-the-stairs wall space and a ledge into a showplace for a poster and vignette of baskets, giving guests in the entry below something to look up to.

FIVE: A passageway becomes more than a means to an end in this old-world home. By design and function, it's a walk in the garden with faux ivy stenciled on the walls and a real garden for blooming pleasure. A mirror on one wall expands the narrow space by reflecting light.

KITCHENS

AT THE HEART OF EVERY HOME IS THE kitchen. Be it galley or open, today's kitchens are truly "living" rooms, hubs for family gatherings, homework, entertaining, and, of course, cooking and dining. Necessities aside, your kitchen's personality is up to you. How about a kitchen where everything stays perfectly in place? Then brush on fool-the-eye art like the garden items here. Whether it's a big-scale remodeling or a weekend facelift on your kitchen plate, this chapter has lots of ideas.

ADD A DASH OF COLOR

When it comes to choosing cabinetry and appliances, classic white is the universal favorite and, in many kitchens, the best choice. It's as popular as ice cream and as easy to work with as pasta. White sets a timeless mood, provides a solid-color backdrop to showcase other hues, and visually expands space—something many kitchens lack. However, too much white can be glaring, clinical, and boring, so fix that by adding color to the menu.

THE RIGHT WHITE

All white cabinetry isn't alike. Some whites have undertones of blue, pink, yellow, gray, or brown. Lighting and surface materials can make the same tints look different. Take home paint chips in different tones to see how light changes the look through the day.

WHITE PLUS WHAT?

When white is predominant, the rest can be varied as your lifestyle and tastes change. Colorful paints, wall coverings, fabrics, artwork, and accessories make kitchens friendlier, more inviting, and more comfortable.

- *Painted furniture,* stenciled wall borders, and faux wall finishes help personalize a white kitchen.
- *Solid colors*—say, a sky blue ceiling or delicious peach-hued walls—add contrast. Consider natural and artificial light in making color choices.
- *Visual texture* in fabrics and wall coverings can warm up white and cue easy-to-coordinate color schemes.

ONE: *This vintage kitchen's old-fashioned cabinetry sports design details in a fresh green hue. Cabinet doors are stenciled in a one-color motif, and the same green is repeated in the diamond-shaped tile of the backsplash and miniprint wall covering.*

THREE: *Picking up blue accents from a new granite countertop, the designer generously and dramatically splashed the color around this French country kitchen. Walls are covered with subtly textured wallpaper, and painted counter chairs have floor-length slipcovers for an upholstered look.*

2

3

TWO: *Accent colors don't have to be bold to make an effective foil for the everlasting whites. Earthy sage green paint on the backdrop, natural pine window trim, and checkerboard flooring in a muted green and white add up to a space-expanding solution for this compact, but comfortable, kitchen.*

CABINET COLOR

Lobster bisque, limesicle, pineapple fluff, salmon mousse, banana split. Who could resist brushing color over kitchen cabinets with paint names like these? If you'd rather buy cabinetry with color than create it, your choices range from basics to luxury custom lines.

READY-MADE OPTIONS

Look at custom cabinetry for the widest range of finishes—solids, two-toned or antiqued, lightly glazed pastels and naturals, and opaque color over wood grains. Colors can be dramatic and range from barn red and black to glazed mint and green over red-brown. Wood and wood veneers come in colors, too, from peach or blue to pickled white.

DIP INTO PAINTS

• **Expand small spaces** with paints in lighter colors. In large kitchens, conjure coziness and intimacy with darker hues.

• **Create special effects** on cabinetry with sponged, rag-rolled, antiqued, or crackled finishes. Prepackaged kits are available.

• **Choose durable paints** such as alkyd or latex enamel for kitchen surfaces. It's easy to wipe up the inevitable spills and spatters.

• **Update wood cabinets** with semitransparent stains in an array of colors or with pale pickled finishes to lighten the look and mood.

ONE: *Walls and accents in Chinese red and cabinetry finished in black lacquer transform this kitchen into a high-energy space.*

TWO: *In this freshly painted old kitchen, white trim sets off the cabinets' glossy blue doors. A beaded board backsplash is a nostalgic touch.*

THREE: *Vivid hues highlight the natural woodwork in this kitchen and help set its Scandinavian style.*

PUT ON A HAPPY FACE

Your dream kitchen may not be an impossible dream after all. This sunny updated space is just the inspiration you need. It once had orange countertops, dark cabinets, dim lighting, and stingy windows. The handy homeowners pitched in on most of the work, consulted pros when necessary, and did it all on a limited budget.

LET'S DO A MAKEOVER

The crew subtracted half-walls by the eating area, worn parquet flooring, and some of the countertops. Cabinets shifted to squeeze in two garden windows. Take a look at some of their other slick moves:

• *New sunny yellow backdrops* include painted beaded paneling on walls and the grid-pattern ceiling with molding trim. The floor is a pinelike laminate.

• *Stained plaid cabinetry* was stripped and sanded, then a one-step stain-and-finish product—in light, medium, and dark hues—was brushed on to create the plaid effect on the doors; cabinet frames were stained white. With doors lying flat, 3-inch squares were taped off, and colors were applied one at a time and allowed to dry. New countertops are laminate, and new backsplashes are tile.

• *Built-in display shelves* and a window seat were added to create a focal point for the eating area. The homeowners painted an unfinished table and chairs, then made cushions and window valances to unify the working and eating areas. Recessed lighting and the new window visually expand the long, narrow space.

ONE: *With fewer cabinets, this updated kitchen has room for two deep garden windows that transformed the space with sunlight to highlight the fresh yellow walls. Cabinetry doors were redone with a three-stain plaid finish, and the work core sports new hardware, lighting, and countertops.*

TWO: *The same white laminate that was used for the cabinet countertops covers the new island that corrals food preparation, the cooktop, and the microwave. It*

2

3

offers open-basket storage on one end and has an overhang to accommodate stool seating at the handy snack counter.

THREE: Diners at the painted table and chairs have a view of new built-ins—packed with favorite collectibles and dishware—that frame one of the garden windows. Casual fabrics in stripes and an oversize plaid show up as valances, accent pillows, and cushions for chairs and the window seat.

SOFTEN WITH FABRICS

In an empty kitchen, sound bounces off bare walls, and appliances take on a hard-edged look. Fabrics, however, can absorb the sounds and soften the architecture. They also infuse a space with color, pattern, and texture while boosting the overall mood.

TRY A LITTLE SOFTWARE

Crisp curtains, charming valances, seat cushions, rugs, and other fabric accents may be the style statement your kitchen needs. With coordinated collections of wall coverings and fabrics, it's easy to create your own designer kitchen. If you're creating your own mix, almost any type of window treatment works as long as it's cleanable. For fun, stencil a valance or stitch one from vintage dish towels or tablecloths for a retro 1940s look. Choose patterned fabrics—botanicals, foods, florals, or country prints—with textures and motifs that nicely gather or drape, or gently pleat. Upholstered furniture absorbs sound and adds comfort.

STITCH A SINK SKIRT

To make a two-section sink skirt like the one in the kitchen, *opposite*, cut fabric into two equal portions, twice the width of your opening, to gather onto a tension rod as you would curtains. Sew a top rod pocket into each section; hem fabric with iron-on tape. Spray with a fabric finish.

ONE: *A bucket of paint, 2 yards of fabric, and a roll of wallpaper turned a series of brown doors into a kitchen worth savoring. After they had the cabinets painted white and outlined with crisp blue stripes, the homeowners punctuated them with blue hardware and added a plate-print fabric skirt to hide old plumbing and break up the wood. For continuity, the fabric repeats in the tailored valance.*

TWO: *A trompe l'oeil wall border of painted-on collectibles and scalloped valances trimmed in rows of succulent cherries unify this kitchen that once seemed segmented by appliances. Fabric echoes the soft pastels of antique plates displayed on the walls.*

A freestanding island in the middle of a kitchen isn't a new idea. However, if you're looking for something out of the ordinary or downright spectacular, consider an antique twist.

BEYOND THE BOX

The standard square kitchen island is functional, but a piece of furniture can be just as hardworking and offers immense charm and character. For example, a handsome oak table placed in the center of the room handles food preparation, buffet service, and informal dining—all with warm style.

• *Tables to turn* into kitchen work surfaces include old rectangular farm tables, drop-leaf tables that work efficiently in small spaces, and any sturdy period table that fits the style of the

A LET YOUR ANTIQUES TAKE CENTER STAGE

rest of your home. Even a chunky old sideboard can be customized for use as an island. Before integrating an antique piece, make sure it can withstand the rigors of daily use and that its height is right for dining, chopping, and other kitchen chores.

• *Age a standard island* with vintage-look hardware and crown moldings to make the piece look more like furniture than standard cabinetry. One advantage of making islands out of today's cabinetry is you can customize them to your height and add special features such as eating counters, stepped levels, and inset cutting boards.

• *Design an island* so that it works efficiently for your kitchen. A ready-made butcher's block on legs makes it easier for two cooks to work in a small kitchen. U-shaped and L-shaped kitchens benefit greatly from islands that direct traffic and shorten distances between work centers.

ONE: The star of this French country kitchen is an old marble-topped table with a curlicued metal base. The table extends the work surface and serves up buffets. The gathered sink skirt and Roman shade are made from peach toile.

TWO: This mix-and-match table and chairs work comfortably for dining, but if the cook needs more space to prepare food, the English antique table can scoot even closer to the cabinetry. The table also fits the mood of this 1800s-style kitchen.

THREE: Collectors made this 19th-century Canadian cabinet the showpiece of their kitchen. Clad in red and green paint, it's inherently functional with a wide top, deep side drawers, and open display niches at the bottom for a bevy of baskets.

TILE IN STYLE

One no-fail ingredient of kitchen decorating is tile. There's an array of shapes, sizes, finishes, and colors you can mix and match for a backsplash masterpiece. Shop tile showrooms to examine different types: glazed and unglazed, matte and glossy finishes, and pebbly and smooth textures. You don't have to settle for plain squares either. Rectangles, octagons, rounds, and diamonds are among the shapes available. Or, smash tile with a hammer to create irregular shapes for a mosaic. Measure first; tile is priced by the square foot and installation may be extra. Imported, hand-painted tiles are priced per piece. Although they cost more, they have dramatic impact, even if used sparingly.

ONE: *Dark grout and special edging set off this creamy white tiled wall behind the cooktop. Tiles painted by artists, more costly than the plain ones, are sprinkled over the wall. Using a few well-placed one-of-a-kind tiles is a good way to stretch your budget.*

TWO: *If the tiles' motif is dramatic, you don't need many. Just three oversize tiles, painted with a woolly sheep in a country landscape, create a charming mural on this kitchen wall.*

THREE: *Using patterned tiles in a room-wrapping border links areas of a big kitchen. For definition, the border is underscored by smaller tile in matching green and white hues.*

FOUR: Patterned blue tiles define special areas in this European-style kitchen, creating focal points such as the cooktop. Plaster tiles were even added to the cooktop hood.

FIVE: Three types of durable ceramic tiles combine on the wall and range hood of this kitchen for personality.

SIX: Matte and glossy tiles were smashed into irregular shapes and studded with marbles for this wall mosaic. A tile checkerboard takes the high road above the random mosaic motif.

MIX & MATCH NATURALLY

Kitchens at work are filled with sensual pleasures—the aroma of simmering chocolate and the silky feel of kneading dough. Plan design elements so that even when your kitchen is at rest, it will still delight the senses. Here are tips on choosing functional, and marvelously touchable, countertop materials:

• *Mix surface materials* for a custom look. Contrast colors such as light woods with dark marble. Capitalize on optical illusion: Slick, shiny finishes lighten a small room; nubby, rougher textures make large kitchens feel cozy.

• *Mimic the look* of marble, granite, and stone with synthetic solid-surface materials. They come in many colors and resist damage from knives and hot pots.

• *Inset specialty materials.* Wood butcher's block insets are ideal for chopping but are ruined by water, so should not be near the sink. Because marble is susceptible to stains, it's not good as a countertop; inset a slab for rolling out pastry. Stainless steel withstands hard wear and is good by the cooktop and oven.

ONE: In this sunny kitchen baking center, a 24×36-inch piece of granite is set flush into the countertop tile and offers a spot for rolling out pastries and kneading bread dough. Storage below the counter holds baking supplies.

TWO: The mirrored backsplash brings unexpected shine to an otherwise understated mix of natural woods, stonelike countertops, and brushed stainless steel. Combining materials imparts function and sophistication.

THREE: Opposite this kitchen's work triangle, a built-in cherry wood hutch, a second sink, and black granite countertop enhance function and drama. Use more expensive surfaces such as granite for niches like this.

FOUR: Durable slate plays a primary role in this kitchen's textural scheme. Rough-textured, square slate tiles range from red-brown to gray-green. They pique interest in the countertops and the backsplash.

FIVE: Hand-worked finishes and seasoned materials charm this high-performance kitchen. The backsplash derives its timeless aura from custom-designed, tumbled marble tiles and makes the cooktop a focal point.

T he warmth and charm that make a kitchen irresistible builds upon the personal decorative touches you add and collectibles you display.

SHOW-OFF SPACE

One of the easiest ways to extend displays and lighten a room's mood is by replacing solid cabinet doors with glass-front doors. Then wallpaper the cabinet interiors before filling them with Grandmother's colorful china. Select only a cabinet or two for glass so you'll have fewer to keep neat.

• *Look high and low* for display options. Parade collectibles along the tops of cabinets and hang burnished copper cookware from a ceiling rack. Glass shelves attached to a kitchen window frame can transform it quickly

A PLACE TO DISPLAY

into a greenhouse. Then line the shelves with the cook's choice of herbs in terra-cotta pots.

• *Move in more storage,* such as an antique hutch, wicker baskets, fabric-covered boxes, hand-painted tins, and old jars from the flea market. Allot a few open shelves for your cookbook library that could add instant color. Don't line up objects at the back of the countertop; group them in arty vignettes as you would in the living room.

• *Display the unexpected.* Bring out your family's heirlooms—art, framed letters, dishes, old kitchenware, and other treasures. If it's fragile or especially valuable, place it on a high shelf or under glass.

ONE: Architectural moldings integrate new floor-to-ceiling storage units with cabinetry. Only 6 and 8 inches deep, the two freestanding units have open shelves that adjust for books, birdhouses, and about any size collectible these flea-market-loving homeowners might cart home.

TWO: An antique pine hutch in the breakfast room displays a variety of old pitchers and pictorial china. The chicken coop at the bottom is the painted masterpiece of the artist in residence.

THREE: New glass doors, wallpaper, and paint give one section of cabinets the look of a built-in hutch. The deep blue background of the wall covering echoes in solid-hue paint on the wall beneath the cabinet. Botanical prints in antique frames carry on the theme.

FOUR: In this small kitchen, a skinny, end-to-the-counter wall is put to work with a 12-inch-deep built-in cupboard for open display. There's also a work spot, cook's stool, and storage cabinet for stowing baking supplies within reach in this niche.

WHY NOT A KITCHEN FIREPLACE?

Cozy fireside suppers aren't only for pioneers and campers. Just add a focal-point fireplace to your plans for building, remodeling, or updating your kitchen, and dining beside a warm hearth and crackling fire can be yours.

• ***Choose an outside wall*** for installing a new fireplace. A new flue and chimney also can be added to a room with a vaulted ceiling. Prefab fireplaces come in various sizes, shapes, and designs. Make sure installation follows the manufacturer's guidelines on clearances and ventilation.

• ***Enjoy the glow*** by choosing a fireplace with a glass door. These units are energy-efficient, spread the heat around, and keep sparks from damaging furnishings. Consider a two-sided fireplace that warms the kitchen on one side and the family room on the other. Gas makes building a fire easier, and there are no messy ashes to clean up. If you don't have storage for firewood, try gas logs.

• ***Dress up your hearth*** in materials and motifs that fit your kitchen's style. In mantels, rugged stone and scrubbed English pine are more informal options; elegant marble is more formal. If you find an antique mantel in good repair you want to use, you may need to have it customized to fit today's larger fireboxes.

ONE: *Although its main purpose is to provide ambience, this raised masonry fireplace is a much-enjoyed kitchen amenity. Edged in stool seating, the counter is used as often as the breakfast table because it's a cozy place for casual meals, snacks, and chats.*

TWO: *Country as can be, this fireplace creates a homey and functional focal point on the dining side of the open-plan kitchen. There's even enough room hearthside for two*

armchairs. You can create a fireplace effect without the fireplace by hanging a mantel on a flat wall and topping it with framed art.

THREE: A bump-out made way for a new wood-burning stove when this Scandinavian-spirited kitchen was remodeled. The little warmer is set into a niche, once a doorway, that's faced in white ceramic tile with dark grout.

FOUR: A counter-height kitchen fireplace echoes the clean, elegant lines of this home's modern design. Lighted display cabinets and strips of beveled granite-look, solid-surface material complement the fireplace.

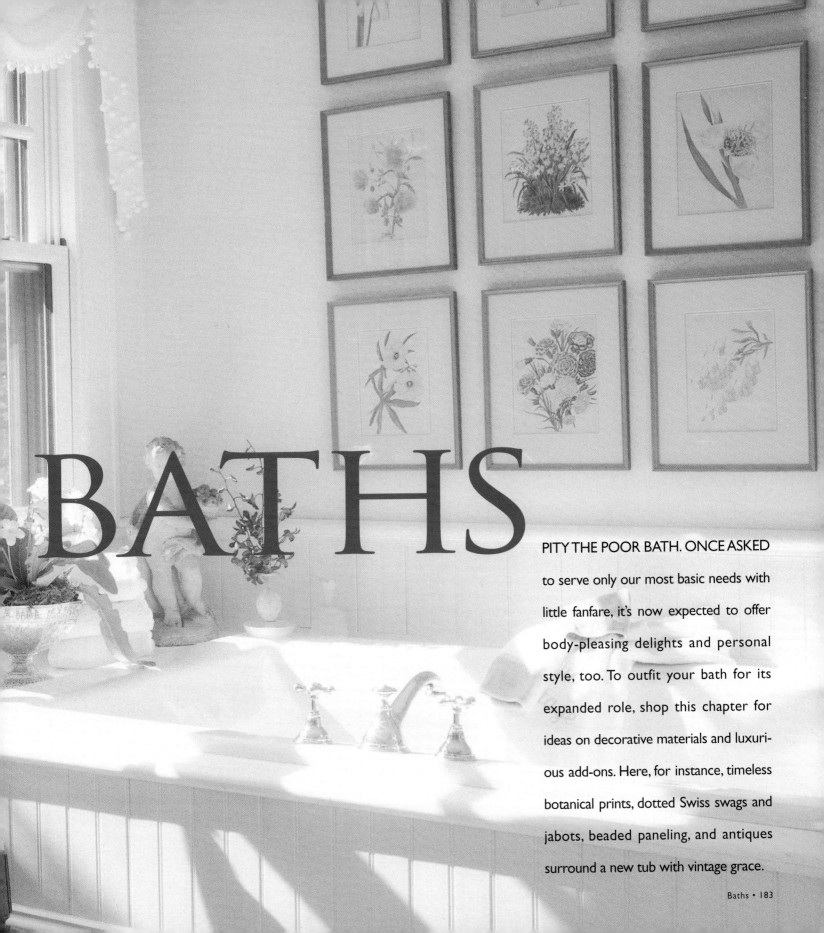

BATHS

PITY THE POOR BATH. ONCE ASKED to serve only our most basic needs with little fanfare, it's now expected to offer body-pleasing delights and personal style, too. To outfit your bath for its expanded role, shop this chapter for ideas on decorative materials and luxurious add-ons. Here, for instance, timeless botanical prints, dotted Swiss swags and jabots, beaded paneling, and antiques surround a new tub with vintage grace.

What to do if your bath is small but your dreams are grand? Relax. No matter what the size of your room, you can pamper yourself with quality materials, fixtures—and *style*.

• *Splurge on materials.* A small bath offers you the chance to indulge in materials that might break the budget in a large bath. After all, it takes only a few marble floor tiles to add luxury to a half-bath.

• *Replace fixtures.* If your room's layout works well, you can spend your money on quality fixtures—not on moving plumbing lines. A new whirlpool tub can turn a basic bath into a spa.

• *Improve the lighting.* Flank a mirror with lights for a shadow-free makeup spot or replace a single ceiling fixture with track lights for better general lighting. Don't forget the dimmer. Bright lights may be necessary for grooming, but you'll want to dial down the wattage for a leisurely, after-work soak.

LITTLE LUXURIES

- *Be sensual.* Fill a basket or an over-the-tub rack with loofahs for scrubbing, and scented soaps and oils for relaxation. Wire in some extra speakers and let yourself get carried away by music.
- *Give walls an illusion of depth.* Instead of a small mirror above the sink, dramatically expand the look of a small bath with a mirror that runs from wall to wall and countertop to ceiling. Add depth to walls with layered paint treatments, such as combing or sponging, and with semigloss or gloss (versus flat) paints.
- *Use vertical space.* Stow grooming supplies on floor-to-ceiling shelving or a slim étagère, or craft a shallow, between-the-studs cabinet.

ONE: *Sculpt the space in a small half-bath. A textured, tone-on-tone wall covering, rounded lights, and a framed mirror give depth to flat walls. Because it allows the floor and walls to flow uninterrupted beneath it, the pedestal sink also fosters an illusion of space.* **TWO:** *For today's comfort in yesterday's space, replace a basic tub with a standard-size whirlpool. White tiles and fixtures keep things light and airy;*

contrasting blue tiles and a miniprint wall covering add extra snap. **THREE:** *Wisely resisting the temptation to modernize, the owners enhanced the charm of this bath with scenic toile de Jouy fabric on the walls, a filmy voile sink skirt, and an antique pine chest.* **FOUR:** *With or without the new tub, a rich mix of dark wood, a granite countertop, and gray tile turns a bath into a serene oasis.*

GRAND COMFORTS

reating a grand-size master bathroom can be fun but taxing. Choosing the materials for such a bath can make you feel like royalty, but it's hard to keep the extra square footage from feeling cold and cavernous. Solve this by defining the area into zones for bathing, grooming, dressing, exercising, and relaxing. Here are other good ideas:

• *Fixtures come first.* For spa appeal, consider a whirlpool or oversize tub, and, perhaps, a steam shower. In a large bath, you should have plenty of space for a generous two-sink vanity.

• *Surface matters.* If you have the space, help set the bath's mood with dramatic hand-painted tile, a run of colorful laminate cabinetry, shapely marble or granite vanity counters, and elegant wall coverings.

• *Make it safe.* Choose carpet or nonskid flooring. Add a telephone, childproof latches on storage, tub-and-shower grab bars, and ground-fault circuit interrupters on outlets.

• *Indulge it.* Treat your bath to heated bars for toasty towels, lighted makeup mirrors, a television, a massage table, and an after-bath easy chair near bookshelves.

In this old house redo, vintage fixtures stayed put, but fresh fabrics now dress the roomy bath. Double-stick Velcro tape—it adheres to sink and fabric—secures the vanity skirt.

PERSONAL TOUCHES

Sure, your bath must be functional, but it's also a place in which you can use the colors, motifs, and objects you love to create warm ambience.

• **Use contrasting textures** to take the edge off stretches of cold tile and fixtures. Weathered flea market finds and antiques play off beautifully against slick porcelain, ceramic, and glass. An aging pine or wicker chest or a small mahogany table can double as storage and a spot for a mood-enhancing lamp.

• **Watch the humidity.** With no tub or shower to add humidity, a half-bath can make a wonderful showcase for a treasured painting or limited-edition print. In a full bath, however, it's best to stick with lower-cost prints.

• **Create eye-catching displays** of favorite photos or colorful perfume bottles atop vanities. When arranging, heed three guidelines: Group objects that have a motif, style, or color in common; vary their sizes and shapes; and arrange them so they form overlapping triangles.

• **Look for shapely variety.** Soften hard edges with rounded accents: curvy hampers, plant stands, and gathered curtains of lace or your favorite floral fabric. Skirt an old pedestal sink or romance a newer vanity by replacing under-sink doors with fabric gathered onto a tension rod.

ONE: *There's a relaxed serendipity to this bath's mix of antiques, greenery, and botanical prints. The white backdrop makes each accent more important.*

TWO: *What better place for blooming plants than a bath that already looks like a garden? Here, an airy, plant-filled étagère becomes part of the window treatment.*

REVIVE
AN OLDER BATH

If your bath is aging, but not gracefully, apply the lipstick principle—without the lipstick. Revitalize your bath's looks with clever cover-ups, splashes of color, and a bit of conditioning.

DECIDE ON THE MOOD—OLD OR NEW?

Today's fabrics, wall coverings, and paints can make you a decorating magician capable of taking your bath forward or backward in time. Update a ho-hum bath with bright new colors and geometric prints or take it back in time with romantic florals and lace.

• *Paint it.* Lavish fresh color on walls, ceilings, doors, trim, wood floors, furniture, and cabinetry. Stencil a border or sponge a faux finish on walls. If you dislike the color of tile walls that are still in good condition, have a bathroom facelift specialist paint them. By keeping everything in the same light color family, you can visually expand a less-than-grand space.

• *Cover it with fabric and wallpaper.* When designing curtains or sink skirts, remember that gathered treatments create romance and nostalgia; tailored treatments— Roman shades and straight sink skirts with inverted corner pleats, for instance—imbue a bath with contemporary crispness. Wall coverings infuse color and pattern, too. Look for a scrubbable vinyl print that fits the room's scale. Or, for just a touch of pattern, use a border at the ceiling line or to create a chair-rail effect around the room.

ONE: *This facelift begins with pastel blush for the walls. An old chest, painted with romantic flowers and ribbons, teams with a flowered sink and mirror for unabashed romance. The dressing table? It's a junk store find clad in a lacy new "dress."*

TWO: Oversize elements can actually add a feeling of generosity to a small bath. Here, the owners used a stencil to create the wide fish border at chair-rail height for a room-widening horizontal line. Wide 2-inch blinds with a deep fabric-covered cornice repeat the large scale of the border.

THREE: Stars and stripes in gold and cream tones quickly coaxed this half-bath into a contemporary mood. The strong wallpaper motif draws the eye away from the plumbing to a complement of earthy-hued accessories.

FOUR: Animal lovers of all stripes appreciate this cheery room that uses a trio of patterns and fresh fabric treatments. To mix your own patterns, vary the scale. Here, a mini-stripe and midsize plaid team with a larger novelty print.

FROM COUNTRY TO CONTEMPORARY

2

ONE: *If you like to redecorate frequently or you're face-lifting a bath with resale value in mind, stick with basic whites and rely on accessories to set the style. Fabrics and small-scale accents carry the French country air into this space. At the window, ruffles and flourishes in provincial prints set the scene. Underfoot, a hooked rug picks up the floral motif. A fanciful lace panel (hung on a ceiling-mounted rod) takes the modern glass tub divider back in time.*

TWO: *It's out with the old, in with the new, as the bath switches to color-blocked contemporary style. In this context, the timeless tile floor takes on a modern look. The clean-lined window treatment layers striped, angled valances over a trim cafe curtain that's gathered at the top and bottom on tension rods. A white-framed poster print replaces the traditional painting, and the double vanity holds sculptural glass accents. Flowers, wicker, and loofahs add warm texture.*

SETTING THE MOOD

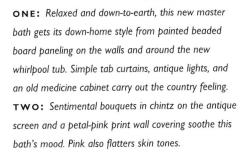

Working from the walls in, you can create a background to soothe away the stress of the day and rejuvenate the spirit. Tile makes a beautiful and practical wall covering, but, as you can see here, it isn't your only choice. In areas where splashing is at a minimum, you're free to set the scene in a variety of ways.

• *Warm with wood.* Add white-painted wainscoting, perhaps with new vintage-style lighting, and the tone is farmhouse fresh. Walls of natural pine or cedar, protected with polyurethane, can set a contemporary sauna mood.

• *Let color change your mood.* You can cloak bathroom walls in durable vinyl wall coverings, scrubbable paint, and even fabric. The trick is to choose the right palette for your personality. Energizing bright hues will get you off to a fast start in the morning; depending on your personality, they may either revive you or jangle your nerves at day's end. Wake up with brights? Relax with cool blues, greens, and violets? If you're undecided, a neutral backdrop with colorful, easy-to-change towels and accessories may be best. (For more information on setting the mood with color, turn to the "Color" chapter, page 279.)

ONE: *Relaxed and down-to-earth, this new master bath gets its down-home style from painted beaded board paneling on the walls and around the new whirlpool tub. Simple tab curtains, antique lights, and an old medicine cabinet carry out the country feeling.*

TWO: *Sentimental bouquets in chintz on the antique screen and a petal-pink print wall covering soothe this bath's mood. Pink also flatters skin tones.*

THREE: *Simple rolled-on stripes and a fanciful trompe l'oeil canvas runner jazz up this attic bath.*

$\mathbf{A}$ll vanities are not created equal. Some just have more personality. Some succeed on the unexpected. They all do the job, but a splash of style and imagination always helps. These one-of-a-kind vanities, in small and large baths, are the personal masterpieces of homeowners who just wouldn't settle for off-the-rack pieces.

NOT YOUR USUAL VANITY

ONE: *A soothing, natural aesthetic reigns at this maple vanity, which was redone with a French granite countertop and backsplash, and a concrete bowl on top for the sink. A variety of bowl sinks are commercially available.*

TWO: *Chunky farmhouse dressers are easy to find at flea markets. Fresh paint, updated hardware, and sink and plumbing pipes gave this one new life as a vanity.*

THREE: *A medley of materials makes this pickled-maple vanity a star. The countertop is limestone, and the backsplash is creamy glazed tile, framed in khaki matte-finish squares.*

3

FOUR: A simply crafted classic, this wood vanity fits beautifully into the mood of the Shaker-style bath. The mirror is set between traditional peg racks, and the tile floor suggests the vivid geometry of antique quilt blocks.

FIVE: With vanity space at a premium in this contemporary bath, the homeowner made a strong style statement with scaled-down fittings. The 12-inch round sink and bar-type faucet are made of stainless steel.

SIX: A discovery of bargain-hunting homeowners, this old buffet went from dining room to bath vanity with a new mirror, two sinks, and coats of polyurethane sealer.

TURN AN OLD CHEST INTO

For lots of charm in the same old space, turn a vintage chest into a vanity. To be sure your project is feasible, consult with a plumber or a skilled do-it-yourselfer about the placement and the condition of existing plumbing lines. Also remove any attached mirrors that could keep the chest from being placed flush against the wall.

ONE: Start with a self-rimming sink to help keep water off the chest top. If your sink does not come with its own template, draw your own and tape it to the chest's top. Drill a 1/4-inch hole on the inside of the outline, then use a jigsaw to carefully cut along the inside of the template.

TWO: Cut holes for pipes and seal drawers shut. Or, to retain storage space, adapt drawers to fit around pipes, making cutouts for the pipes and piecing in new wood as needed. Refitting the lower drawers requires average skills, but you may need a pro to reshape top drawers (see above).

THREE: Waterproof the dresser. For natural wood, sand the wood top lightly using sandpaper with a very fine grit; use a tack cloth to remove all dust. Apply a coat of high-gloss polyurethane. If your piece is painted, protect the top with one or two coats of high-gloss acrylic.

A CHARMING VANITY

FOUR: *Once the plumbing has been hooked up by you or a professional, and before the sink has been cemented, replace the drawers. Slightly adjust the position of the sink as needed. To provide a good seal between the sink and countertop, apply a thin bead of caulk.*

FIVE: *To complete the installation, bolt the mirror (which you will have detached at the beginning) directly to the wall. Finally, be sure to provide adequate grooming lights on either side of the mirror. You can have lights wired in or use wall-mounted plug-in lamps.*

OUTSIDE

PORCHES, DECKS, AND PATIOS HAVE BECOME OUR THREE- AND FOUR-SEASON living rooms, demanding furnishings as functional and beautiful as those inside our homes. In this chapter, you'll find inspiration for creating fresh-air spaces, such as this front porch with nostalgic wicker. With a gathering of plump cushions, cheery fabrics—and a few fair-weather friends— an outdoor spot like this becomes a sublime setting for dining alfresco.

MIDSUMMER NIGHT'S DREAMING

Approach decorating an outdoor room—whether it's a screen porch or a corner of yard—as you would an indoor living space. First decide how you will use the space. You're not limited to the usual activities, such as sunbathing and barbecuing. With a few simple luxuries—an ample chaise, a fan for languid summer nights, or a quilt for crisp fall evenings—a screen porch or deck can become a peaceful oasis for snoozing. These ideas can help you envision ways to decorate your personal patch of the great outdoors.

• ***Design a garden "room."*** It's the most natural approach to outdoor living. Pull seating out beside your perennial bed or deep into your lush shade garden. Define your new "room" with walls consisting of a tangle of tree limbs, a weathered wood railing, or flower-filled trellises. Underfoot, try cool pavers or a carpet of moss. Overhead, string paper lanterns, scatter "stars" into the trees with a few white holiday lights, or simply relax under a canopy of real stars.

• ***Make it entertaining.*** Why not drag the television out to the "screening room" for sitcoms by moonlight? Weather-protected speakers make it possible to equip a porch or deck with sound—but keep the volume low to avoid disturbing neighbors who prefer a symphony of crickets and tree frogs.

• ***Include space for hobbies.*** Outdoors, nobody will fret about paint fumes or spills. If you have a yen for model building or decoupage, set up a worktable in a covered porch. Transform an upper deck into an observatory for stargazing; bring out a telescope, patio chair, and binoculars.

ONE: *This screened porch recalls one of life's great pleasures—sleeping outdoors. For even more versatility, substitute a daybed for the conventional bed; it will serve as a sleeper by night and casual seating by day. Old-fashioned white wicker, clothesline-fresh cotton linens, and fragrant herb topiaries are sure to inspire sweet dreams.*

TWO: *No room for a bed? Hang a hammock that can be rolled up and stored when not in use. Rope hammocks like this one with wood stretchers at either end are the most comfortable. Secure it with S-hooks and heavy chain to solid wood trim or porch framing.*

FAIR-WEATHER

ONE: *Divide a large porch for different purposes. Placing this table near water's edge treats diners to a view; a glider and rockers provide for relaxing conversation.*

TWO: *Antique furniture feels at home on this riverside porch. Easy-clean cotton cushions and the straw mat camouflaging the concrete floor can be removed in foul weather.*

LIVING

A front porch facing a quiet residential street is even more welcoming when furnishings are arranged to embrace neighbors strolling by. In addition to such public spaces, also plan for privacy. Even if your surroundings are lovely, privacy may mean more to you than communing with the neighbors. If so, head to the backyard and shut out the world with screening, such as a lattice wall, fabric curtain or roll-up shade, or a border of vegetation. Flowers, climbing plants, and herbs all work well as natural, airy screens. To give great-outdoors spaces a more intimate feeling:

Once you've settled on the functions for your outdoor room, start planning. The same interior design principles apply outdoors. Arrange furniture to facilitate dining, conversation, quiet contemplation, and especially traffic flow since spaces outside a home usually double as entries and exits.

OUT OF BOUNDS

With outdoor rooms, more so than indoor areas, what lies beyond the actual boundaries often plays an important role in design. On a deck with an ocean or lake view, place furniture to take advantage of the natural wonder.

• *Gather furniture* into cozy groupings or turn seating pieces toward the house. Add window boxes or vine-covered trellises to the house itself to create a colorful focal point.

• *Pick porch-friendly furniture.* Sturdy materials such as treated woods, plastics, and rustproof metals will withstand the elements but may do little to promote a feeling of comfort and livability. Consider indoor furniture for protected outdoor areas. Often an extra coat of paint or varnish and fluffy cushions made with mildew-resistant fabrics and fillings are all that's needed to make these pieces weather-hardy.

BRIGHT SPOTS AMID THE SHADE

The cool greens of shady woodland porches may be refreshing, but they also can seem a bit chilly unless you "plant" some sunny reds and yellows. Here red fabrics turn up the heat, and old-fashioned, painted wicker creates a bright white counterpoint to the cool green background. Tossed over the sofa, a star-studded blue and white quilt injects a shot of bold color as do the other snappy accents—a framed flag and fire engine red metal chair and pillows.

ONE: *Ocean blue, cabana-striped curtains give this suburban porch a pool-house feel and keep you cool when summer days sizzle. Curtain rings, stitched to both the top and bottom of each weatherproof panel, gather onto rods to make an unflappable shield from the sun along the hot west side. Mismatched porch chairs, painted white and softened with cushiony pillows, entice passing neighbors to stop for a chat.*

CONTROL THE ELEMENTS

Y ou'll enjoy your outdoor room more often if you plan for those times when the weather is less than ideal. Overly bright sun, a strong breeze, and even light rain won't spoil the day if you incorporate some protection from the elements into your open-air deck or patio.

LOCATION, LOCATION, LOCATION

If you're planning an outdoor structure, build it where it will get indirect light or shade for at least part of the day. A grove of trees is the perfect spot for a gazebo or detached pavilion. When location isn't ideal, consider other ways to keep Mother Nature at bay. Look for a spot that's shaded by the house, a detached garage, or a garden shed for part of the afternoon. Or, install an adjustable market umbrella to shade your patio and add bistro charm. Deflect sun and rain with a retractable awning, or stitch simple curtains or roll-up blinds from new, weather-resistant materials.

SHOP FOR TODAY'S SUPER SYNTHETIC FABRICS

Gone are the days when slippery vinyl was the only outdoor fabric. Newer synthetic materials simulate the look and feel of natural fibers—but weather the elements beautifully. Here's a sampling:

TWO: *Open on three sides, a backyard pavilion makes a great outdoor room. Furnishings sit atop a plank floor; the quilt-block pattern was created with colored stains.*

THREE: *Retractable acrylic cover-ups fend off sun and light rain. Curtains open or close as needed; overhead, flat panels fitted with large grommets slide back and forth on sturdy wire.*

• *Woven vinyl-coated polyester*—a popular material for cushions, slings, and umbrellas—is waterproof and resists fading.

• *Acrylics* sew up easily into soft furnishings and curtains. They dry quickly, don't mildew, and look and feel like indoor fabrics. Check tent, awning, and fabric stores for acrylics.

• *New laminated-cotton* yard goods are intended for outdoor use. Or, waterproof your own fabrics with iron-on vinyl available at fabric stores. Natural fabrics fade and mildew with time so reserve them for sheltered areas.

ONE: *A come-hither grouping of light and airy wicker chairs set on angle anchors half of this divided front porch. White walls and flooring, lightly scaled accents, and a wrap of checkerboard windows all help expand the look and feel of this long, skinny space.*

TWO: *Turning this sofa crosswise, instead of placing it against the long wall, helps visually widen this porch. Shared greens and whites pull the two seating areas together.*

RESCULPT THE TUNNEL

Coming up with a functional furniture arrangement for the typically long and skinny porch may seem like an impossible dream. But, break the porch into two or more separate groupings and place some furnishings on the diagonal, and you'll have the problem licked in no time. Here are the details:

BREAK IT UP

• *Create separate but equal halves.* A central door often provides the natural dividing point between two porch groupings. To create balance, anchor one side of the porch with a single large piece of furniture, such as a porch swing, glider, or settee. On the other side, assemble a grouping of lounge chairs or dining pieces that carry approximately the same visual weight. Balance a tall chest or étagère on one side with a low bench or table on the other. Color also affects your porch's balancing act. A large piece of furniture painted or upholstered in a light color is less imposing than the same piece in a darker hue.

• *Square up with paint.* Paint short end walls a bright, advancing color and longer side walls a light, receding color.

• *Use color to unify furnishings.* Even if your furniture is a jumble of secondhand chairs and tables, paint them white or another single hue for a smooth blend. Keep accent colors flowing on cushions, pillows, fabric shades, and table coverings.

• *Add a rug—or two.* Let a large round area rug or long runner laid in the center of the porch link the halves. Or, use matching rugs to anchor separate groupings.

TRY A NEW ANGLE

Placing a sofa or settee on the long wall only adds to a porch's tunnel feeling. Instead, add a look of width by placing it crosswise or on the diagonal. Because a diagonal is the longest line through any space, such placement helps you visually widen a narrow porch—and squeeze in more furniture. For example, a settee might barely fit across a narrow end wall, but set it on an angle in the corner, and you can add a chair at one or both ends. If your grouping consists of three or four chairs, rearrange them into an on-the-bias cloverleaf for increased width. Emphasize the new angle with a diagonally laid area rug, too.

2

Year-long Porch Style

E ven if rain or snow drives you indoors for part of the year, you *can* have your place in the sun. Well, you can fake it, anyway. Always adaptable—and welcome—alfresco-style furnishings can help you turn any room into an outdoors-style getaway. Pop in an audiotape or CD of woodland birds or ocean waves, close your eyes, and let your imagination wander beyond the room's actual boundaries. We've only just begun to transport you to summery climes. Here are more ideas:

ENJOY THE GREAT INDOORS

With a thoughtful approach, you can conjure up the ambience of an open porch for any room in your home.

• ***Make it casual.*** Set the mood by bringing outdoor standards, such as wooden Adirondack chairs and metal-and-glass dining tables, indoors. Add plump cushions with removable, washable covers so you—and Fido—won't be afraid to put your feet up. Choose a fearless floor covering, too—resilient tile, wood, or vinyl accented with a brightly colored rug. Now, do a general survey: Does the space encourage you to slow down, take a deep breath, prop your sneakers on the coffee table, and contemplate the universe?

• ***Invite the outdoors in.*** Opt for minimal window treatments—perhaps honeycomb shades that let sunlight flood the space in the daytime but help insulate the room at night. Choose bright accents that energize like summer flowers, rugged textures that speak of wild places, and painted woods with comfortably worn surfaces. Contrast new and rustic pieces.

ONE: *Simple neutral furnishings complement nature without upstaging it in this sunroom. Furnishings are fuss-free leather, canvas, and wood.*

TWO: *A cool green color scheme makes this porch feel as inviting as a summer lawn party. The peeling paint of a vintage metal chair is a charming foil for the fresh whitewashed wicker.*

THREE: *Rustic woods and wicker bring tree-trunk texture to the otherwise slick space. In this four-seasons solarium, light-filtering shades roll back for moonlight and stargazing.*

3

RELAX IN THE OPEN

Furniture for your patio or deck can be as big an invest-ment as those for your home's interior. That's why it pays to know about materials and construction, since the pieces are exposed to the elements. Our list will help you choose wisely.

- **Aluminum is lightweight,** durable, and rustproof. It comes in wrought or cast forms with a baked-on enamel or textured fin-ish. Cast-aluminum pieces are more expensive. Look for thick, heavy-gauge alloys and smooth seams on welded parts.
- **Iron is good for windy climates.** Made from cast or wrought steel, iron furniture is heavier and less expensive than aluminum but may require more care over the long run. Iron rusts and needs frequent paint touch-ups when exposed to water and air.
- **Wicker should go undercover**—inside or on a covered porch—unless you buy synthetic all-weather wicker. When buying wicker for porches, look for aluminum frames and a baked-on polyester finish.
- **Most wood species** require at least a yearly coat of paint or varnish. Pressure-treated lumber is a low-cost alternative for the do-it-yourself furnituremaker.
- **Plastic is virtually indestructible** and comes in two forms: *PVC* (polyvinyl chloride) is made of plastic piping that's joined together. *Resin* furniture is molded into a variety of shapes.
- **Cushions need to weather** the storm. To leave them outdoors, be sure fabric covers are waterproof, not only mildew resistant, and that the covers and foam filling allow water to drain. Otherwise, you'll need to take them indoors during storms.
- **Paint designed for outdoors** protects furniture. Oil-base paints will hold up better than latex, and gloss or semigloss finishes are preferable to flat. Industrial paints contain more binders to adhere paint to surfaces and are more fade-resistant. For bright colors, ask for industrial safety paints.

ONE: *This gracious outdoor living space is classic California style, with a palette that embraces ocean blues and a sweep of brick rising from the patio into a fireplace—a true outdoor room luxury. Freestanding fireplace units of metal or clay also work outdoors. The patio, set with durable teak furnishings, is used as an everyday family room and for entertaining.*

TWO: Like indoor rooms, outdoor spaces need a focal point around which furnishings revolve. Here, a compass medallion, made of stone and concrete, is set into a patio of salvaged fireplace brick. The intriguing art naturally draws guests to the patio's trio of shapely wicker and wood seating.

THREE: The garden theme of this partly sheltered patio makes the tulip-back Adirondack chairs a playful choice. Not content with an ordinary—and ugly—concrete slab floor, the homeowners disguised it with a marbled-paint finish.

MAKE FUSS-FREE
ACCENTS

Now that you've got the basics covered, it's time to find those one-of-a-kind accessories, art, and accents that will infuse your porch or patio with personality and warmth. Almost anything you'd display inside works outside, but use common sense; keep valuable art and sculpture, fragile textiles and furnishings out of the weather and heavy traffic. Since outdoor rooms are intended for comfort, choose accessories that welcome use, things that can be walked on, touched, or even tipped over without being damaged. They should be easy-going, washable, and just plain fun.

ACCENT ON PERSONALITY

Think durable outdoor accents the next time you head for the flea market. Have fun doing your own Picasso thing, too. Here are a few do-it-yourself ideas:

• *Create a patterned floor cloth* to boost the color quotient of a concrete patio or wood deck. Sketch a simple geometric pattern onto grid paper (check out old quilts for inspiration). Cut 54-inch-wide painter's canvas to desired length; prepare it with gesso. Transfer the geometric design to the cloth with pencil and yardstick. Use masking tape as a guide as you add colors, one at a time, to the design. Oil-base paint works best for outdoors; use acrylics for protected areas.

• *Paint a tabletop design.* Brush a well-sanded, unfinished piece with two coats of background color. Then use the techniques outlined above for the floor cloth.

• *Work pillow magic.* Energize a ho-hum space with weather-resistant acrylic fabric. Choose neutral seat cushions for porch furniture, then stitch up a wardrobe of lively accent pillows to change on a whim. Neutrals quiet the scene; primary hues rev up the mood.

ONE: *Classic white wicker is the canvas for this Mad Hatter's mix of cabana stripes, garden florals, country checks, and ethnic prints. It works because the scale of each pattern is different.*
TWO: *A do-it-yourself floor cloth puts patchwork underfoot in this farmhouse porch. With a protective coat of polyurethane, this funky cloth is easily cleaned.*

CHAIR REMAKES

REBORN REDWOOD

Give an old redwood chair fresh paint and a new patchwork cover. Prime and paint frame. The stripes and solid seat slipcover consists of two squares, each with four triangles. To determine the squares' dimensions, measure the circumference of a cushion and divide by 2 (this will be the length of each side of the square). Make a paper pattern, adding $\frac{1}{2}$-inch seams. Draw a second square; divide diagonally into quarters. Cut apart triangles; trace one onto paper, adding $\frac{1}{2}$-inch seams. For the back cover, cut two squares from plain fabric. With right sides facing, join squares along one side. For front, cut six striped and two plain triangles. Join short sides of two striped triangles; repeat with a striped and plain triangle. Join long sides of these two pieces to make a square. Repeat for a second square. Join, leaving plain edge open for inserting cushion; hem and baste opening shut.

NAUTICAL ACCENT

A director's chair can sail through the summer in style, if you rig it with a new canvas seat that's machine-appliquéd with bright nautical flag designs. Appliqué existing canvas seats or buy or sew new ones. To make your own, copy measurements of old seats onto paper, adding $\frac{1}{2}$-inch seams to sides only. Note sewing line for casings with felt marker. From heavy white canvas, cut out back and seat rectangles, adding $\frac{1}{2}$-inch seams to top and bottom. Turn seams under twice; hem. On paper, draw four $1\frac{1}{2}$-inch-wide stripes, two the height of the back and two the depth of the seat. Cut and align stripes on right side of chair. Draw diagonal lines across both pieces; unfold casings. Lay tracing paper on top of patterns and trace appliqué triangles. Secure appliqués to fabric with fusible web using zigzag-stitch machine setting. Turn under, sew casings, and attach to chair.

FOR SUMMER FUN

REWEBBED FLORA

Replace an aluminum chair's ho-hum webbing with a floral sundress. Just stretch a splashy fabric over the frame and lace up the sides. Remove the old seat and save screws. For a pattern, measure the height of the back; add ³/₄-inch for seams and several inches for wrapping around the top frame. Measure seat depth; add several inches as you did for the back. Add the two measurements for total length. Measure seat and back width inside frame and subtract 3 inches for ropework. Transfer measurements to paper. Cut two rectangles from fabric, adding 1¹/₂-inch seams to long sides. Place wrong sides together and topstitch at 1³/₈-inch seams. Turn under top seam. Mark fabric for 1-inch-wide grommets spaced 2 inches apart; install with grommet tool. Align short ends of fabric to chair top and front; attach with screws. Pull ¹/₄-inch rope laces through grommets.

CELESTIAL REDO

This aging Adirondack has a bright future in an old-fashioned crackle finish with a celestial seasoning of paper-star appliqués. For a painted chair, don't strip the original paint; wipe on liquid sander. Sand raw wood pieces, apply sanding sealer to prevent knots from bleeding through, and prime. Apply a base coat with blue exterior latex paint; allow to dry. To prepare crackle finish, mix two parts hide glue to one part water in a disposable container; stir. With nylon brush and long strokes, apply glue mixture evenly over the chair; let dry overnight. Apply green exterior latex paint evenly over dried glue, drawing each stroke down the length of area to be crackled. Don't brush over areas already painted. Paint will begin to crackle in about 20 seconds; dry overnight. Adhere paper stars with vinyl-to-vinyl paste. Finish with two coats of polyurethane.

BEGIN

NINGS

WHAT DO YOU SAY TO AN EMPTY room? Warm, welcoming spaces rich in personality, like this living room, all start with a plan. This chapter's successful step-by-step strategies will help you outfit a room, shop smart, reach for a few stars, and turn your decorating dreams into reality.

GETTING STARTED

Whether you're planning to spruce up the den or treat the living room to a professional makeover, write your room's script first. What's its story line? How do you want it to live, look, and feel? Can you afford everything on your decorating wish list? If not, what are the priorities and compromises? Only you and your family know the answers.

WHAT SUITS YOU?

Let everyone in the household speak about design ideas, practical needs—and dreams. Don't worry about what the neighbors will think; your furnishings should be strictly personal, based on your family's size, lifestyle, and design tastes.

• *Assess your room's natural resources.* A rugged fireplace, a bay window view, or a wall of sleek built-ins could become a focal point. Don't let a floor plan dictate room roles; if a dining area has a better view than a living room, make the switch.

• *Do a furniture reality check.* List your needs, setting priorities for what goods you need to buy now and what you can buy later. Is your family formal, casual, neat, or rough-and-tumble? How do you entertain? Factor your answers into your furniture selection. For multipurpose spaces, consider double-duty pieces—sofa beds, coffee tables with storage, and generous-size tables for dining and desk work.

• *Set an affordable budget.* How much can you do yourself? Will you hire some expert craftspeople? If the project isn't doable all at once, phase it in—buy the new bed first but wait awhile on carpet, wall coverings, and accessories.

• *Call in a pro?* Interior designers can prevent costly mistakes and give you access to special products. Some set fees on a per-project basis, others charge hourly rates for their advice, and some design services are free at furniture stores.

ONE: The two homes shown on the next page have the same basic open floor plan with a focal-point fireplace. **TWO:** New built-ins give the fireplace wall depth and function. Contemporary modular seating on the angle separates living from dining areas. **THREE:** This home takes a different tack: Sofas face off at fireside and add color. A glass-topped basket forms a casual dining spot.

2

3

PLAN ON PAPER

Your home's comfort and convenience don't depend on its square footage. Space is a coveted commodity in today's homes, but it's how you arrange and furnish your rooms that counts. Even small rooms live big if you put the right pieces in the right places. But forget tugging furniture here and there to see how it looks. Measure your room and furniture, pull up an easy chair, and explore your room's options on paper. Get started with the following tips, then turn to the "Room Arranging" chapter, page 242, for more advice and a *Better Homes and Gardens*® arranging kit.

MADE TO MEASURE

• *Draw a to-scale plan on graph paper.* Transfer measurements, making one square (¼ inch) equal to 1 foot. Using the same scale, cut templates of furniture from sturdy paper; note height, depth, and width of each piece. Because color carries visual weight, shade templates with colored markers.

• *Note architectural and fixed features.* Pencil in closets, built-in cabinetry and window seats, fireplaces, electrical outlets and switches, lighting, and heat sources. Note the clearances and opening directions of doors and windows.

• *Site major pieces first on your plan.* Seating was the priority for the living room here. It's pulled in toward the room's center to free up a perimeter walkway, but there's still room to move comfortably between pieces.

• *Zone for traffic.* For traffic lanes, allow 3 feet for interior doors, 4 feet for entries, and at least 30 inches for walkways. For conversation areas, group sofas and chairs a maximum of 8 feet apart. Leave 14 to 18 inches between a sofa and coffee table and at least 3 feet of pull-out space behind dining chairs.

• *Try a do-it-yourself, life-size plan.* If it's difficult to visualize your room from to-scale templates, tape newspaper sheets together into full-size templates or stack empty cardboard boxes to approximate furniture sizes.

ONE: *Traffic to the handsome corner desk skirts the living room's conversation area because the pulled-in sofa sets the boundary.*

TWO: *Floating on a space-defining rug, lightweight seating and a sofa gather around the room's two focal points—the fireplace and an armoire with a television tucked inside.*

THREE/FOUR: *To make furnishings fit, arrange your own cut-to-scale templates on graph paper, or use our arranging kit, which begins on page 258.*

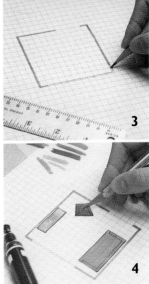

BUILD A WARDROBE

You'll find one of the best decorating strategies right in your own closet. There's that little black dress or that classic navy blue blazer that, when dressed up or down with accessories, can go anywhere and always look great. Start putting together your home's wardrobe of versatile, well-designed basics that you'll be able to mix, match, and move around today and in future homes.

FLEXIBLE PICKS

To nail down your personal style and vision for a room's design, clip magazine photos of rooms you love. Even if a photo looks nothing like your home or style, clip it if it grabs your eye—and heart—in some way. After you've amassed a dozen or more clippings, spread them out to see what they have in common. Chances are a particular furniture style, color scheme, or intriguing mix of textures or materials, such as pine with wicker, will turn up again and again. To fill in the specifics of your design plan:

• *Choose simple upholsteries.* When you're just starting out, use durable fabrics in neutral colors and subtle patterns and textures that don't steal the show. Later on, you can always pop on a slipcover or add an array of colorful toss pillows to change the palette.

• *Buy future-perfect seating.* Love seats and upholstered chairs, instead of conventional long sofas, offer more room-arranging options. They can face off around a coffee table, form a right angle in a corner, float inward to define a conversation spot, or split up to serve two rooms.

ONE: *Furnishings gathered in this new home's dining spot are an easy-going mix that can be reshuffled later on into other roles in other rooms. Countrified ladder-back chairs pull up to a clean-lined glass-top table that could become a desk for a home office/guest room. The love seat's creamy white upholstery makes it a go-anywhere piece.*

• *Rely on whites, woods, and wicker* if you're timid about mixing. They always make congenial companions and work as beautifully in the living room as they do in the bedroom.

• *Buy a few good pieces one at a time.* Whether new, antique, or fresh from a flea market, well-designed furniture pieces, old and new, that can stand on their own merits make wiser investments than matched suites. The more basic the lines of a piece, the easier it blends in. Disparate furnishings should share a unifying mood, such as formal, casual, contemporary, or country.

TWO: New, but classic, this white-on-white rolled-arm camelback sofa is elegant enough to move right into the living room, but here it adds extra curl-up comfort in the den. Natural-finish twig chairs, a wicker coffee table, and textured accents are hardworking staples of this home's flexible wardrobe.

THREE: Functional favorites—an old dresser, trunk, wicker chair, rustic accents, and a new spindle bed of timeless styling—warm up this new-home bedroom. Painting the headboard wall sky blue was an inexpensive way to fill in the blanks.

ONE: An imposing armoire makes an industrious and dramatic addition to this living room. It adds architectural impact, creates vertical interest, and stows everything from table linens and dishes to books and office supplies behind its carved doors.

TWO: There was nothing special about this new-house bedroom until the dreamy canopy bed took center stage. This showstopper dresses in citrusy hues for summer and in snug plaids for winter. Another endlessly versatile building block, the wall-hung, pine-framed mirror opens up the bedroom today—but could move to a future living room.

ONE GREAT PIECE SETS THE SCENE

Don't wait to give your rooms drama. As you build your wardrobe of furnishings, be brave. Resist the temptation to fill every nook and cranny with dull, small-scale furnishings and accessories. Instead, pare down and scale up with fewer but more high-impact pieces—items that offer grand size and unique character. Stately armoires, modular wall units, superstar beds, and such accents as oversize posters or paintings, for instance, can set a room's decorating style and become the flexible centerpieces for future decorating projects, wherever you might live.

PLAY WITH BUILDING BLOCKS

When you shop for furniture, never buy a major piece without knowing where you'll put it; take along your to-scale floor plan, a tape measure, and fabric and color samples. Don't forget to:

• *Select flexible pieces.* Make sure they can function in different ways and in different spaces. Select classic lines so they'll fit into casual or dressy, country, or modern schemes.

• *Create instant focal points.* Using large-scale furniture is a good strategy for adding character to otherwise plain-Jane rooms. Gather seating around an armoire (tuck a television inside) or a low chest topped with a large mirror or painting, or add the feeling of a vintage library with a book-filled wall unit.

• *Surprise small spaces.* Overstuffed seating drawn in around a tall, handsome cupboard actually makes a diminutive room look larger than if you squeeze in a lot of tiny tables, a lightly scaled sofa, spindly chairs, and a clutter of small accessories.

• *Think big.* And that doesn't just mean furniture. A large Oriental or woven rag rug gives a room definition and impact. Wall-hung artwork can become the dramatic focus of a seating group. When buying artwork, remember that a good print is much better than a bad original. On a tight budget? Order an especially large stretched canvas from an art-supply store, paint it whatever solid color you love, then display it proudly.

THREE: *It's hard to believe that this living room once had the blahs. Lacking a fireplace or any inherent character, this room gained a focal point with a bold red wall and new but classically styled wall units. Today, the three-piece bookcase serves as a natural magnet for the room's seating, but it can easily move to a den or bedroom later on.*

LET YOUR ROOM EVOLVE

Decorating a room, or a whole house, should be an open-ended process. The most comfortable and personal rooms continually evolve to keep pace with changing lifestyle demands, activities and jobs, interests—and, of course, tastes. Decorating an entire room all at once isn't wise, and it's hard on the budget. Satisfy your basic comforts and functions first, then phase in a room's other design elements over time. For example, invest in a bed before bedroom carpet and wall covering. Buy seating for the living room before a formal holidays-only dining table.

HAVE FUN ALONG THE WAY

What fun is a room that doesn't welcome that antique rug or painting you found at a bargain price or the Victorian wicker rocker you carted home from an auction? Your rooms should love the things you love, and if you set the scene for change, they will. To do that:

• *Adopt an easy-does-it approach.* Add elements little by little so you don't obscure a room's character. Prop framed art on the mantel before you decide where to hang it or let a wicker rocker settle into its surroundings before choosing a cushion fabric.

• *Keep it simple.* Instead of boldly patterned upholstery, complicated window treatments, and overheated colors, stick to basics, such as solid fabrics and neutral backdrops, when you're starting out. They'll make it easier for you to make changes as your decorating taste and confidence grow.

• *Know when to stop.* Don't overdecorate and don't feel compelled to fill every inch. Take a periodic

inventory to see if furnishings are meeting your needs. If a room seems claustrophobic, pare down furniture and accents to make the space look and feel larger.

• *Mix price points.* You can afford high-quality pieces when you take your time and use budget fill-ins. With a mix of your own money-saving creations, refurbished secondhand finds, and a well-designed but lower-cost unfinished piece or two, you'll actually create more interesting schemes.

ONE: *Functional, versatile, and easy to rearrange, neutral sofas and minimal accents made a great beginning for this living room.*

TWO: *Over time, some quick-and-easy weekend projects warmed the room with fresh paint, new framed prints, pillows, and tie-on tab curtains. Rearranging the seating and adding a louvered screen also gave the room more inviting intimacy.*

SHOP SMART

Browse first, buy later, should be every furniture shopper's credo. With today's dizzying array of retailers, discount stores, custom shops, and catalogs, it doesn't pay to be impulsive with high-ticket items. Peruse books and magazines to learn about styles and construction, then compare items in all price ranges.

UPHOLSTERY AND WOODS

Here are a few tips for judging furniture quality:

• ***Test-drive upholstered seating.*** Sit on it, lean on it, lift it up, and turn it over to check comfort and construction. Frames should be kiln-dried, seasoned hardwood joined by dowels or interlocking pieces, not butted together. Tempered-steel springs are coil or sagless; eight-way hand-tied coils denote good quality. Polyurethane foam is the most common filling; softer down is more expensive. (Consult the "Fabrics" chapter, page 302, before selecting upholstery fabrics.)

• ***Know your woods.*** When shopping for case goods, the industry term for hard furniture, check hangtags and labels to learn which woods or veneers are used in them.

Look for strong construction where pieces bear the most weight—legs, shelves, braces, drawers. Doors and drawers should open and shut easily, and finishes should be hard and smooth with no visible imperfections.

• ***Bone up on history.*** If you're buying reproductions, know period details and craftsmanship. Reproductions are exact copies of antiques, usually with the same materials and detail; adaptations are loosely based on original pieces; visual reproductions are made with modern shortcuts to hold down costs.

ONE: *A mix-don't-match philosophy and snappy neutral colors weave together this living-dining room's diverse pieces—new upholstery, wall units, and Shaker chairs and chest. Curtains on the French doors would give a home office privacy.*

TWO: *A classic wing chair tweaks tradition—and plays up the sassy mood—by dressing up in bold contemporary stripes.*

THREE: *Simple Shaker reproductions infuse this dining spot with historic character, but their clean lines blend them into the slick scheme.*

IN WITH THE OLD

Antiques, quirky-but-sturdy flea market furnishings, and vintage handcrafted pieces lend unrivaled character to your home. But you don't have to be an avid collector to enjoy the boost in personality that a few aged pieces can give your rooms. Scout secondhand stores, quaint shops, and auctions for treasures, keeping these shopping tips in mind:

• **Know your dealer.** If you're looking for antiques, generally defined as objects more than 100 years old, consult a reputable dealer. A piece is more valuable if it has a known maker and date, fine design, original hardware and finish, and no damage or repairs. Antiques are a major investment; you don't want to pay top dollar then discover you bought a reproduction, not an original.

• **Know the market.** Whether you want Louis XV, Shaker, American primitive, or some other style, study up on history, construction details, and most recent auction and retail prices.

• **Is it a good buy?** Wood frames should be sound with no sign of termite damage or dry rot. If legs are wobbly, finishes are marred, or upholstery is worn, factor repairs into the total cost before you decide to buy a piece.

• **Is it true love?** The antiques market is mercurial, so buy for love, not money. Whether its price is high or low, you'll always find a place for something you love. And don't worry about mixing woods and finishes; the variety builds character.

ONE: *In this charming almost alfresco dining spot, a dark-hued cupboard joins lighter-toned painted chairs and an old table. Combining woods—antique pieces and some not-quite antiques—in different colors makes the space more interesting. The cupboard is filled with bright new pottery for needed color and a spirited modern accent.*
TWO: *It's hard to resist browsing—and buying. Enjoy the thrill of the hunt but take time for close inspections of your finds.*
THREE: *A mix of antiques, acquired over several years, gathers in this rustic family room. An interplay of black and white patterns and upholstery, from sheets to vintage chenille, blends the varied pieces.*

HOUSE DRESSING

U NDAUNTED BY AN EMPTY APARTMENT AND A TIGHT BUDGET, CATHLENE VANDAFF WENT LOOKING FOR FURNISHINGS IN ALL THE RIGHT PLACES.

It's true—when the going gets tough, the tough *do* go shopping. From flea markets to salvage shops, and the like, Cathlene ("C.J.") VanDaff toted old furniture and pretty yet practical accents to a sunny apartment in a stately Greek Revival home. Then she creatively married her trove of unlikely treasures with fresh fabrics and colors, turning opposites into an attractive wardrobe of mix-and-match pieces.

LIGHTHEARTED COTTAGE

"I'm a hopeless romantic," says C.J., a designer. "I'm attracted to pretty, but not necessarily fancy, things. I gather what I love rather than what's expected." She's not totally ruled by her heart, however. She chooses many of her furnishings for their practicality as well as their charm. Her step-back cupboard—$50 at a church sale—is functional in the dining room; a bootjack bench serves as a sofa table for displaying collectibles; and a painted drop-leaf table adds a dining and sewing spot in the den. "I like the energy of contrasts, of pairing something rough with something more polished," she explains, noting that these mixes work best when one piece is subtle and doesn't compete with a more eye-catching partner. Color is her secret ingredient for successfully linking diverse finds, from primitives to her more elegant Chippendale love seat. "I love a neutral room," she says. "You can take it any way you want to." Creamy white cover-ups blend seating, and warm white walls display antique artwork, dishware, and, on the den wall, a lipstick pink and white quilt. Patchworks aren't the only color shots, however. She used floral, plaid, and gingham fabric remnants to upholster an old easy chair and toile to cushion a rustic twig seat. "You have to check out all venues and keep your eyes open," says this seasoned sleuth, "because you never know where the deal will be."

Textiles with personality, vintage furniture, and a few bold accents bring character to C. J. VanDaff's Michigan apartment.

ONE: *Unexpected old finds forge beautiful new relationships in C. J.'s at-ease living room, where a prim Chippendale love seat cozies up to a porch-style wicker chair still wearing worn paint. Canvas white walls and upholstery create the perfect backdrop for her collections of expressive, eclectic accents—old books, art, and a wall-hung platter and plates. "I want the big elements to showcase my special pieces rather than compete with them," C. J. says. Always looking for ways to introduce color and pattern, she tops bland beige carpet with an elegant hooked rug, which also defines the sitting area.*

TWO: *Although vintages vary, the objects of C. J.'s affection have at least one thing in common: a timeworn, touchable look. In this living room vignette, a slipcovered chair makes a subtle partner for the more colorful furnishings of an old chest in well-rubbed paint, an aged needlepoint pillow, and bright-hued pottery accents.*

ONE: To relax more formal elements in the living room, the shawl-back wicker chair and an old footstool wear colorful sundress florals. Basketry and aged woods enrich the textural mix.

TWO: French iron garden chairs gather for dining at a homemade plywood table topped with easy-mix and easy-care cotton prints. Flea market shutters, hinged together, create a rich-looking floor screen that divides living and dining spaces.

THREE: Picket fencing for a headboard was salvaged down on the farm. A lineup of cottage garden-style pillows and botanical art perks up the room's white walls and simple linens.

FOUR: C. J. favors painted furniture over polished woods. One of her most prized finds is the tall, handsome step-back cupboard—complete with original mouse hole—that serves the dining spot. She outfitted top shelves with self-adhesive strip lights to showcase her majolica collection.

ARRANG

ING

IMAGINE EASY-LIVING SPACES, THEN FIT your furnishings into the vision. Use this chapter's ideas for reshaping space to solve your own room-arranging puzzles.

FLOOR PLAN
BASICS

How do you define comfort? Do you like to curl up, stretch out, or put your feet up on the coffee table? Do you prefer a room that accommodates hobbies or videos so the clan can get together? Do you usually entertain for a crowd or just a few friends? Before you arrange your furnishings, decide what you want your room to do and how you live. For more on floor plan basics, see pages 90–91 in "Bedrooms," pages 44–45 in "Living Rooms," page 71 in "Dining," and page 225 in "Beginnings."

ARRANGE TO SUIT YOURSELF

Successful arrangements don't depend on the style or status of your furnishings. What matters is how your pieces work together and relate to the overall space. For example:

• *Find the focal point.* It's the all-important cornerstone of your arrangement. A fireplace, a spectacular view, and a wall of built-ins are obvious possibilities. In rooms without natural architectural focus, be creative—group furnishings around a dramatic painting, freestanding shelves, a tall cupboard or armoire, or a wall hung artfully with collectibles.

• *Subtract to add; divide to multiply.* Could you create floor space by deleting some nonessential furnishings? Would the room be more livable if you added more furniture to divide it into activity centers?

• *Break the rules.* Every sofa doesn't need to be anchored to a cocktail table. Dining tables don't need to be centered, and beds don't have to hug walls. Different plans might be more comfortable.

• *Make room for personality.* Surrounding yourself with furnishings and collections you love is the key to making a room satisfying.

ONE: *This luxurious master bedroom takes its architectural eccentricities into account. The old brass bed floats out from the wall to give the covered radiators clearance. That leaves room in the corner to showcase an heirloom clock.*

TWO: *A blend of sophisticated comfort and Scandinavian charm, this living room's lace-dressed bay window is its focal point. The sofa placed in front of it shares the spotlight. Instead of the expected coffee table, a higher tea table serves snacks comfortably. Seating ushers traffic around the grouping.*

DIRECTING TRAFFIC

The party's over, but don't ignore the messages your guests left behind. Did they pull lightly scaled chairs and an ottoman off the beaten path and into a corner for undisturbed conversation? Did they edge modular seating closer to the television so they could watch the game without people traipsing by the screen? Both situations should clue you in to how you can make your everyday furniture arrangements more comfortable and convenient. After all, entertaining is the best test of the suitability of your home's traffic patterns.

GO WITH THE FLOW

Making your home convenient means grouping your furniture to promote traffic flow and encourage whatever activities you've planned for your rooms. Use furniture as curbs to funnel traffic around seating or a hobby or homework table, or to channel it through a family room/dining spot to the backyard.

• *Halt cross-traffic.* If pedestrians are conversation stoppers as they constantly cut through the main sitting area, rearrange your room. This family room, *opposite*, uses seating to help wall off three sides of the conversation zone, buffering the spot.

• *Eliminate speed bumps.* Locate secondary sitting or work spots so they don't impede across-the-room traffic. Make sure electrical cords aren't underfoot and secure area rugs along routes with tape or nonskid backing.

• *Create an entry.* If your front door opens directly into the living room, create an entry with a love seat or tall screen. Just back either piece up to the boundary.

Rooms broken up by many doors and doorways only seem like a nightmare. Here grouped seating and end tables create clear traffic lanes that lead around—not through—the fireside conversation area to the dining area, patio, and hallways beyond.

• *Keep lanes in line.* Allow about 2½ to 3 feet for major traffic lanes. For other furniture placement measurements, refer to page 225 in the "Beginnings" chapter. Custom-size certain pathways, for instance, widening the space between sofa and cocktail table for long-legged comfort.

Maintain your Equilibrium

What makes a photograph or painting intriguing is the same secret ingredient that makes space configurations successful. It's composition—a well-balanced mix of large- and small-scale furniture, accessories, accent colors, and patterns throughout a room. Coax the eye off a single plane with interesting furniture and art high and low. Give the eye a rest now and then with breathing room—not clutter—around furnishings. With appropriate composition, spaces avoid that uncomfortable, listing-ship feeling. (For more on balance, scale, and proportion, turn to the "Elements" chapter, page 265.)

FORGING GOOD RELATIONSHIPS

Balance works on the teeter-totter principle. If a large sitting group at one end of a living room lacks a counterweight such as built-ins, the room seems lopsided. You needn't match a chunky sofa pound for pound with another hefty piece; just group a couple of chairs, a table, and an area rug that together are in the same visual weight class. To create equilibrium:

• *Practice your scales.* The scale of individual pieces contributes to a room's overall balance. Next to massive upholstered seating, a delicate tea table with slender legs looks spindly, but a heavy marble-topped coffee table holds its own. A small lamp gets lost on a large table, and an oversize painting overwhelms any small furniture beneath it.

• *Count color in.* Dark upholstery grants importance to seating, but covering a sofa to match wall color blends it into the background. If you anchor an area with strong, dark colors or bold patterns, scatter colorful accessories around the room for balance.

In this narrow 1880s row house, four inviting armchairs provide for comfortable conversation while allowing traffic to flow by. Working together, the weighty quartet balances the bay window and built-in sofa on the front wall. A tall tea table and a wall-hung print anchor the four chairs, the loftiness of the print balancing the height of the front door and windows.

PULL FURNISHINGS AWAY FROM THE WALLS

Most rooms have a few architectural eccentricities that may foil your room-arranging plans. But don't despair. Rooms that are boxy, tunnel-like, or have walls broken up with doors and windows will benefit from easy solutions that are literally off-the-wall.

RESHAPE YOUR SPACE

Instead of lining furnishings around the room in waiting-room fashion, float or angle your groupings. The two rooms shown here illustrate these points:

• *Arrange on the diagonal.* A diagonal is the longest line through any space; arrange a sofa on the diagonal, and you will widen a room visually while also making room for more seating. In the narrow room *opposite*, the sofa angles across the corner between two windows, creating a room-stretching line and making way for a pair of slipper chairs.

• *Place a sofa crosswise* to emphasize the width, not the length, of the room. Placed perpendicular to the long wall, the sofa *at right* makes a wide cut across the room. Two chairs opposite the sofa emphasize the new width and round out the conversation area. The sofa also divides the "living" from the "dining" areas. The front window, dramatized with fabric, serves as a bright focal point.

• *Float furnishings.* When seating is tied to the walls, conversation groupings often become awkwardly far-flung. Move sofas and chairs away from the walls and into tighter groupings to facilitate conversation and coziness. Floating the groupings also frees up perimeter space for storage, desks, and walkways.

• *Change proportions.* Refer to the "Color" chapter, page 279, to learn how light and dark hues visually reshape your rooms. Furniture can help, too. Square up a long, narrow room with bookshelves across one end; they'll seem to advance to shorten the space.

ONE: *Simply dressed windows are the backdrop for this striped love seat that angles between the panes despite the dictates of convention. Now the small, square room is blessed with eye-pleasing proportion because the sofa accentuates room width.*

TWO: *In this traditional living room, seating anchored by a colorful kilim rug is placed crosswise to square up the long and narrow space. The sofa serves as a low wall, separating the intimate conversation area from the dining area behind it.*

Factor flexibility into design schemes, and rooms will satisfy your family's needs today and meet tomorrow's demands with comfort and convenience. A room never risks getting stale and set in its ways if its furnishings are versatile and easily reworked for a fresh outlook and updated function. Multifaceted spaces are more livable—always ready for entertaining or even day-to-night and season-to-season use.

ON-THE-MOVE ROOMS

From upholstered seating to stackable chests and wall units, modular furniture is the handy solution for hard-to-arrange spaces. It's sized and shaped to fit together in numerous ways,

CHANGE HAPPENS

so regrouping components is easy. Scaled-down pieces are available for compact spaces. Also consider these ideas:

• *Opt for double duty.* Choose furnishings with multiple functions. A drop-leaf table can be an everyday sofa table that pops up for dining when occasional chairs are pulled around it. Look for sleek sleep sofas, Murphy-style beds, and wall units customized for home offices and entertainment centers.

• *Make it movable.* Include easily moved sitting pieces— lightly scaled chairs, ottomans, small benches—and even tables on casters to meet your changing needs. If a television can't be placed close to the fireplace, include swivel chairs that will let you shift your attention as needed.

• *Recast your characters.* Your furniture may be more adaptable than you realize, so rethink its function before buying anew. Armoires and cupboards stow entertainment gear, daybeds serve as settees, dining tables work as desks, and ottomans, trunks, and benches make interesting coffee tables.

• *Watch the clock and calendar.* A home's traffic patterns change after the children go to sleep, so tuck a desk/study area into a playroom corner or the foyer. In winter, scoot a comfy chair in front of an unused patio or porch entrance.

Flexible furnishings help this living room rise to the occasion for an intimate dinner party. The love seat and overstuffed armchair, usually focused on the fireplace, now angle toward a round table that's moved into the spotlight and dressed up for company. When the party's over, the table can resume its role as an oversize end table.

ARRANGE FOR YOUR LIFESTYLE

A room's major furnishings usually dominate your attention, budget, and design strategies. But don't miss a chance to provide function with a little change here and there. Place a bistro table and chairs in an alcove for morning coffee. Tuck a pull-down desk into kitchen cabinetry for homework. No matter how small the room, you can increase its function by reclaiming slivers of space and selecting furnishings that do the job.

GETTING PERSONAL

Your rooms' roles aren't carved in stone. You decide how you want to live in your space

• **Arrange a dinner date.** If you require an everyday den and only occasionally a formal dining room, design one room to do both. With a table and chairs pulled up to the upholstered daybed, this den, *right*, entertains guests, then gets back to business the next day.

• **Invite an entry to tea.** As you look for new function, think small—alcoves and stair landings for seating and under-stairs nooks for desks. The entry, *opposite*, becomes a dining spot with the addition of a drop-leaf table. Overlooking the living room, it's ideal for tea and small parties.

• **Have a seat.** Dressed-up daybeds or long, low lounges turn unused space in bay windows into reading and relaxing spots. Replace the ubiquitous end-of-the-bed blanket chest with a small-scale love seat.

ONE: *When guests are due, the upholstered daybed and living room armchairs team up as seating around the table. Because this elegant apartment's rooms are open to one another, they're visually linked with the variations of striped silk on the daybed and chairs.*

TWO: *This small home's space isn't wasted on a separate dining room, because the homeowners drafted their high-ceilinged entry for the job. The antique drop-leaf table accommodates up to six diners comfortably, and seating brought from other rooms supplements the Victorian-style chairs on casters.*

THREE: *When at ease, the entry's drop-leaf table folds down on one side and scoots back against the wall so it's out of hallway traffic. Topped with a bouquet and a few collectibles, the table offers a gracious greeting to arriving guests and is a handy spot for tossing keys and shopping bags.*

DIVIDE AND CONQUER

Rambling great-rooms and open floor plans are more the rule than the exception in contemporary homes. Even in renovations, it's likely walls will fall as homeowners update with multipurpose spaces that keep families connected no matter what they're doing—reading, cooking, enjoying a hobby, dining, or watching television.

TAME YOUR SPACE

Although the great-room here boasts a spectacular vaulted ceiling and views, the well-planned furniture arrangements and design elements make the long, narrow space cohesive and livable. Here's how it's subtly subdivided into comfort zones:

• ***Talk comes first.*** At midroom, the dramatic fireplace is the conversation area's natural focus. Leather chairs backed up to the walkway establish the outer limits. A flooring change—from hardwood to tile—also sets off this zone. Wired-in floor plugs for the lamps eliminate the hazard of snaking electrical cords.

• ***Define activities.*** The room's windowed corner is a secondary sitting spot with backless upholstered lounges instead of traditional sofas that would have blocked the view and light. The focal point here? The piano.

• ***Leave breathing room.*** The wide-open stretch behind the main conversation area is a generous corridor for all three living zones, and it affords access to the grand French doors and terrace beyond.

• ***Link with design elements.*** On the airy backdrop, a taupe stripe wraps the entire space. A carpet runner is the visual bridge between dining and secondary sitting areas. Grid patterns repeat in floor tile, mullions, and fireplace design.

ONE: *Clean-lined furnishings, earthy colors, and warming textures—all with substantial visual weight—bring this two-story great-room down to earth. The fireplace is the focal point for major seating that rests on an island defined by tile flooring and a colorful kilim. Floor plugs allow lamps to shine where needed.*

TWO: *The same open-plan great-room is subdivided into three activity areas. A room-size dining alcove and a secondary sitting spot gathered around the piano flank the living space (also seen above).*

ROOM ARRANGING MADE EASY

Creating an inviting room has less to do with what you have than how you use it. By following these guidelines, you can design a room from scratch or rearrange what you have to make the most of your furnishings and space. How would you like the room to function? Do you want places for desk work, hobbies, kids' games? Do you want to watch television, play the piano, dine, read? What about storage or display space? Look at your present furnishings and decide what pieces you'll have to add and which ones you can eliminate to meet your needs.

MAKING ARRANGEMENTS

Using the *Better Homes and Gardens®* floor plan kit and templates, *opposite* and *on pages 260–263*, work through the following steps.

• *Measure your room.* Plot it on the kit's grid—or graph paper—using one square for each square foot of floor space. Determine the length of each wall, and draw it onto the floor plan. Mark windows with a double line, leave an open area for doorways, and indicate door swings. Include architectural features such as fireplaces, sliding glass doors, stairways, and bay windows.

• *Use furniture templates.* Measure each furniture piece. Trace or photocopy the kit's corresponding templates and cut them out with a crafts knife. *Hint:* If you need to make your own special templates, outline them on graph paper or cut them out of self-sticking Post-it notes so you can position—and reposition—them as needed.

• *Find a focal point.* Physically, this is the cornerstone around which you build a grouping; visually, it's the dramatic element that draws you into a room. If your room doesn't have a natural focus—a fireplace, built-in bookcases, or expansive window—substitute a large-scale or boldly hued accessory or use freestanding wall units.

GET MOVING

Once you've found the focus, arrange your furniture templates on the graph paper floor plan. Keep these tips in mind:

• *Direct traffic.* If traffic passes through a room, it doesn't have to run through the center of it. Think of your furniture pieces as walls or guideposts that can funnel traffic around your conversation areas.

• *Float furnishings.* A lineup of furniture around a room is as inviting as a waiting room. Pull pieces away from walls into close-knit groupings with major seating no more than 8 feet apart.

• *Keep convenience within reach.* Set a handy resting place for drinks or books close to every seat. It can be a true end table, a stack of books, or simply a piece of glass atop a decorative basket or cube. Just be sure the surface is roughly the same height as the arm of the chair or sofa next to it.

• *Do a balancing act.* Combine furnishings of different heights and hefts for interest, but avoid placing all of your tall or weighty pieces on the same side of the room. It will look lopsided if you do.

• *Forget room labels.* Use space creatively, letting your furniture determine the room's function. Who says your L-shaped dining area can't function as a TV spot? Why not dine in the living room?

• *Try a fresh angle.* Because a diagonal is the longest line through any room, an angled grouping creates an illusion of width. On-the-bias seating also takes advantage of two focal points—for example, a fireplace and window view—at once.

• *Cozy up a big room.* Divide and conquer. Break the room into two or more groupings for coziness and better function.

• *Maximize a small room.* Include a large-scale piece, such as a vintage armoire or a fat love seat, for a feeling of grandeur. Use vertical storage in tight spaces.

• *"Widen" a long, narrow room.* Place major furniture crosswise or on the diagonal to break a skinny room into a friendlier time-out spot.

• *Fix low or high ceilings.* "Raise" a low ceiling with floor-to-ceiling window treatments and tall furniture. "Lower" a ceiling with a colorful area rug and low-level lighting; play up the floor-hugging look by hanging artwork so that it's at eye level when you are seated.

When planning your room schemes on paper, use these symbols to profile your space and see it with more dimension. Copy or trace the templates that best reflect your furnishings and begin experimenting with different arrangements.

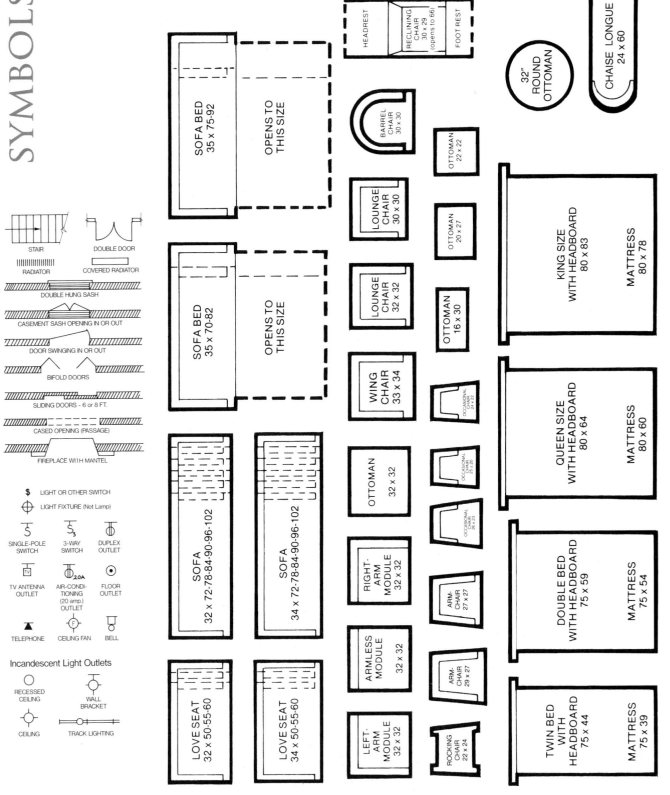

SYMBOLS

STAIR

DOUBLE DOOR

RADIATOR

COVERED RADIATOR

DOUBLE HUNG SASH

CASEMENT SASH OPENING IN OR OUT

DOOR SWINGING IN OR OUT

BIFOLD DOORS

SLIDING DOORS - 6 or 8 FT.

CASED OPENING (PASSAGE)

FIREPLACE WITH MANTEL

$ LIGHT OR OTHER SWITCH

LIGHT FIXTURE (Not Lamp)

SINGLE-POLE SWITCH

3-WAY SWITCH

DUPLEX OUTLET

TV ANTENNA OUTLET

AIR-CONDI-TIONING (20 amp.) OUTLET

FLOOR OUTLET

TELEPHONE

CEILING FAN

BELL

Incandescent Light Outlets

RECESSED CEILING

WALL BRACKET

CEILING

TRACK LIGHTING

SOFA BED 35 x 75-92

OPENS TO THIS SIZE

SOFA BED 35 x 70-82

OPENS TO THIS SIZE

SOFA 32 x 72-78-84-90-96-102

SOFA 34 x 72-78-84-90-96-102

LOVE SEAT 32 x 50-55-60

LOVE SEAT 34 x 50-55-60

HEADREST

RECLINING CHAIR 30 x 29 (opens to 66)

FOOT REST

BARREL CHAIR 30 x 30

LOUNGE CHAIR 30 x 30

LOUNGE CHAIR 32 x 32

WING CHAIR 33 x 34

OTTOMAN 32 x 32

RIGHT-ARM MODULE 32 x 32

ARMLESS MODULE 32 x 32

LEFT-ARM MODULE 32 x 32

ROCKING CHAIR 22 x 24

OTTOMAN 22 x 22

OTTOMAN 20 x 27

OTTOMAN 16 x 30

OCCASIONAL CHAIR 24 x 22

OCCASIONAL CHAIR 25 x 20

OCCASIONAL CHAIR 26 x 23

ARM-CHAIR 27 x 27

ARM-CHAIR 29 x 27

32" ROUND OTTOMAN

CHAISE LONGUE 24 x 60

KING SIZE WITH HEADBOARD 80 x 83

MATTRESS 80 x 78

QUEEN SIZE WITH HEADBOARD 80 x 64

MATTRESS 80 x 60

DOUBLE BED WITH HEADBOARD 75 x 59

MATTRESS 75 x 54

TWIN BED WITH HEADBOARD 75 x 44

MATTRESS 75 x 39

TEMPLATES FOR UPHOLSTERED FURNITURE AND BEDDING

TEMPLATES FOR OCCASIONAL TABLES AND SPECIAL PIECES

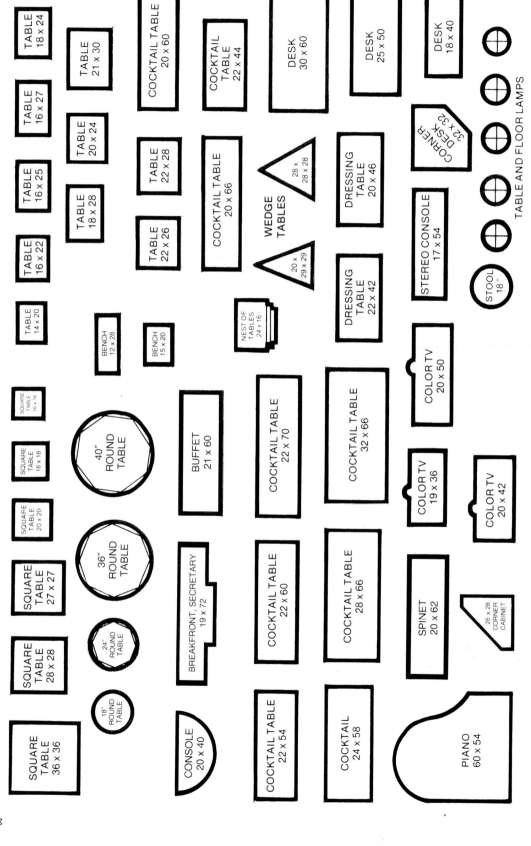

TABLE 18 x 24

TABLE 16 x 27

TABLE 16 x 25

TABLE 16 x 22

TABLE 14 x 20

TABLE 21 x 30

TABLE 20 x 24

TABLE 18 x 28

SQUARE TABLE 16 x 16

SQUARE TABLE 18 x 18

SQUARE TABLE 20 x 20

SQUARE TABLE 27 x 27

SQUARE TABLE 28 x 28

SQUARE TABLE 36 x 36

COCKTAIL TABLE 20 x 60

COCKTAIL TABLE 22 x 44

TABLE 22 x 28

TABLE 22 x 26

COCKTAIL TABLE 20 x 66

WEDGE TABLES

28 x 28 x 28

20 x 29 x 29

DESK 30 x 60

DESK 25 x 50

DESK 18 x 40

CORNER DESK 32 x 32

DRESSING TABLE 20 x 46

DRESSING TABLE 22 x 42

STEREO CONSOLE 17 x 54

STOOL 18"

TABLE AND FLOOR LAMPS

BENCH 12 x 28

BENCH 15 x 20

NEST OF TABLES 24 x 16

40" ROUND TABLE

36" ROUND TABLE

24" ROUND TABLE

18" ROUND TABLE

BUFFET 21 x 60

BREAKFRONT, SECRETARY 19 x 72

CONSOLE 20 x 40

COCKTAIL TABLE 22 x 70

COCKTAIL TABLE 32 x 66

COCKTAIL TABLE 22 x 60

COCKTAIL TABLE 28 x 66

COCKTAIL TABLE 22 x 54

COCKTAIL 24 x 58

COLOR TV 20 x 50

COLOR TV 19 x 36

COLOR TV 20 x 42

SPINET 20 x 62

26 x 28 CORNER CABINET

PIANO 60 x 54

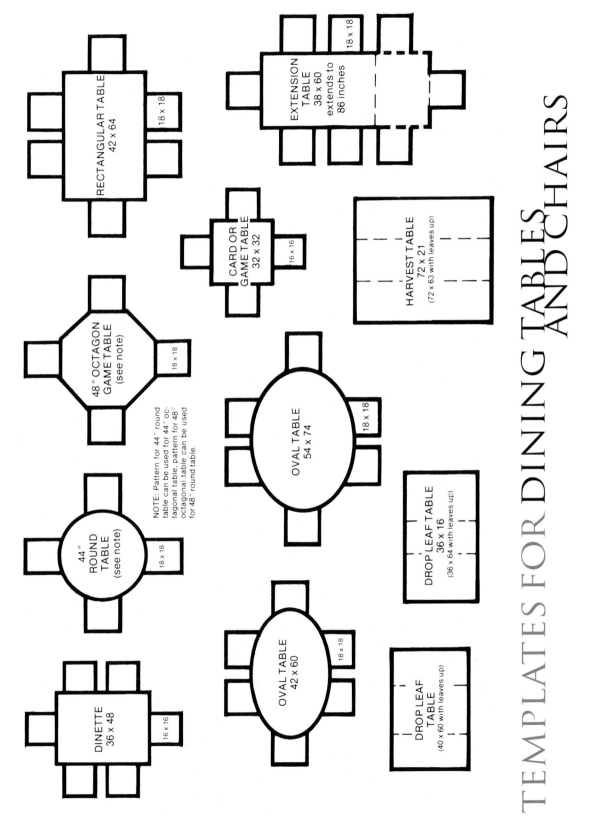

RECTANGULAR TABLE
42 x 64

18 x 18

EXTENSION TABLE
38 x 60
extends to
86 inches

18 x 18

CARD OR
GAME TABLE
32 x 32

16 x 16

HARVEST TABLE
72 x 21
(72 x 63 with leaves up)

48" OCTAGON
GAME TABLE
(see note)

18 x 18

OVAL TABLE
54 x 74

18 x 18

NOTE: Pattern for 44" round table can be used for 44" octagonal table, pattern for 48" octagonal table can be used for 48" round table.

44"
ROUND
TABLE
(see note)

18 x 18

DROP LEAF TABLE
36 x 16
(36 x 64 with leaves up)

DINETTE
36 x 48

16 x 16

OVAL TABLE
42 x 60

18 x 18

DROP LEAF
TABLE
(40 x 60 with leaves up)

TEMPLATES FOR DINING TABLES AND CHAIRS

DIAGRAMS FOR INTERCHANGEABLE STORAGE AND SPECIAL PIECES

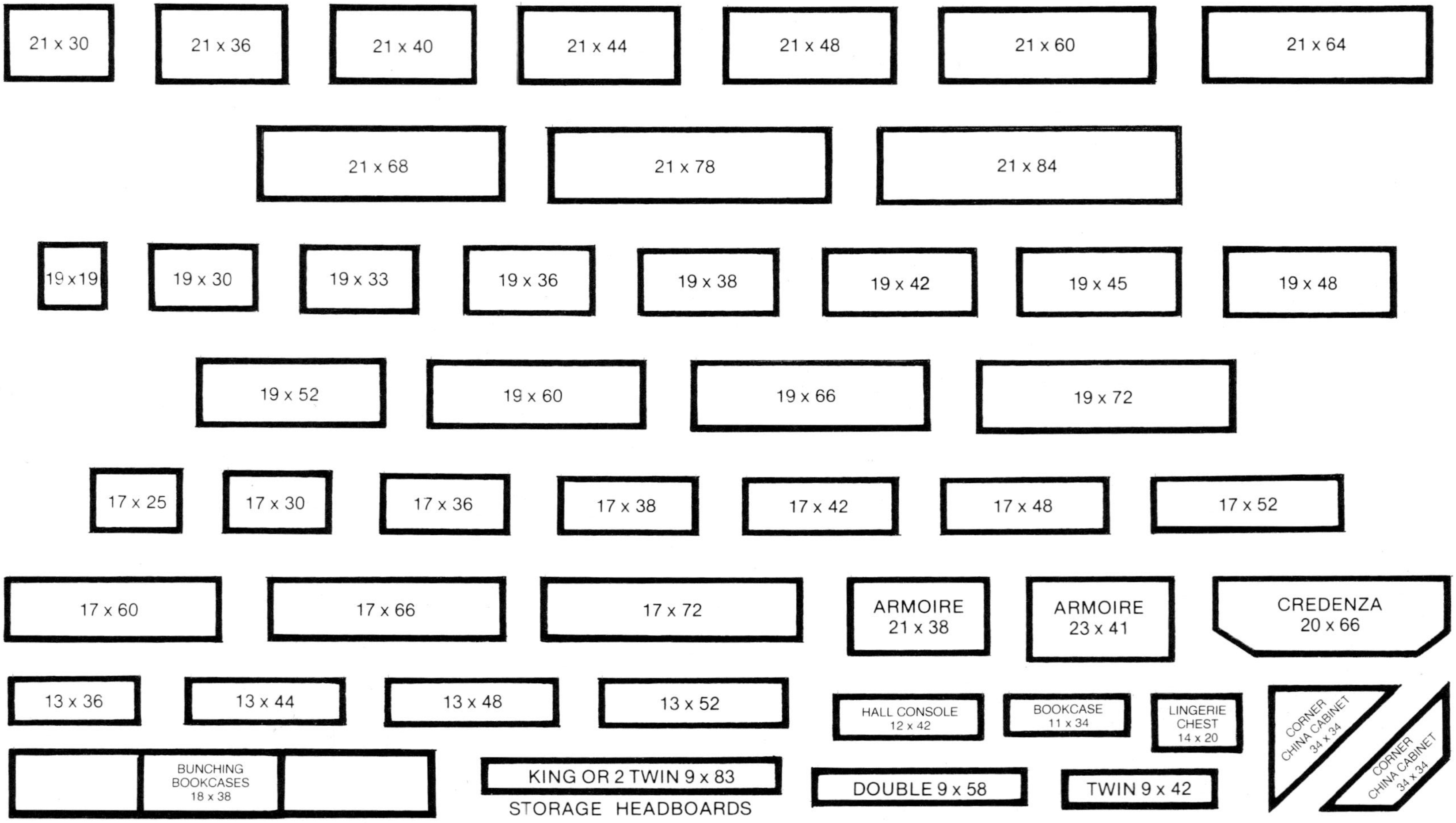

21 x 30
21 x 36
21 x 40
21 x 44
21 x 48
21 x 60
21 x 64

21 x 68
21 x 78
21 x 84

19 x 19
19 x 30
19 x 33
19 x 36
19 x 38
19 x 42
19 x 45
19 x 48

19 x 52
19 x 60
19 x 66
19 x 72

17 x 25
17 x 30
17 x 36
17 x 38
17 x 42
17 x 48
17 x 52

17 x 60
17 x 66
17 x 72

ARMOIRE 21 x 38
ARMOIRE 23 x 41
CREDENZA 20 x 66

CORNER CHINA CABINET 34 x 34
CORNER CHINA CABINET 34 x 34

HALL CONSOLE 12 x 42
BOOKCASE 11 x 34
LINGERIE CHEST 14 x 20

13 x 36
13 x 44
13 x 48
13 x 52

BUNCHING BOOKCASES 18 x 38

KING OR 2 TWIN 9 x 83
DOUBLE 9 x 58
TWIN 9 x 42
STORAGE HEADBOARDS

These templates can be used for charting chests, dressers, serving carts, buffets, china cabinets, credenzas, consoles, hutches, tea carts, bars, stereo cabinets, hope chests, window chests, secretaries, and many other pieces of furniture onto your floor plan.

ROOM ARRANGING GRAPH GUIDE
1 SQUARE EQUALS 1 SQUARE FOOT

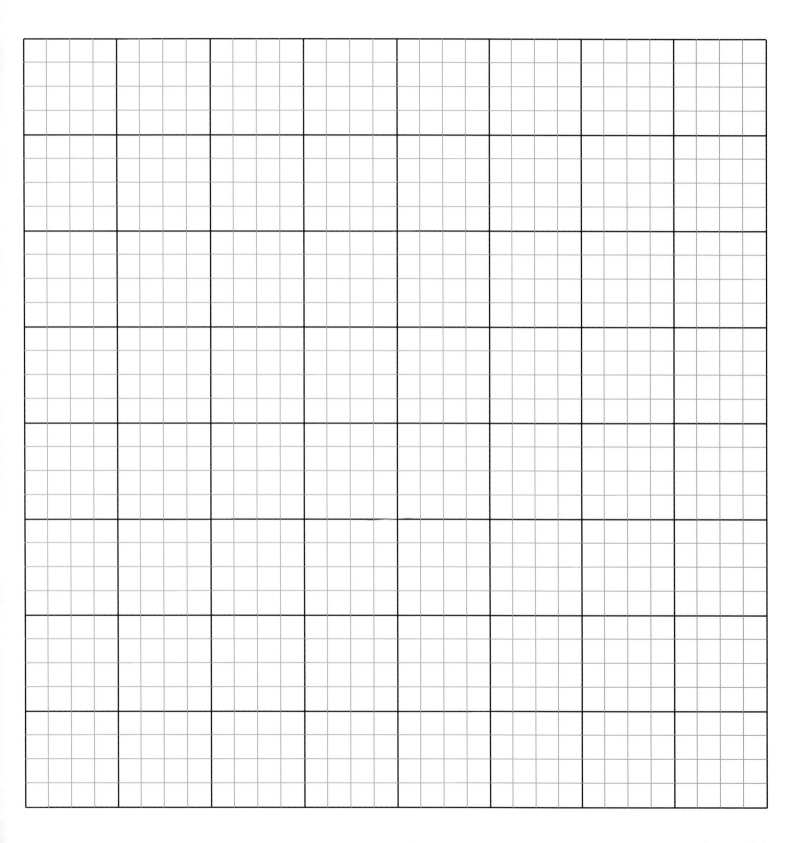

ELEMENTS

THE KEYS TO GOOD DESIGN AREN'T SECRETED away by professional decorators. You follow the same principles they do when you select your day's attire each morning. So just think of the decorating process as dressing your home. Used wisely, texture, pattern, visual rhythm, proportion, and balance produce the artistic arrangements that will stamp any room with personal style.

VARY THE TEXTURES FOR IMPACT

2

exture is one of the more subtle, but most important, design tools. Though not as dramatic as bold color or lively pattern, its presence makes the difference between a merely well-designed room and one that resonates with richness. The key lies in diversity.

MIX IT UP

Think of pairing opposites: hard and soft, nubby and smooth, rough and slick, fuzzy and silky, coarse and fine. This means using a little creativity when selecting your furniture and accessories. Matched suites won't do. Mix things up by encircling your smooth wood table with rippled wicker chairs. Pull a rough-hewn iron lamp and nubby throw close to a petal-soft sofa. Experiment with textiles of different "feels," from crisp chintzes to feathery velvets, with a few nubby weaves tossed in as wake-up calls. It's also important that you:

• *Texture your backgrounds.* Play rough against smooth, shiny against matte when planning floors and walls. Plop a fuzzy or woven rug atop a floor of smooth, gleaming hardwood to intrigue the eye. Contrast a rough brick or stone wall with a shiny framed mirror or warm a flat, painted wall with a textured-plaster dado.

• *Weigh the effects.* The use of certain textures goes a long way in defining a room's mood. It's really just common sense. Grouping soft, fine textures casts a romantic, feminine spell; rugged, hard surfaces create a more masculine mood. When planning your mix, pick the mood you want and rely on the textures that will express that feeling for a majority of the room's materials. Then look for ways in which you can diversify.

ONE: *Use textures to add warmth. Here an elegant sofa and glossy wood-look laminate floor serve as a stage for textural drama played out by rugged woods, weathered iron, and woven wicker.*

TWO: *A medley of earthy textures enhances this cottage dining spot. The coarse sisal rug anchors wavy wicker chairs to the wood table, and satiny chintz cushions contrast pleasantly with rough stone walls.*

PUT PATTERN IN ITS PLACE

Because pattern is a powerful design tool, it can be intimidating. Use these simple guidelines for choosing and mixing patterns, and you'll remove the guesswork—and restore the fun. (For more on using pattern, see the "Fabrics" chapter, page 303.)

PATTERN HAS WEIGHT

To keep a room in balance, it's usually best to distribute pattern evenly around a room. The exception? You can place all your pattern in one part of a room—say, to draw the eye to a seating grouping—as long as that cluster of pattern is balanced by weighty furnishings or architectural features elsewhere.

KEEP SCALE IN MIND

Consider a room's size when choosing patterns. Small prints may look insignificant in a large room; a large print may overpower a small room. Then consider how the pattern will be used. A large-scale print in tall draperies has room to repeat its pattern, but it won't work on a little cushion. Smaller furnishings need smaller prints. Upholstery patterns should complement the lines of furniture.

When mixing patterns, vary the size of the prints from large- and medium- to small-

ONE: *A rooster and sunflower print on seating is strong enough to balance the visual weight of the stone and log wall. Checks on the chair make a soft complement.*

TWO: *The love seat's chintz establishes this room's palette, with plaid rose chairs and pillows in assorted prints based on colors in the dominant floral pattern.*

scale designs. If you're new to pattern mixing, add a fail-safe geometric mixer, such as a check or stripe. Wake up a floral sofa with a couple of striped toss pillows. Still timid? Investigate today's worry-free, premixed collections. As you create your own fabric blends, keep the following in mind.

• *Select patterns within a color family* for pleasing harmony. Patterns don't have to be the same color, but there should be a thread of continuity.

• *Maintain the right attitude* of casualness or formality. Don't mix a formal silk damask with a country gingham. Do mix damask with moiré stripes or gingham with ticking.

GET SOME RHYTHM GOING

Rhythm isn't restricted to poetry and the performing arts. Some living spaces almost sing and dance with a beat of their own. By repeating colors, patterns, or shapes, you can create the kind of visual rhythm that grabs the eye and leads it through a room.

SET THE TEMPO

Sometimes you want a room's tempo to seem brisk, lively, and playful. In other rooms, the pace needs to be waltzlike, graceful, and slow. Whichever rhythm you choose, select and place the colors, patterns, shapes, and textures carefully. For example, the lineup of square checks and hard-edged artwork *opposite* produces a sharper, staccato look; the rounded plates and platters at *left* set a softer, more languid pace.

GO FOR THE FLOW

• *Scatter a dominant hue* throughout the room, because color repetition keeps the eye moving along and weaves the space together. Don't forget color and pattern for walls and floors.

• *Punctuate with accent colors,* placing them around a room in spots where you want the eye to pause and linger.

• *Use bold patterns* for windows and upholstery. Geometrics and viney florals have natural rhythm. They bring neutral walls to life and make seating a focal point. Throw pillows in several patterns add staccato rhythm to a sofa.

• *Draw the eye to texture.* A rough-hewn stone urn displayed in a corner grabs your attention when surrounded by soft colors, textiles, and seating.

• *Group objects for impact.* Small objects strewn about a room don't facilitate visual movement. Displayed together, however, they captivate the eye.

• *When in doubt, subtract* patterns, colors, or objects to lower a room's energy level and prevent the eye from working overtime.

ONE: *A parade of blue-and-white pottery sets this primitive hutch pulsating with rhythm. Color creates the flow; the varying shapes and sizes slow the pace.*
TWO: *The eye can't help but keep time to the beat created by contrasting colors on the graphic buffalo-check fabrics. Echoing the boxy checks, a trio of black-framed prints marches across the wall, leading the eye toward the smaller framed print on the table.*

ONE: *The size and shape of pieces in this room work in harmony, proving the importance of proportion. The pair of wing chairs holds its own alongside a chunky sofa. Large but lightly scaled, the end table and lamp balance but do not overpower the airy Windsor chair diagonally across from them.*

TWO: *Small-scale rooms can benefit from large-scale furnishings. This whimsical cottage bed brings grand height and architectural presence to a bedroom of postage-stamp size. The bed doesn't overwhelm the space, however, because it's painted white to blend into the background.*

KEEP THINGS IN PROPORTION

One of the easiest ways to understand proportion is through negative examples. Who hasn't seen a lamp that was much too large for its tiny table? Or who hasn't noticed a willowy, slim-lined chair that seemed to be swallowed up by the heft of a nearby sofa? In furniture design, proportion is about the relationship between the parts of a piece—how the shape and size of the chair arms look when compared to the shape and size of the legs and seat. In room design, it's about how furnishings look in relation to each other and to the room itself. Getting proportions right means working out the relationships among your furnishings—choosing and arranging pieces so they appear compatible in scale.

RELATIVELY SPEAKING

• *Group small furnishings* or they get lost in large-scale spaces. However, don't limit petite rooms to small-scale pieces. A single oversize piece adds surprising architectural interest and makes a room feel larger.

• *Forget mirror images* when trying to create pleasing proportions with furnishings at the ends of a sofa. Tables and accessories don't have to match. A lower table at one end could have a taller lamp.

• *Check the visual weight* of furnishings because it's just as important as height. Even if chairs are the same height, a reed-thin one looks awkward beside a bulky one.

• *Compose tabletop displays* that span at least one-third the table's diameter. For impact, groupings should be a few inches taller than one-half the table's height.

• *Think big,* starting with your largest piece of furniture—usually the sofa. Then add other furnishings that visually fit. A table and lamp may be proportionate to each other, but placed next to a sofa, may look too large or too small.

2

DO A BALANCING ACT

Even when a room's furnishings have the right proportions, the overall effect still may not be quite right. The balance may be off. Even if furnishings are compatible in scale, unless they're arranged in balance, the eye won't be content.

JUGGLING THE ELEMENTS

Several forms of balance within a room increase the space's overall impact. For example, a symmetrical grouping of sofas flanking a fireplace will be more interesting if the mantel grouping begins with an off-center painting. Consider the following major types of balance before deciding which works for you.

• *Formal symmetry* is created with mirror images on either side of an imaginary line that goes through the middle of a space. Objects don't have to be identical on either side—just close enough in size and shape to create the idea of a perfect match. Symmetry soothes the eye but risks boredom unless you add one off-center item, such as a mantel scarf that dips to one side.

• *Asymmetrical arrangements* don't pretend to be mirror images. Instead, this informal balance evenly distributes visual weight. Five objects grouped on one side balance a massive piece on the other. A fat, squat object makes a pleasing counterpoint to an array of tall, thin objects.

• *Radial balance* is like the dial on a clock. To add interest to a boxy painting or straight mantel, for instance, radiate objects an equal distance from, and around, a central point.

ONE: *Like the colorful flea market tableware on the shelf, objects displayed on the upper reaches of a wall must be balanced among themselves and in relation to the furnishings below. For vertical balance, artwork bridges the gap between shelf and table.*

COLOR WEIGHS IN

In balancing your room's design, remember that color wields great influence. Warm colors and bright patterns advance toward you, visually consuming more space than their cooler colleagues. When using two paint colors or patterns on one wall, apply the warmer or brighter one to the lower part as an anchor. Apply the receding color or quieter pattern on top, just as you do with fashion apparel. Otherwise, the space looks top-heavy, disrupting balance. Consider the effect of color when arranging accents. Group more objects to balance items with greater visual weight due to color.

TWO: *This elegant entry achieves near symmetry and sets a formal mood. The various curves and novel shapes make provocative yet congenial companions.*

THREE: *Symmetry and asymmetry work together. The love seat is centered; kitchen stools and above-the-counter artwork at one side balance modular storage cubes at the other.*

2

1

3

ARTFUL ARRANGING MADE EASY

Now that you have the various tools of design snugly under your belt, it's time to put them to work—to have fun and build confidence by playing with design principles in small ways. Create a new tabletop or shelf grouping, or rearrange an existing one. When selecting items for vignettes, keep in mind that an odd number of objects in a grouping has more visual appeal than an even number of pieces. For an asymmetrical informal look, use a one-third/two-thirds guideline; start with the tallest object one-third of the way in from one side of your display, then work down and out with smaller items. Use unequal negative (or blank) space between items to add more visual interest.

KITCHEN GARDEN

• *Group like objects.* Containers don't have to match; in fact, it's more interesting if they don't. For easy mixing, remember that you can't go wrong if you choose items that share the same color and material. *Opposite*, green glassware filled with white baby's-breath and Queen Anne's lace creates a mini meadow.

• *Vary the heights* from low jars to tall bottles, then arrange the containers in overlapping triangles to create movement.

• *Add depth.* Instead of a flat lineup, stagger glassware in a front-to-back zigzag pattern to plant a deep forest of green.

PITCHER PERFECT

• *Create a focal point.* The framed photo with its wide mat and the wooden shelf form the nucleus of this grouping, *above*.

• *Use an odd number of objects.* A display of two objects can be static and formal; add a third to get a display moving.

• *Be repetitious.* Unified both by color and the green foliage, this line of white ironware, with its progression of shapely handles and lips, carries the eye along.

• *Leave some breathing room.* Instead of cramming too many objects together, allow some space between them so that shapely pieces can show off their curves.

ALL IT TAKES is a little courage and confidence to create color schemes that please your eye and psyche. To build your confidence, we'll lead you through the basics of choosing and mixing colors. For a high-energy but low-risk start, take a cue from these settings. Grab some paint and contrast one or two solid colors with lots of white. If you tire of it later, simply repaint.

COLOR

PRIMARY TERTIARY

SECONDARY MONOCHROMATIC

WHAT COLORS SPEAK TO YOU?

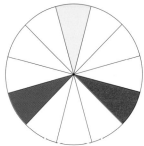

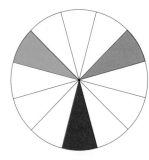

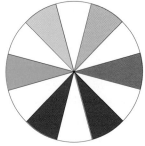

It's easy to pick a favorite color for your rooms. For the visual tension that makes things interesting, however, a single color isn't always enough. Mixing colors takes some skill, but it shouldn't intimidate. Begin with your favorite color, then use the simple color wheel lessons on the next few pages to find compatible accents for it. For starters, you can prevent color clashes with a palette from one of four color groups: primary, secondary, tertiary, and monochromatic.

A STRONG FOUNDATION: PRIMARY COLORS

For rooms that come off feeling strong and solid, a scheme of primary colors—red, blue, and yellow—is an ideal choice. Each is a pure color that can't be created by mixing other hues. Use them in pairs or combine all three; they work equally in country, traditional, and modern rooms.

THE NEXT STEP: SECONDARY COLORS

Secondary colors—green, orange, and purple—are created by mixing two primaries in equal amounts. Green is made from blue and yellow, orange from yellow and red, and purple from red and blue. Like all colors, each secondary hue can be tinted with white or shaded with black for variations. If you can't envision a bold orange and green room, think about pairing up their paler tints of peach and sage. The primary and secondary colors illustrate that you can make a compatible triadic scheme by choosing any three colors equidistant on the wheel.

INTERMEDIATE PLAYERS: TERTIARY COLORS

These colors are an equal mix of a primary plus its closest secondary color: blue-green, yellow-green, red-orange, red-purple, and blue-purple.

SINGLE-SHOT COLOR: MONOCHROMATIC

What prevents a monochromatic scheme from being bland is subtle variation of a single color's intensity. For instance, orange, coral, peach offer variety within the same family.

Use examples of the color wheel, left, to experiment with color combinations for your rooms. It is a rainbow in the round, representing the brilliant bars of color that light produces as it passes through a prism.

HOW COLOR AFFECTS YOUR MOOD

The colors you live with really do influence your emotions. Some palettes lighten and brighten your mood, and others pacify or purify. We respond to color with our hearts, not just our heads, so it's important to choose wisely. Understand that colors behave in three basic ways—active, passive, and neutral—and you can easily match every room's colors to your personal desires and taste, and to how you intend to use the room.

ACTIVE COLORS

On the warm side of the color wheel, active colors include yellow, orange, and red. Extroverts, these advancing hues step out in the room to greet and sometimes dominate. They inspire conversation and an upbeat attitude. Red, the most intense, pumps the adrenaline like no other hue. Small doses of the fire-engine hue wake up an entry or turn up the heat on a hearthside den. Golden or lemony yellows—good for home offices and kitchens—unleash creative juices.

PASSIVE COLORS

The cool colors—blue, green, and purple—will pacify, staying quietly in the background to calm and restore depleted spirits. They're ideal for bedrooms or private retreats, but if yours is a cold climate, you may want to work in some decidedly sunny accents for warmth and contrast.

NEUTRAL COLORS

Neutralizers are the "uncolors"—browns, beiges, grays, whites, and taupes. They neither activate nor pacify but combine and cooperate, bridging together different rooms and colors. They're good transitions on woodwork, trim, hallways, and functional spaces such as kitchens and baths, but even living rooms can benefit. Darker neutrals tone down other colors; crisp white intensifies them.

COLOR LANGUAGE

• *Pink:* soothes, acquiesces; promotes affability and affection.

• *Yellow:* expands, cheers; increases energy.

• *White:* purifies, energizes, unifies; in combination, enlivens all other colors.

• *Black:* disciplines, authorizes, strengthens; encourages independence.

• *Orange:* cheers, commands; stimulates appetites, conversation, and charity.

• *Red:* empowers, stimulates, dramatizes, competes; symbolizes passion.

• *Green:* balances, normalizes, refreshes; encourages emotional growth.

• *Purple:* comforts, spiritualizes; creates mystery and draws out intuition.

• *Blue:* relaxes, refreshes, cools; produces tranquil feelings and peaceful moods.

ACTIVE

PASSIVE

NEUTRAL

GOOD NEIGHBORS

Choosing neighborly colors is as easy as a glance at the color wheel. Compatibility is guaranteed when you choose similar, or analogous, colors—those located side by side on the color wheel.

START WITH YOUR FAVORITE COLOR

Analogous schemes can be created from any point on the color wheel. The slice of colors you select doesn't have to be strictly warm-family or cool-family hues. They can span both hemispheres, with warm hues accenting a mainly cool scheme or vice versa. Start by choosing a favorite color as your main color, then look on either side of it. Like both colors? Include them. If you only like the color on one side, select that one and use the color adjacent to it as your third choice. Divide the palette into major and minor accent hues to work with the main color.

THREE'S A PARTY

Why limit the kindred colors to only two next-door neighbors? The true spirit of an analogous scheme is expressed best using three or more adjacent hues. Don't get too carried away. Use no more than half the colors on the wheel for your palette.

ONE: *Accent an analogous scheme for more drama. Here oranges, orange-reds, and yellows gain intensity when paired with complementary accents of lime-green and blue.*

TWO: *Analogous periwinkle blue, green, and purple create this restful scheme. Flowers and linens add warm contrast.*

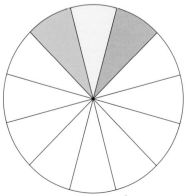

HOW OPPOSITES ATTRACT

The adage "opposites attract" applies to color as much as it does to any other kind of relationship. Known as complementary colors, hues opposite each other on the color wheel make dynamic duos, creating stimulating, high-energy spaces. Complements, including red and green, blue and orange, and yellow and purple, allow warm and cool hues to play off each other, producing palettes that enjoy the best of both worlds.

Opposites are riveting because, when warm and cool colors are viewed together, they intensify one another, bringing out the best in both. That means red is redder and green greener, more so than when each is used alone or in combination with another hue. For best results:

• **Choose a star.** That's the only real rule when you're working with complements. Let the other color serve in a supporting role as an accent. If you don't, the complements struggle for attention or even neutralize one another. Provide some air, such as white space or any neutral, to prevent overkill.

• **Easy does it.** Complementary schemes are among the easiest to implement because you're dealing with only two colors. When optimum contrast is desired, this combination shakes things up.

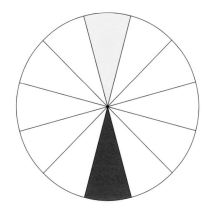

ONE: *In complementary reds and greens, floral curtains and a vintage tablecloth inspired this exuberant room. Instead of sticking with a strictly red and green scheme, the owner added a trio of accents analogous to green: yellow-green, yellow, and yellow-orange.*

TWO: *Use the wheel as a guide, not a dictator. This high-energy blue and yellow scheme is a variation of complementary blue and orange, with blue dominating.*

COZY UP WITH WARM COLORS

When you want a room to embrace and cheer, decorate it in one of the warm colors from the right-hand side of the color wheel—red, orange, yellow, yellow-green, and all their variations. Like the sun itself, these fiery hues visually heat up any space and take the chill off emotions at the same time.

HOW WARM COLORS WORK

Warm colors are known as advancing colors, because that's exactly what they do. A red or yellow wall visually advances, hugging the viewer. Knowing that, you can use warm colors to cozy up an entry, provide guaranteed sunshine in a breakfast room—or to perform decorating tricks. For instance, reshape a long, narrow room by painting the end wall yellow or red; the wall will visually advance to help square up the space.

TURN UP THE HEAT

Consider using a warm color or a combination of warm colors in your palette when:

• **Windows are few.** This keeps natural sunlight out, so color is needed for warmth.

• **Northern exposure** admits only cool light.

• **Woodsy views** create a cool greenish cast to the space, especially if windows are expansive.

• **Night life** is the room's main function. That's when the high energy from alternative sources such as warm colors is a plus.

ONE: *Sunny yellow cheers this bedroom, even on a dark wintery night. Teamed with white for contrast, the warm color becomes even brighter than if it were used alone. Blue adds a serene touch.*

TWO: *Warm coral walls advance toward the eye of the beholder, providing a mood of intimacy that's ideal for a dining room used frequently for entertaining. The hue also stimulates appetites and convivial conversation, but not at the fevered pitch of pure red.*

RELAXING Cool COLORS

Draw an imaginary vertical line down the middle of the color wheel. On the left are the cool colors. These are the hues of nature at its most refreshing and soothing—the watery blues, restful greens, and dreamy-sky violets. They make rooms seem cooler and spirits less ruffled.

SPACE EXPANDERS

Unlike advancing warm colors, cool colors retreat, keeping a low profile by visually receding. This makes them ideal for small rooms—or any room where you want a restful, replenishing break.

SOOTHING HUES

Cool palettes cool things down and slow the pace in the following areas.

• *Serene spaces* such as bedrooms, sitting rooms, or porches often use cool colors to conjure a tranquil mood where the mind can drift and dream.

• *Where leisure reigns,* cool colors encourage the family and your guests to kick back and slow down. The palette can keep spaces from feeling too lively. For instance, you may want the vitality of warm accents in the kitchen but the calm of cool colors in the adjacent family dining spot.

• *In sunny spots,* such as south- or west-facing rooms with ample natural light, cool colors can work together to keep a space's visual temperature in check.

• *Splash on cool blue,* even in small accents, when any palette feels too warm.

• *Barriers dissolve* between indoors and outdoors when you use lush variations of leafy greens in a porch or family room that opens directly onto a terrace. In such cases, you may want to take the chill off dominant greens with warm accents of yellow, red, or orange.

ONE: *Walls with a glazed and striated finish, done in a pale lettuce green paint, transform this bedroom into a serene retreat. By visually receding, the green walls make the room look and feel larger than it is.*
TWO: *With the inky-blue magic of the moonlit sky, the walls of this dramatic dining room step back. The hallway beyond was painted cheery yellow to visually pull it into the dining room.*

PUT IT IN NEUTRALS

Easy on the eye (and psyche), neutrals—blacks, whites, and grays in all their variations—are actually noncolors. Mix them together or build a room around variations of one neutral.

THE NEW NEUTRALS

In today's understated and elegant room schemes, neutrals have come to mean much more than black, white, and gray. A neutral can be any color so subtle that it mixes easily with other hues in a room and allows those colors to dominate. Even grayed-down mauves, greens, and soft peaches can play the neutral role.

LET NEUTRALS HIGHLIGHT COLORFUL ACCENTS

Although they didn't make it onto the color wheel, neutrals enjoy more popularity than their flashier chums. That's because they blend into any palette and serve as quiet backdrops. You can create an entirely neutral room or use demure neutrals as supporting players to highlight a colorful collection of quilts or artwork.

KEEP AN ALL-NEUTRAL ROOM LIVELY

When invited center stage, these noncolors offer relaxation that's anything but boring. Consider the unabashed romance of a white-on-white cottage-style bedroom. Or how about the snug appeal of a den decorated with tranquil beiges and taupes or grays and gray-mauves? And, for dynamic visual rhythm, nothing keeps the beat better than a combo of black and white. To be sure your neutral scheme keeps the eye fully occupied, follow these tips:

- *Vary the tonal range* of furnishings and accessories from light and medium to dark to create drama.
- *Decorate with diverse textures* from smooth to rough. To keep your textural mix in line with your room's style, remember that smooth finishes suggest formality; rough textures lend a more casual feeling.

Darker furniture stationed around the edges of this neutral space draws the eye around the room. A progression of sofa pillows—with darker pillows at the ends and lighter ones in the middle— also invites the eye to travel. A slick mirror, nubby and soft textiles, coarse baskets, and hardwoods mix textures.

CHANGE YOUR MOOD

When the mercury rises in summer, you want a room that's airy and expansive. In the frigid depths of winter, a toastier look is comforting. Start with a neutral backdrop and a wardrobe of quick-change accessories, and you can create rooms that play to your emotions no matter what the season. Plumped with ticking cushions, wicker seating bespeaks the joys of summer. Citrusy accents, a sisal rug, garden cuttings, summery art, and a green plant on the hearth keep their cool.

WITH COLOR

Flip the calendar ahead, and the same room is dressed for some serious cocooning. When temperatures drop outside, snuggling with a steaming hot chocolate at fireside is a favorite pastime. The same wicker seating wraps up for winter in woolly red and black cushions, a buffalo-plaid rug warms the hardwood floor, and an antique table sheds its lacy summer cloak. Above the fireplace, posters replace the summery painting, and a small lamp adds a spot of welcome "sun."

Mix
WITHOUT
MATCHING

WITH A POND THIS PLEAS-
ING, IT'S LITTLE WONDER INTERIOR DESIGNER SUZY STOUT
ABANDONED PLANS TO SELL AND MOVE ON. INSTEAD, SHE
RESURRECTED HER AGING HOME WITH JOYFUL COLOR.

More than 20 years old, Sam and Suzy Stout's suburban Chicago home keeps pace with the times thanks to vibrant colors that Suzy chose when she redid the interiors. She used a complementary palette of green and red to unify the first floor but avoided boring sameness by emphasizing different colors in different rooms.

ENJOY FLOWING COMPLEMENTS

Take Suzy's lead and pull your home together easily using two main hues in varying tones and proportions. In her home, one room is mainly green, another predominantly coral or rose. Suzy has even managed to work in some additional colors. But the eye flows smoothly through the spaces, thanks to the presence of the two main hues and consistent use of white woodwork.

Of her upbeat and dynamic high-contrast palette, she says, "For me, colorful paints and fabrics are like tonics. They have a great restorative effect on old belongings."

WELCOME GUESTS WARMLY

The vibrant coral of the entry is a warm color that visually advances to extend an appropriately wholehearted welcome. A bit of it can be seen from the living room, where the mood remains friendly and warm but less intense with more subdued variations of the same color. Fabric makes the major color statement here with a mix of florals and stripes and even a solid blue, cooling things down to encourage relaxation. The complementary hues of upholstery fabrics link Suzy's collection of vintage furnishings.

ONE: *The suburban Chicago home of interior designer Suzy Stout and her husband, Sam, has its own pond and a woodsy setting.* **TWO:** *Suzy wears the colors she loves to live with—cheery roses, greens, and Bristol blue.* **THREE:** *True to its fresh palette, the living room mixes greens and a shot of blue for a quiet complement to the entry's coral.*

*Decked in cheery coral, the
entrance hall makes a bold
declaration of welcome.
Here's how Suzy turned
contrast into a great asset:
Knowing that the rich coral
color is too strong for much
more than a cameo appearance,
Suzy accented the entry with
green—a link that shows up in
facing spaces as the dominant
hue. The result is that the eye
is intrigued, gravitating from
the initial warmth of the high-
intensity entry to the cooler-
looking depths of the oasislike
rooms beyond. For further
contrast, creamy white paint
coats the woodwork, and
the area rug and fabrics
echo the palette.*

USING COLOR AS THE LINK

When two rooms visually open to one another and are meant to work as one, let color pull them together. Here apple green visually links the kitchen to its adjoining dining area.

• To forge the transition, green is even splashed on the ceiling for impact.

• Refreshing white woodwork and cabinets keep the saturated greens from overpowering the spaces.

• For variety, yellow-green cheers the kitchen and opens the door to neighboring yellow and blue accessories.

FABRICS

IT'S A MATTER OF MATERIAL WEALTH.

With such an irresistible array of fabrics on the market, how do you even begin to narrow the field? In this chapter, we'll help you choose the right fabric for the job—and you'll learn how easy it is to mix patterns, too. In this eating spot, for instance, six patterns coexist beautifully because they're color-related and vary in scale.

FABRIC BASICS

Think of fabrics as character you can buy by the yard. Pick the right pattern, and a room can easily assume whatever personality you choose.

MAKE AN ATTITUDE ADJUSTMENT

Fabric patterns, like people, have distinct personalities; some have a more formal attitude than others. Before you can select a fabric, decide how formal or casual you want your room to be. (If you're in doubt about your decorating attitude, refer to the quiz on page 26.) If you're a formal traditionalist, a rich damask or brocade will quickly convey that personal preference. If, on the other hand, you're the feet-up type, country gingham or casual awning stripes could be your choice. As you shop, consider these tips:

• *Check out the sources.* The do-it-yourselfer may head for fabric shops, but if you plan to have a professional do the work, drapery and upholstery shops, furniture stores, and interior designers are all good sources.

• *Buy decorating fabrics,* not garment fabrics, because they're durable but not intended to be washed or dry cleaned often like clothing. They are typically sold in 54-inch widths. Order all the fabric you need at one time.

• *Collect swatches.* Take samples of carpet, wall coverings, paint, and other fabrics along as you shop. Once you've found a fabric or two that you like, borrow samples—as large as possible. Put samples in the room where you want to use them and observe them in changing light over a day.

ONE: *Surprise! Usually formal toile de Jouy fabric takes on a decidedly casual tone when contrasted with homey checkered trimmings and cushions.*

TWO: *Bandanna-inspired cotton florals and a coordinating plaid give this weekend home its bright and casual atmosphere. Naturally durable, the cotton fiber also holds colors well.*

THE RIGHT FIBERS

Q *My husband and I are shopping for fabrics and carpeting. We are concerned about durability, care, and cost. What should we look for in furnishing our living room and family room?*

A Because different areas of your home receive different types of use, consult this handy guide to determine which fabrics are the smart choices. You don't want to make a mistake and put a linen fabric on a sofa in a high-traffic area such as a family room. Instead, cover the sofa in a nylon fabric for durability.

THE NATURALS

	Comments	Advantages	Disadvantages	Care/Cost
Cotton	Creases easily; absorbent; breathes well; easily treated; highly flammable; fair resilience and elasticity.	Strong fiber; takes color well; blends well with other fibers; versatile.	Wrinkles easily; affected by mildew and sunlight; shrinks and stretches unless treated; yellows.	Machine washable; must be ironed. Inexpensive.
Wool	Very elastic and resilient; good absorbency; does not burn easily.	Strong fiber; insulates; takes color well; handles and drapes easily.	Attracts moths unless treated; needs careful cleaning; weakened by sun; shrinks unless treated.	Must be dry-cleaned. Moderately expensive.
Linen	Low resilience and elasticity; natural luster; burns easily; absorbent.	Very strong fiber; nice texture; somewhat resistant to sun and mildew.	Wrinkles easily; inconsistent in quality; somewhat stiff; shrinks unless treated.	Needs special cleaning to preserve appearance; colors may run; must be ironed. Expensive.
Silk	Lustrous; elastic, resilient; good absorbency; does not burn easily.	Colors have jewel-like tone; strong fiber; drapes beautifully; resists mildew.	Colors may run or change with age; weakened by sun; water spots show unless treated.	Most are dry-cleanable unless label indicates hand washable. Very expensive.

MAKE A DIFFERENCE

THE SYNTHETICS

	Comments	Advantages	Disadvantages	Care/Cost
Rayon	Creases easily; versatile; high absorbency and moderate elasticity; not flammable.	Drapes well; blends well with other fibers; takes color well; can be made to look like natural fibers.	Weak fiber; shrinks and stretches unless treated; weakened by sun; needs special care.	Dry-clean unless label indicates it can be hand-washed; must be ironed. Usually inexpensive.
Acetate	Moderately good resilience and elasticity; fair absorbency; burns readily and melts.	Appears lustrous and silklike; drapes well; resistant to mildew; somewhat wrinkle free.	Weak fiber; weakened by sun; colors fade from atmospheric fumes.	Dry-clean unless label indicates it can be hand-washed; use a cool iron. Moderately inexpensive.
Acrylic	Low absorbency; good resilience and elasticity; does not burn easily.	Wool-like in texture; resists mildew, moths, and sun; holds color well; fairly strong fiber.	Tends to pill; stretches somewhat; not as durable as some fibers, especially when it's wet.	Hand-wash unless labeled otherwise; hang to dry. Moderately expensive.
Polyester	Very good resiliency and elasticity; not absorbent; melts under high heat.	Strong fiber; resists wrinkles, moths, and mildew; blends well; doesn't stretch or shrink.	Slick to nubby textures; difficult to dye; gradual loss of strength from being exposed to sun.	Most items can be machine-washed and dried. Moderate cost.
Nylon	Very good resiliency and elasticity; low absorbency; melts under high heat.	Very strong; can be sponge-cleaned; blends well; lustrous; resists abrasion.	Tends to look glassy; fades and weakens from being exposed to sun.	Most items can be machine-washed and dried. Moderate cost.
Olefin	Low absorbency; lightweight with good bulk; somewhat resilient and elastic; not flammable.	Strong fiber; good insulator; resistant to stains, sun, and mildew; resists abrasion.	Best as blend or lining due to appearance; easily damaged by heat.	Machine-wash; dry at low heat. Moderate cost.

TERMS TO KNOW

Before you shop for fabrics, brush up on some of these most common fabric terms:

• **Brocade:** Used in fine, formal upholstery, it has raised surface patterns resembling embroidery.

• **Chenille:** The thick needle-punched designs on this fabric have gone from bedspreads and robes to casual upholstery.

• **Chintz:** Plain-weave cotton with high-luster glaze and usually floral motifs. It sets a traditional mood.

• **Damask:** In a variety of fibers and weights with textural contrast between satiny and dull, damask makes lush, durable draperies and upholstery. Inherently formal, it can take on a more casual look when used for washable loose-fitting slipcovers.

• **Matelassé:** The double weave of this fabric gives it an embossed look. Long used in elegant bedcovers, it now appears throughout the home.

• **Moiré:** Noted for a shimmery finish that looks like watermarks or wood grain. It has a very traditional appearance.

• **Plissé:** Puckered stripes give it the look of overscaled seersucker. It has a casual feeling but can blend into traditional schemes.

• **Toile de Jouy:** A tightly woven fabric with a pictorial printed in one color on a neutral ground. Toiles show off best on large seating, walls, and flat drapery panels.

• **Strié:** Slightly varied warp-thread colors produce an irregular streaked effect. The subtle pattern makes it a good mixer in casual or more formal schemes.

• **Taffeta:** Crisp plain-weave fabric that's an asset in window coverings because it retains its shape with little support.

- *Tapestry:* Due to thickness and pictorial designs, woven tapestries suit simple upholsteries and flat window panels.
- *Twill:* Tightly woven with a diagonal ridge, twills, such as denim and herringbone, are ideal for casual upholstery.
- *Velvet:* With a furlike feel and a cut pile that shimmers in the light, velvet creates a mood of formal elegance. Newer "eco velvets" can be made of recycled plastics.

ONE: *Made of durable and easy-care cotton, eye-catching floral slipcovers bring traditional style and modern ease to this living room. At the windows, gilded starfish pull back draperies of unlined taffeta.*

TWO: *The sofa and antique French bench at fireside are clad in creamy white linen. Both have welting in a raspberry hue; the bench gets extra accent with tricolor fringe, which helps define its shapely lines.*

THREE: *Fabric can change the mood of a furniture piece. Here a casual ticking slipcover relaxes a classic open-arm chair.*

WHICH FABRICS GO WHERE?

Before you make final selections, consider whether the fabrics suit the roles you want them to play. Are they in the mood to enhance your room's style? A lustrous moiré is unmistakably formal, a tweedy homespun more rustic, and a watercolor print more lighthearted and romantic. Is the fabric right for your application? A heavy canvas, for instance, won't have the ability to drape required for pinch-pleated curtains, but it could make a great roll-up shade. Similarly, filmy gauze can't hold up as upholstery on the sofa, but it makes wonderfully gossamer curtains.

CHOOSE FABRICS THAT FIT YOUR ROOMS

The array of natural, synthetic, and fiber blends makes it possible for you to match fabrics to very individual needs. What's your climate? This is especially important in choosing drapery fabrics because of their insulative potential and sunny locations; natural fibers trap heat, and light-hued, tightly woven opaque fabrics reflect sun's rays. If humidity is a factor, look for fibers with less absorbency. Do you want easy-care, soil- and stain-resistance in, for example, family room upholstery? Then look for fabrics that are cleanable and have protective finishes or apply a spray-on finish yourself. If a fabric will be used near a wood stove or fireplace, ask for fabrics with flame-resistant finishes. Use these additional tips and consult the chart in this chapter to match a fabric to your specific use:

• *Fabrics for upholstered furniture:* Chintz and cotton, used for light upholstery; brocade, corduroy, damask, used for heavier upholstery; chenille, flannel, jacquard, homespun tweed, tapestry, ticking, toile de Jouy, twill, velvet, and wool.

• *Fabrics for draperies:* Lightly glazed chintz, light- to medium-weight cotton, lightweight corduroy, damask, dotted swiss, faille, flannel, homespun tweed, linen, plissé, silk, taffeta, toile de Jouy, and velvet.

RELAX WITH ONE PATTERN

Sometimes, it's love at first sight. You find a can't-live-without-it print and can't resist splashing it everywhere. So, what's wrong with that? Nothing. With one pattern, there's no mixing and matching to worry about. Use these tips to choose and show off that one great pattern:

• *Choose a bold pattern.* One-pattern schemes succeed with a single pattern that's strong enough in color or large enough in scale to carry the room. (If the pattern you love is a miniprint, turn the page to find out how to support it with some decorative companions.)

• *Paint the walls a saturated color.* Using a single strong pattern usually requires an equally strong background color, so paint the walls in a dominant or secondary hue picked from the fabric's palette. As you can see *at right*, the wall color you choose can create a warm, gregarious mood or a cool, more serene one. Once you've picked your wall color, go back to the fabric and find a second color to put on large upholstered pieces and window treatments. Finally, look for the sharpest hue in your fabric and use it for a few accent pillows and accessories.

• *Add variety with vintage textiles.* An heirloom patchwork quilt or an Oriental rug, for example, can provide a dash of contrasting pattern without upstaging the room's starring motif.

• *Spread pattern around* your room for unity and balance. Don't gather all of the floral chintz-covered seating pieces at one end of the room without a counterweight at the other end.

• *Factor in textures.* Textures can add subtle pattern to a room for a well-balanced mix. Smooth finishes, such as glass, brass, and polished woods, lend a more formal look and also lighten a small room. Rough textures, including homespun fabrics and hand-hewed woods, bring more casual ambience to a room and also help to warm up an overly large space.

ONE: A floral-patterned slipcover on the sofa inspires this room's design elements. To create a warm mood, walls are painted in the fabric's dominant sun-drenched coral hue.

TWO: The same fabric inspires a dramatically different mood by picking a secondary color—a cool shade of green—from the floral pattern for the painted walls.

THREE: In this one-pattern scheme, garden-print chintz covers major seating pieces and is used in the window treatments for balance and vertical interest. Accents pick up the pinks and floral theme of the fabric, and walls are in yellow, an airy secondary hue of the print.

MIX THREE SCALES FOR HARMONY

Creating your own pattern mixes really is as easy as 1-2-3. Start with one print you love, then work in color-related fabrics in two other scales. Love a narrow stripe? Mix it with a boldly scaled floral and a midsize stripe. Love a miniprint floral? Try mixing it with a midsize gingham check and a large floral. The three-scales rule remains the same—but the beautiful specifics are up to you.

VARIETY IS THE SPICE

Most people are comfortable with the concept of mix-and-match in their personal wardrobes but less so in their furnishings. If you follow a few easy steps, it's not as difficult as it initially seems.

• *Why vary the scale of patterns?* Too many small prints can be dull, while two or more large prints fight for attention. A family of large, medium, and small patterns coexists without that kind of sibling rivalry. Where to start? Large-scale patterns are perfect for large-size furnishings. Here sweeping bed curtains call for a grand paisley fabric lined with a stripe. Smaller-scale prints go on accents such as the pillow shams. Put medium prints on medium-size pieces; striped fabric on the duvet is a good example.

Color and a casual attitude make the design connections in this blue and white master bedroom. Following the basics for mixing prints, small- , medium- , and large-scale patterns are distributed around the room for balance. Easy-mix striped fabrics make coordinating the patterns less daunting.

• *Link with color, mood, and weight.* Color can successfully marry two or more disparate patterns. Stick to patterned fabrics of approximately the same weight, texture, and degree of formality.

• *Mix in geometrics.* A color-coordinated geometric—a stripe or gingham check, for instance—often works as well with other prints as a solid-color fabric.

• *Explore ready-made coordinates.* Furnishings manufacturers have taken the guesswork out of pattern mixing with coordinated collections of fabrics, wall coverings, accessories, window treatments, and linens.

KEEP BALANCE IN MIND

Once you've found the perfect fabrics for your room, there's still the question of how and where to use them. Assuming you've given some thought to the appropriate pattern scales for each of your furnishings, you need to start putting things in balance.

THREE WAYS TO BALANCE

These simple methods will work magic:

• *Try the 60/30/10 rule.* If, for instance, you're working with three patterned fabrics, some simple mathematics come into play. To balance the patterns in the room, follow the 60/30/10 rule: Use your favorite fabric in 60 percent of the room, your second favorite in 30 percent of the room, and the third fabric as an accent in 10 percent of the room.

• *Multiply by 3.* It's another way to get the balancing act right. Use each patterned fabric at least three times. For example, your dominant pattern may be used on the window treatments, an armchair slipcover, and a decorative pillow.

• *Focus on pattern.* Instead of spreading pattern around the room, cluster it in one area to draw the eye to a comfy bed or sitting spot. The visual weight of a fireplace or armoire balances patterns clustered elsewhere in a room. Because pattern attracts the eye, use it to reshape awkward spaces. Bold patterns in advancing colors square up tunnel-shaped spaces; bright accent pillows placed on a sofa in a long, narrow living room pull it toward you visually.

ONE: *Covered in the same oversize plaid fabric, a daybed and the wall behind it draw the eye to this end of the bedroom, giving the area increased importance. For visual rhythm, the lattice-look back on the armchair echoes the fabric's grid pattern.*

TWO: *Tucked neatly into a sunny bay window, this sitting spot is an attention-getter, thanks to the blue and white toile curtains framing the alcove and the complementary blue and white striped fabric that softens the leggy armchairs.*

DO A QUICK FABRIC MAKEOVER

ONE: *Comfortable? Yes. But this window seat was just sitting down on the job. It needed more privacy, a little mood adjustment, and more work to do. In this "before" shot, the scheme is cool blue and white with pillows in demure prints.*

A weekend can make all the difference if you devote it to a quick-and-easy update of a spot in your home. For success without frustration, pick just one area that needs work, adapt these strategies to your taste, and plan ahead so all materials are on hand by Friday night. A new room is only two days away....

READY, SET, GO

How can it seem like anything but a sunny day when you're surrounded by citrus hues? Pretty in pastel blue, the original window seat brightened up with sprightly patterned fabrics and a warmer palette. A mood change comes naturally with this color shift, but the patterns created a change of attitude, too. The fanciful mix of a harlequin print with stylized scenic and floral patterns gives the spot a more fun-loving spirit.

- **Sew a fresh outlook.** For fuss-free ease, use coordinated fabrics—even ready-made curtains—or sew a treatment like this one with simple straight seams. Scenic cafe curtains are clipped to rings; side panels simply gather on a rod. Accent pillows are done in several fabrics, including harlequin remnants.
- **Make carbon-copy cushions.** Carefully remove the foam from existing window seat cushions, rip out seams in cushion covers, and use the fabric pieces as patterns for cutting the new cushion fabric. No measuring!
- **Add new function.** With a new tea table, the sitting spot is set for casual dining. A mix of chairs creates more coveted "window seats."
- **Plant an indoor window box.** This one thrives in the sunny window. A small one is easier to transport to the dining table for a centerpiece or outside where blooms can get an extra dose of sunshine.

TWO: *Fabrics in fresh tropical hues turn the once-cool bay into an especially warm time-out spot. At the windows, casual easy-sew curtains create newfound privacy. A glass-top table and wicker chairs—import store finds—pull up to the bay window for dining with a garden view.*

A HOUSE WHERE FABRICS PLAY

KATHY CUROTTO HAS NEVER MET A VINTAGE FABRIC SHE DIDN'T LIKE. SHE USES HER COLLECTED REMNANTS OF THE PAST TO CHARM HER FAMILY'S HOME.

Maybe it's the garden-fresh patterns, the happy colors, or the settle-back comfort of every charmingly designed room, but Kathy and Frank Curotto's suburban St. Louis home beckons you in—and invites you back again.

IN WITH THE OLD FOR NEW STYLE

Once truly a country cottage before suburbs encroached, the vintage two-story with the rambling porch touched their hearts. They filled it with the antique furnishings and past-perfect accents they love. One of Kathy's passions is the vintage fabrics that infuse her rooms with character but also with color, pattern, and visual energy. She masterfully mixes the old, extravagant floral prints with new fabrics that share the same nostalgic spirit. But turning this bevy of prints into a cohesive whole takes a practiced eye. Kathy astutely picks color threads—bright reds, rosy pinks, and soft blues in the living room, for example—to tie patterns together. She carefully combines patterns of different scales and, like any good gardener, spreads a variety of blooming fabrics throughout each and every room. Her varied-vintage philosophy applies to furniture, too—the dining room pulls reupholstered art deco chairs around a Sheraton table. "Mixing styles helps create a more casual feeling," says Kathy, an antiques dealer. Her vintage fabrics play accent roles due to their fragility. She'll toss a paisley shawl over a chair arm for a color shot and sew oldies into napkins and accent pillows with traditional trims, and let old linens enliven her dining spots. For upholstered pieces that need to be durable, however, she picks new fabrics that reprise Victorian-era florals. And that porch they love? It's dressed up as an outdoor living room—in old fabrics, of course.

Antique wicker and colorful old fabrics offer an irresistibly shady invitation to sit a spell on this suburban St. Louis front porch—a gracious prelude to wonderfully warm interiors. It's the creative haven of Kathy and Frank Curotto, here with daughter, Libby; son, Taylor; and family dog, Addie.

ONE: *Stepping into the Curottos' living room is like walking into an English country cottage. Old and new fabrics and colorful patterns abound, tied together by the major colors: rosy reds and pinks and cool blues against a snappy white backdrop. New sofa upholstery has a nostalgic spirit, but the pillows on board are made from old textiles.*

TWO: *Kathy cushioned the window seat with a medium-scale floral, then she tossed on large-scale print pillows for an unstudied look.*

THREE: *The bookcase's red-painted back wall balances the bold floral fabric used to slipcover this easy chair. Kathy turns vintage textiles, such as this old paisley shawl, into decorative accents.*

Fabrics • 323

ONE: *A beautiful counterpoint to livelier patterns in the living room, the elegant dining room does an understated rendition of mix-and-match. Chair upholstery is a subtle blue-on-blue fabric with yellow trim, and old table linens follow suit. Red walls show off collected blue and white ware.*

TWO: *Son Taylor's toy boat was the color cue for his room that began with blue striped wall covering. Then Kathy worked in two plaids— one red, one blue—and varied them in scale. The bed linens are a merry mix-up of color and classic prints.*

2

WINDOWS

WINDOWS ARE THE EYES OF A home, not only framing views to the outside but also revealing the character that lies within. Working with the walls, your window treatments can express your decorating personality, whether casual or formal.

&WALLS

BUILD CHARACTER

Whatever your design style is, window dressings and wall treatments can form the decorative framework—the guts—of your decorating scheme. Even if you prefer your walls snowy white and your windows unadorned, you're establishing your room's character and mood—swept-clean, uncluttered, and contemporary. Run through the following checklist of considerations before you choose a treatment style.

• *Be practical.* Window dressings can monitor light, save energy, and ensure privacy. For instance, a chilly room may require insulating honeycomb shades or heavy tapestry curtains. In a south-facing room, you'll want to layer shutters or miniblinds beneath decorative curtains so you can fend off midday glare without totally blocking your view and light. A bedroom requires more privacy than mere sheers can deliver. You may want to add privacy to a room facing a busy street or sidewalk with sheer curtains or half-curtains.

• *Set a mood.* Decide the mood you want, then assess whether your windows are assets worth featuring or oddly shaped and sited liabilities to camouflage. Decking out the windows in sumptuous, floor-to-ceiling fabric that puddles on the floor adds instant elegance. Wooden shutters and vertical blinds bring linear interest for a more subtle, graphic look. Gauzy curtains with delicate wall stenciling romance a room. Creative treatments add color, pattern, and texture. Whether you knot it, swag it, pleat it, shirr it, tie it back, or just let it hang softly, versatile fabric can set any mood.

• *Alter the architecture.* Extend treatments beyond the bounds of small windows to make them look taller or wider. Raise a low ceiling by treating short windows to floor-length curtains and walls to vertical stripes. When a window is too high, lower it with a floor-length curtain. To get nondescript walls in a traditional mood to match windows, add crown molding at the ceiling line.

ONE: *A layered window treatment of valances over sheer side panels and simple wood blinds gives this living room privacy and a romantic contemporary look. Pale walls are intentionally understated.*

TWO: *Wrapped in rich toile, this home office is anything but cold and high-tech. Creamy draperies break up the busy wall pattern, and cornices topped with crown molding lend height and vintage style to modern windows.*

WHAT'S YOUR ATTITUDE? FORMAL

When a formal statement is what you're after, give windows the first chance to deliver it. With the right dressings, they make a more dramatic declaration of formality than any other element. Walls play an important backup role, supporting the windows' statement through color, coordinated or matching pattern, or subtle details such as texture, border trims, and moldings.

WINDOWS TAKE SHAPE

Though even the most casual fabric can be shaped into a formal drapery, starting with a formal fabric ensures communicating the right attitude. Fabrics with sheen such as silks, damasks, and taffetas—or their synthetic look-alikes—are clearly formal. Given the right treatment, as explained below, gauzy sheers are, too. Heavier-weight fabrics that fit a formal approach include velvet and tapestry. (Consult the "Fabrics" chapter, page 303, for selecting fabrics.)

• **Choose classic designs.** In general, a formal room is the place for symmetrical treatments. For example, formal looks include valances plus side panels, swags and jabots, and swagged valances with rosettes and silk fringe. Highly tailored valances alone can have a formal edge.

• **Pay attention to details.** Elegant braids and fringes can dress up even plain linen draperies. The fun is in subtlety, such as drapery linings in contrasting colors and unusual hardware.

• **Dress up for today.** Some decidedly modern rooms also can be formal. Consider, for example, the cool elegance of matched Barcelona chairs facing off across a travertine floor. In such a setting, utterly simple blinds, Roman shades, or no window treatment at all contribute to a formal feel.

ONE: *In this living room, floor-to-ceiling draperies in a golden damask fabric have the commanding presence and symmetry that's important in formal style. The treatment is simple—side panels topped with fringed valances. Walls support the windows by echoing the damask color in a lighter shade of butter yellow.*

TWO: *Light-touch window and wall treatments give this gathering of Scandinavian country pieces an air of formality. Sheers cleverly mimic the forms of traditional swags and draperies, but they allow light to bathe the living room.*

WHAT'S YOUR ATTITUDE? CASUAL

Fun, fuss-free, and, more often than not, affordable are the hallmarks of casual window dressings. Unlike formal treatments, fabric isn't essential. Shutters, blinds, or even folding screens pulled up to the window work just fine and may be your best option for hard-to-treat panes.

EASY-GOING WINDOWS

• ***Relax with fabrics.*** Make sure the fabric in casual window treatments is durable and easy-care. Cotton is a popular option, as are denim and other sailcloth-weight fabrics. Polished cottons such as chintz have a more relaxed look if you launder them first to remove the sheen.

• ***Shutters, shades, or blinds?*** Though they come in different styles, sizes, and materials, they fill the same practical role. They're also a smart starting point for your windows; you can enjoy light control and privacy now and layer more elaborate draperies or curtains over the blinds later.

• ***Get in shape.*** Colorful Roman shades, valances, cafe curtains, tiebacks, and draperies are among the many casual options. Balloon shades and complicated symmetrical treatments may be too fussy.

• ***Improvise for personality.*** Casual schemes welcome color, pattern, and fun hardware from flea markets and antiques shops. Top your windows in a teacup print like the one, *opposite,* or fashion old finials, door knobs, even branding irons into rods and tiebacks.

ONE: *With a casually draped valance and side panels, the color-confident living room celebrates this collector's passions—vintage textiles, trims, and teacups.*
TWO: *Custom shutters painted to blend with the wall solved this attic bedroom's pane problem— a divided sunburst window.*
THREE: *A wide cabana- striped Roman shade creates a lighthearted alfresco look. Layered beneath it, a shade that combines miniblinds and sheers unifies and masks the dated windows.*

MAKE IT EASY ON YOURSELF

Ou don't need a home economics degree or design maven status to do window treatments that look custom-made. Often, you don't even need a sewing machine. Just get creative with materials you have on hand.

INSTANT DRESS-UPS

• *Toss it on.* What could be easier than draping an heirloom bedspread or a colorful 1940s tablecloth over a tension rod for a fresh look? Tea towels and napkins create instant valances. Scout garage sales and flea markets for similar finds to fit your windows.

• *Do custom touch-ups.* Curtains don't have to look like typical department store fare even if they are. Painted rods and decorative finials set off plain panels. Hang tab curtains with festive ribbons. Tie back panels with napkin rings or bandannas. Add ornaments—dangly earrings or seashells—to curtains with a glue gun.

• *Sew a little style.* It's easy to stitch flat curtain panels. The secret to great style is in the gathering; make the panels three times wider than the window for fullness.

ONE: *This handsome dining room treatment only looks costly. Ready-made pleated shades diffuse the rays and offer privacy. For softness, easy-sew curtains simply gather at the sides of the windows. An extra sleeve of fabric shirred onto the wide rod above the shades pulls it all together.*

TWO: Dressing up windows in lace couldn't be simpler: Use ready-made panels or hem your own yards of lace and stitch to drapery rings. For the swagged look, space rings at least 12 to 14 inches apart. Accented with flowery finials, the black wrought-iron rod is a key to this custom look. Age new hardware with black or verdigris-look paint.

THREE: Loop your own spunky gingham fabric strips over matchstick blinds for a custom touch.

Roll the shade up or down by hand, then bow-tie to secure in place. The blinds provide privacy while allowing sunlight to flood in.

FOUR: A candlewicked bedspread decorated with pom-pom fringe becomes a lighthearted window treatment in this cottage bedroom. It's simply draped over the rod and nipped up in the center with a dried flowers nosegay—a pretty substitute for conventional window hardware.

CURTAIN CALLS

Time was when the basic rod pocket was good enough for most curtains. Today, however, curtain panels are more discriminating. Instead of sliding them into yesterday's rut, hang them by more stylish threads—perhaps bow ties, tab tops, or jaunty grommets teamed with decorative wood or metal rods.

OFF-THE-RACK STYLE

Start with ready-made curtains, then add your own special touches.

• *Instant valances.* Toss a folded tablecloth, lace panel, or even a favorite scarf over the top.

• *Contrasting tiebacks.* Loop long, straight curtain panels over collectible antique doorknobs at the sides. Or, replace matching fabric tiebacks with decorative ribbon, yarn, raffia, or contrasting fabric strips (perhaps braided together).

• *Decorative rods.* Basic curtains take on newfound style when teamed with decorative rods and finials from stores and catalogs.

EASY CUSTOM TOUCHES

Take a look at these curtains, *opposite*, and see what you can achieve with easy do-it-yourself flat fabric panels and a little imagination. The secret's in the personality-packed hang-ups.

• *Use ribbon* to make snappy tabs and bows without sewing.

• *Play with grommets for no-sew ease.* Lace some ribbon, cording, or fabric ties through grommets for easy hanging. Buy small grommets at fabric stores and large ones at marine supply or tent and awning shops.

ONE: *No longer lonely at the top, decorative tabs and other curtain-top treatments now have handsome rods to keep them company. Here custom-made sheer panels hang by spaghetti straps over a hand-forged iron rod. The black iron bed and tiebacks balance the rod's visual weight.*

TWO: *A summery sundress floral gets the hang of casual style with a gingham-ribbon top treatment. To make your own, insert grommets into the curtain header, then tack one end of the ribbon above the first grommet. Loop the ribbon over the rod and pull it back through the same grommet. Lace fabric through remaining holes with rod in place. Tack on a bow.*

THREE: *No fuss and no sew, this curtain is perfect for a kitchen or laundry room. It consists of a tablecloth and napkins clipped to an ordinary clothesline stretched between wood pegs.*

FOUR: *Contrasting plaid fabric adds dash to these leaf-patterned curtains. Insert oversize grommets into the plaid header, then thread the panel onto a ½-inch dowel or tension rod.*

FIVE: *For a fast, no-sew valance, drape colorful fabric napkins over simply shirred curtain panels.*

SIX: *Snappy bow-tie tabs give decorating punch to home-sewn or store-bought curtain panels. To make the treatment, sew your own 1½-inch-wide and 6-inch-long fabric tabs, spaced 4 to 5 inches apart; tack on pretied bows.*

SEVEN: *Perfect for simple tieback curtains, store-bought drapery pins secure curtain panels to a window's molding.*

2

3

4

5

6

7

ONE: *Cheap yet chic, a grid of 1×4s was added to this plain dining room wall to give it architectural interest. The grid frames a scenic wallpaper mural, turning a once-blank wall into a charming window on America's rural past.*

TWO: *Because this bedroom has only a single window, the classic flame-stitch wallpaper is a perfect choice for creating an inner glow. The subtle red-on-red pattern adds depth to the walls, but it doesn't*

BE PLAYFUL WITH WALL COVERINGS

What's your dream? A den wrapped in rugged leather, the formal dining room in scarlet moiré, the kitchen in colonial stenciling? Or how about a book-lined sitting room or a hand-painted mural? With today's array of wall coverings and wallpapers that mimic the real thing, you can have your dream without breaking your budget.

WALLS AT WORK

Before you select a mood-setting wall covering, decide how dominant a role you want the walls to play. In a neutral scheme, for instance, you may only want subtle texture. (For more on choosing patterns, refer to page 269 in the "Elements" chapter.) Also consider what your walls are up against wear-wise. Prepasted, scrubbable vinyl coverings can't be beat in the kitchen and bath.

• *Add color and character.* This is the forte of wall coverings. Create an instant library—and focal point— by papering a wall with realistic books by the roll. Give a plain wall a view with a paste-on mural. Or, enhance any decorating style from traditional to country cottage with the many wall covering prints.

• *Roll on a fresh look.* Wall coverings instantly camouflage damaged walls, so textured grass cloth and string cloth are especially good choices for this job. Applied to lower walls and banded with chair-rail molding or a complementary border, wall coverings can create a wainscoting effect. Pick vertical stripes if you want to visually raise a ceiling, or horizontal designs to help widen a narrow room.

• *Run for the border.* Wall borders can be used alone as wainscoting at midwall and as molding at the ceiling line. To accentuate architectural features such as doors, alcoves, and fireplaces, consider outlining them in a wallpaper border. For fun, look for extra-wide trompe l'oeil (fool-the-eye) borders that mimic the look of everything from plates on doily-lined shelves to landscapes from the past.

compete with the more flamboyant floral print in the draperies. White ceiling, trim, and furnishings set off the red in this high-contrast scheme.

THREE: Let a wallpaper border inspire a new scheme. Here a bold and bright border lifted the dining area's mood and inspired the painted wall stripes. A purposely askew tablecloth valance draws the eye to the border and echoes the room's newfound spirit.

WAKE-UP CALLS FOR WALLS

Sometimes white walls aren't enough. The small "before" shots on these two pages prove that point. If you're longing for a dash of colorful character or architectural interest, use wall coverings or wainscoting to change your room's attitude—without knocking down walls or replacing furnishings. Start with a sure sense of the look you want. Is it the country cottage romance of dishtowel plaids and flowers? Or the more masculine and clubbish look of rich color plus wood?

2

ONE: Sometimes, all you need is a hug—of fresh pattern and color, that is. This sofa offered cold comfort until bright wall coverings and paint stepped in. Since the budget didn't allow for new furnishings, this remake succeeds with a wall treatment that doesn't clash with the room's existing palette and pieces. It leaves a few inches at the top of the wall above the border to paint the upper wall space a deep, contrasting color, thus lowering the ceiling line for a more intimate feeling. The floral border softens the plaid's hard edges.

TWO: New natural-finish pine wainscoting conjures cocoonlike warmth in this once plain white den. Wainscoting, available in paneling sheets and premilled kits, quickly adds a sense of age and architecture. The pine's mellow hue coupled with dark green paint enhances the masculine look created by the leather wing chairs and woods. For best proportion, extend the wainscoting either one-third or two-thirds of the way up the wall; never divide a wall in half. Here the wood covers the lower 32 inches of an 8-foot (96-inch) wall.

WINDOW & DOOR SKETCHBOOK

Browse through this sketchbook, and you'll find ideas for a variety of window and door treatments.

SINGLE WINDOWS

If you're dressing a single window (see illustrations 1–5), consider its size first. Does the window look small compared to the size of your furnishings or the room itself? Add fullness with ruffled tiebacks (4) or flowing curtains (1, 5). If its scale matches other elements, treat it simply with a shade or a top treatment. For the drama of height, mount the curtain rod above the top of the window.

MULTIPLES/MATCHED SERIES

A series of identical windows (6–11) invites the light and beauty of the outdoors inside. These windows also offer you numerous decorating options. First decide whether you want to treat each window in the series separately or treat the entire series as one window. Taking a look at your room's style may give you a clue as to which approach is best. In a clean-lined contemporary setting, the geometric look of a bank of windows can be an asset. To get the full architectural impact, use a top treatment only (6). A valance or cornice adds a punch of interest and color to the expanses of glass without masking the window's design. Do you need a treatment that affords more privacy, light control, or energy efficiency? Shades and blinds (7, 8) mounted inside each window's molding perform those tasks and offer a tailored look. If you prefer a softer, traditional look, fabric options abound. Flowing, to-the-floor draperies (9) lend timeless elegance to spaces. Crown the draperies with a sculpted cornice (10) to add height and formality. In a casual or pared-down setting, simple side curtains flank windows with color and pattern without "overdressing" them. For a lighter look, half-curtains can add French-cafe charm, plus privacy and sunshine.

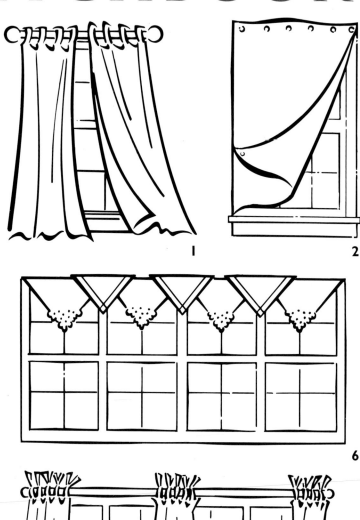

CORNER WINDOWS

Mirror-image dressings (1–5) allow you to treat corner windows separately but achieve the effect of a single design. Be sure draperies or vertical blinds draw to the outside, and blinds raise and lower without clashing. In small spaces, avoid fabrics with busy patterns and contrasting colors; instead match treatments to wall color to blend them into the background and expand the room.

BAY AND BOW WINDOWS

Like the corner window, the windows within a bay or bow may demand separate but equal treatment (6–10). Like the matched series, there are many ways to treat bays, depending on the look you want. To keep things clean, stick with trim shades or blinds (6). Or, outline those tailored treatments with fabric, such as a sweeping swag or a scalloped balloon valance for eye-pleasing softness and color (8, 9). Do you want to fabricate a formal look? Install framing draperies across the front of the window alcove (10), giving the bay even more depth and focus. For a curving bow window, consider hanging curtains on a flexible rod that sweeps around the bow.

SLIDING DOORS

Sliding glass doors present a unique decorating situation. Because they are doors, a covering must allow them to open and close freely. Yet, as windows, they require a dressing that enhances their appearance and provides privacy and light control. Blinds, fabric shades, draperies, and sliding panels are options to consider (11–15). Make sure they mount at the ceiling line or draw totally to the side, keeping the walkway clear. To control light and privacy throughout the day, try a layered treatment of opaque draperies over miniblinds.

HIGH WINDOWS

The goal in treating high windows is to "lower" them with long treatments and/or by placing a piece of furniture beneath them. If you place a piece of furniture under the window, a fitted covering such as shutters, shades, or blinds (16–18) will stay out of the way of the furnishings. If your room is full of horizontal elements—beds, chests, and bureaus—add visual interest with a vertical, to-the-floor treatment (19, 20). To make windows appear larger, install a row of fixed shutters below the windows, and operable shutters on the actual panes (17).

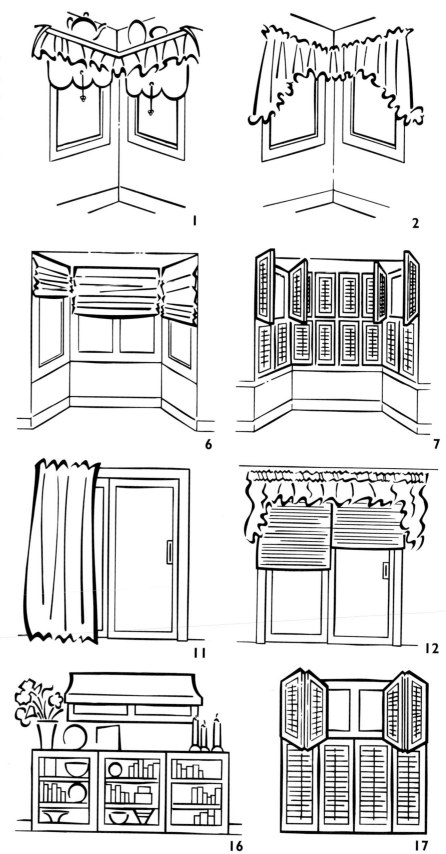

CASEMENT WINDOWS

Standard casement windows open in or out and can be treated similarly to single windows. However, there is one special consideration for casements. The ideal covering should mount to the outside so that it falls over the window's cranking mechanism. Swinging crane rods (1) or fixed curtain rods (3) offer good solutions. If you choose tiebacks, dress each window in a drapery panel that draws to the outer edge of each window where tieback hardware is installed. For inward-swinging casement windows, you'll need a treatment that doesn't interfere with the windows' operation. Inset curtains or blinds on each window section (4, 5) or mount shades or blinds far enough above the windows' molding that they can be raised to let the windows open freely.

FRENCH DOORS

French doors combine the problems of outfitting inward-swinging casement windows with those of covering sliding glass doors. The solutions divide into two groups: Either affix your treatment to each door panel, or opt for a treatment that clears the doors by drawing completely to the side or top. For a look that won't interfere with the architecture, mount blinds or shades on each door (6–8). If your decorating style calls for a softer touch, consider shirred lace panels or door-mounted tiebacks. Traditional drapery treatments are viable options (9, 10). Simply make sure the rod extends well beyond the frame so draperies can be drawn out of the way of the doors. If your French doors are topped with stationary transom-style panes, leave the upper windows bare, or treat the doors and windows as one, with the rod installed at the ceiling line.

SHAPELY WINDOWS

The trick to treating windows with sculptural curves and unusual shapes is to flow with the curves, or bend with the angles, of the opening. Where privacy and light control are needed, use custom-fitted shades, blinds, or even shirred fabric (11–13). Palladian-inspired half-round windows are most spectacular when minimally dressed. For example, in a bedroom add a privacy treatment to the lower part and leave the top half-round bare for maximum natural light (14, 15).

FLOORS

IN EVERY ROOM, WHAT'S UNDERFOOT MATTERS

because the floor is one of a space's single largest areas.

Dressed with an eye for color, pattern, transition, and

texture, as well as function, floors form the foundation

of good design and comfort. In this attic bedroom, car-

pet squares laid on the diagonal make a dramatic deco-

rating statement while underscoring the room's palette.

Nantucket

GARDENS AND HOUSES

PHOTOGRAPHY BY TAYLOR LEWIS
TEXT BY VIRGINIA SCOTT HEARD

MAKE THE MOST OF SIMPLE
TEXTURES

A staple of homes today, wall-to-wall carpet too often is chosen by default, not by design. And that's an opportunity missed. With beautiful weaves and fresh fiber options, such as wool-and-sisal blends, carpet can enrich any room with warm texture. Discover how the texture of carpet can blanket your home with aesthetic value beyond function.

UNIFY BY DESIGN

Instead of changing carpet style and color in each room, consider a single selection to unify your home. It provides visual transition and continuity even if wall and window treatments change, and it works well in homes where the room flow feels choppy.

• *Keep it in the family.* If you use more than one style of wall-to-wall carpet, make your selections within the same color family to minimize contrast.

• *Smooth out the flow.* Even a small area such as a staircase and landing looks larger with a seamless sweep of carpet; using the same carpet in living and dining areas makes a great-room look expansive.

• *Enhance your room's mood.* The more heavily textured the carpet, the less formal the feeling it creates. For a more casual look, choose the nubby texture of berber or other loop-style carpet or the easy-going look and texture of a sisal or sisal-look blend. For a more formal feeling, consider plush pile carpet with its velvety feel.

Carpet with a subtle, raised-diamond pattern adds texture to this neutral living room and sets a subtle backdrop for a mix of natural woods, fabrics, and bamboo.

HOW TO WORK WITH PATTERN

When it comes to choosing a patterned carpet or room-size rug, the only thing you have to fear is fear itself. This flooring option isn't seen everywhere, and there's a mistaken notion that it's a risky choice. But, if you love the pattern of area rugs, why not extend the rug idea virtually from wall to wall? It's one of the most appealing options in flooring, bracing a room with visual rhythm from soothing to snappy.

CONFIDENT CHOICES

A few commonsense tips can erase the fear factor.

• **What's its decorating role?** Do you want patterns to rivet the attention or to serve quietly? Pick carpet with low color contrast between the pattern and the background for the greatest subtlety. For example, pick a rose floral on a paler rose background instead of black stars sprinkled over white.

• **Go easy on the mix.** When your walls, windows, or major furnishings, such as upholstered seating or painted woods, already bear bold motifs or a pattern mix, select a carpet with a small repeat. The small scale and the abundant motif repetition will neutralize the overall pattern, creating an effect similar to that of solid color flooring.

• **Express a mood, a style.** Patterned carpet should fit a room's desired mood or furnishings style. Florals work well in traditional, country, or cottage-style rooms. Geometrics add a clean graphic look to contemporary or Arts and Crafts schemes. Whimsical motifs can work well in eclectic spaces.

• **Vary the scale and motif.** Make the carpet pattern a different scale than those of the other prints in the room. If you have small-print patterns on your furnishings and a medium print at the windows or on the walls, for example, consider a large-scale pattern for your carpet. To prevent confusion, choose a carpet with a different motif from that of the walls—no striped carpet with striped wallpaper. Instead of stripes, consider a small-check carpet with lots of air, or open background, to give the eye a break.

ONE: *Simple, small, and surrounded by white, this carpet's star-studded motif pops out without making a visual nuisance of itself. Above the bed, a recycled gable vent eases the room's hard edges with its gentle curve.*

TWO: *Because it's small and subtle, the grid pattern makes this room-size rug an undemanding companion for true-blue-and-white furnishings.*

ADD A RICH ACCENT

Like a colorful silk kerchief tucked into a blazer pocket, area rugs can give colorful snap to a roomful of furnishings. Whether you lay a rug atop a floor that's already carpeted or clad in wood, your area rug can serve as a room's star or as an important supporting player.

• *Let a rug set the palette.* Finding the right rug isn't easy, so if you find a rug you love, consider making it the first element you choose for your room. Then make everything else fit around the rug's color.

• *Enhance an existing color scheme.* If you've already furnished the room, choose an area rug that pulls together the dominant or accent colors. In a roomful of busy fabric patterns, consider a solid-color rug with a contrasting border.

• *Make it a focal point.* If you want a rug to be the center of attention, choose one with bright colors—in the richest values of hues in the room's palette—and strong contrast between the colors within the rug's design. Also consider shapely variety: A round rug in a roomful of square furnishings can make a bold statement.

• *Define furniture groupings.* One of the best uses of an area rug is to pull together a conversation group. By touching all furniture in the group, the rug visually knits an area together, creating intimacy and

ONE: *A natural rug bridges the gap between formal and casual moods in this eclectic dining room. Not only does the rug let the checked fabric make the room's strong color and pattern statement, but its rough texture works with the fun fabric to take the formal edge off the furniture.*

drawing the eye. Rug size matters here; seating pieces should rest entirely on or off the rug.

• *Shift to neutrals.* Not every space benefits from a bold rug. Neutral rugs add texture and warm a hard-surface floor without disrupting the floor's background role. Use them to subtly separate zones, for example, in an open-plan family room.

TWO: *Vibrant colors and an artistic design make this area rug the uncontested focal point of a modern living room. The rug defines the diagonal, hearthside conversation grouping, and its vivid hues are echoed in small accents.*

THREE: *Providing a solid anchor in a sea of neutrals, this area rug deepens the rose color of the chair upholstery and contrasts it with creamy hues for major impact. It extends under the sofa to link it with the room's other furnishings.*

ARE THESE FAUX REAL?

Striations, or different streaks of color, in wood grain warm up any space, but should you go to the expense of real oak or pine planks, or opt for lower-cost wood veneer over particleboard or newer laminate wood look-alikes?

A WALK IN THE WOODS

Nothing can substitute for the honesty and warmth that real wood imparts—or can it? When you want the look of solid wood floors, but not the expense or its tendency to warp when wet, some great pretenders are worth considering. Also, if you already have wood floors but they need spiffing up, there are some reasons for going against the grain with paint and stain: pure fun and visual delight.

• *Invest in the real thing* if you're planning to stay awhile in your home. It will last not only your lifetime, but also the lifetime of your home. Except when used in wet areas, wood ages gracefully, developing a deeper, richer patina over time. Unlike wood floors of the past, today's floors have polyurethane finishes for easy care. Consider real wood for public or formal rooms because it's hardworking and easy care; lower-priced look-alikes may repel scratches but they won't go the distance of real wood. Real woods are available prefinished, but sometimes it's less expensive to have a new oak floor installed and finished on-site.

• *Add function with faux woods* in kitchens, baths, and family and kids' rooms where you want the wood look without the maintenance. Laminate "wood" flooring planks come in colorful stains or natural "pine"—and look astonishingly real. Prefinished planks of oak veneers over particleboard make budget sense in low-traffic rooms.

ONE: *A rainbow of transparent, semitransparent, and opaque stains can turn a floor into a major design element that makes a room's palette pop. The surprise here? The floor is made of wood-look laminate planks, not the real thing.*

TWO: *Naturally finished, a glowing hardwood floor is the perfect choice for a dining room because it's durable and requires just buffing to undo scrapes.*

SPLURGE ON EARTHY DELIGHTS

In addition to standard carpet, tile, and wood, a whole category known as nonresilients offers natural variety. Clay, tile, slate, brick, marble, terrazzo, and limestone, for instance, bring rich colors, textures, and natural patterns to floors. But how to choose? Different materials can set a variety of decorating stages: creamy travertine for neoclassical or contemporary style, veined marble in sophisticated traditional spaces, random-cut fieldstone for a rugged lodge look, Saltillo tiles for a south-of-the-border flavor, or brick pavers for a yesteryear feel.

CONSIDER THE COST

Is the look worth it? Aesthetically, yes. But these natural wonders generally require professional installation, the materials themselves are costly, they're among the coldest of all flooring choices, they show dust, and they don't provide noise insulation. On the plus side, they add unrivaled texture, mood, and impact to spaces, repel water, and are easy to clean.

HOW TO SAVE MONEY

To enjoy the beauty of one of these natural wonders without breaking the budget, think small. Enjoy a luxurious travertine floor, for example, in a half-bath or a touch of marble in a small entry. Or, create a border of stone or brick around the perimeter of a room, then add a budget inset of carpet.

ONE: *In a collector's home mixing country with traditional and rugged with refined, the baked terra-cotta flooring emphasizes the casual mood the owners prefer.*

TWO: *Cool white marble puts this room in an elegantly understated mood that's just right for the blend of refined furnishings. The creamy sweep underfoot is punctuated with geometric-pattern insets. Today most stone companies will cut stone in any configuration you want, and some major retailers stock stone tiles in their regular inventories.*

TILE RELAXES

Ceramic tile and vinyl flooring are more affordable and easier to find and install than stone or similar natural materials. An ever-growing range of colors, patterns, sizes, sheens, and even grout colors makes ceramic tile flooring an option worth considering for more than the bath. And vinyls have made huge strides in style with custom designs also available.

CONSIDER CERAMICS

Whether in solid colors or fresh hand-painted designs, ceramic tile offers fuss-free durability and style. An expected choice for a kitchen or bath, ceramic tile also makes sense in a high-traffic entry or a family room in which kids continually track in grime from outside. Style-wise, a clean sweep of single-color ceramic tile across a floor creates a streamlined effect that can visually expand a space. But don't overlook other options. Inset a mini area rug of tiles into your floor. Add a patterned tile on the diagonal every few feet. Or, go for the classics with a two-toned tile checkerboard.

VINYL VISTAS

Go for great pretenders—vinyl tiles or sheet vinyls that mimic ceramics, faux lapis paintwork, or other decorative treatments. Classic checkerboard patterns are hard to beat because they fit almost any room style and furnishings mix even if it already has a helping of pattern. Install the checkerboard on the diagonal to add pleasing depth to a room.

ONE: *This new family room creates a gardenlike atmosphere with ceramic tile in a deep forest green. The flooring is less costly and has more intense color than natural stone. Because of its dark color, the green tile helps visually anchor the seating pieces within the tall, white space.*

TWO: *When the budget only covered simple cosmetic updates, this vintage kitchen added bold geometry underfoot with do-it-yourself self-sticking vinyl squares. The tiles are an easy-clean, long-wearing choice for this eat-in hub.*

2

PAINT
YOUR OWN STYLE

A simple square stencil—a paper doily—is the secret ingredient for this do-it-yourself floor, hand-painted with a classic checkerboard area "rug." By using lacy doilies, the pattern is as delicate as a snowflake. The design is long-lasting because it's done in latex paints with a protective polyurethane finish.

ONE: Measure and mark the center of the floor with an X. Place a doily— ours is about 10 inches square—on the X, then lay out doilies in a checkerboard around it. Leave a 6½-inch-wide border, or cover the whole room. Mark grid, using yardstick; note solid-color squares by penciling X at centers.

TWO: To prepare and apply stencils, lay each doily facedown on butcher paper and lightly spray with stencil adhesive spray from a crafts store; dry until tacky, or sticky to the touch. Put tacky side down on floor, lay paper over it, and rub firmly with your hand. Lay out the remaining doilies.

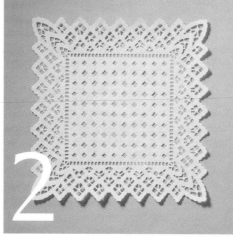

THREE: Tape off the rug border with ½-inch-wide painter's tape that doesn't allow paint to seep under it, but doesn't pull up paint when tape is removed. Lay the first border band around the grid pattern; the middle band is 1 inch beyond that, and the outer band is 4 inches beyond the middle band.

FOUR/FIVE: To stencil, use a 3-inch-wide foam brush and latex paint. First paint solid squares and border nearest rows you are painting. While that dries, paint doily-covered squares with foam stenciling tool; blot paint off tool on paper towel and dab paint on stencils with up-and-down motion until holes are filled in. Paint outer border and allow floor to dry about an hour before adding a second coat of paint. Carefully remove doilies with a razor blade or a heat gun. When floor is totally dry, brush on a coat of polyurethane sealer.

5

FLOORING FACTS
CARPET & RUG CONSTRUCTION

	Characteristics	Advantages	Disadvantages	Care/Cost
Cotton	Soft fiber often used for informal area or scatter rugs.	Easily dyed.	Limited durability.	Cleans very well; some rugs machine washable. Usually inexpensive.
Wool	Deep, warm, rich look; excellent resiliency and abrasion resistance; has a warm and natural feel.	Excellent durability; flame-resistant; crush-resistant; dyes well in a wide range of colors.	Can be damaged by alkaline detergents; needs moth-proofing; not best medium for bright colors.	Resists soil; not cleaned as easily as many synthetic fibers. Expensive.
Coir, Jute, and Sisal	Used for informal matting; available in colors (mainly earth tones); can be stenciled or painted.	Offers textural contrast and a variety of patterns.	Fair to poor durability and resistance to wear and soil; not as soft underfoot as conventional carpet.	Offers little resistance to soil; not easily cleaned. Usually inexpensive.
Acrylic	Closest to wool of the man-made fibers; nonallergenic; resists mildew, moths, and insects; comes in a range of colors.	Crush-resistant; springy; fade-resistant; generates minimal static.	May form pills, or beadlike balls of fiber, on face of the carpet; not as resilient or wear- and stain-resistant as wool or nylon.	Cleans very well; smooth fibers resist soil. Moderate price.
Nylon	Wide choice of colors; excellent color retention; soft and resilient.	Strongest synthetic fiber; resists abrasion, mildew, moths; nonallergenic; continuous filament fibers minimize pilling, shedding.	Static-prone, unless treated; cut-filament loop carpet may pill.	Good cleanability; stain-resistant treatments make nylon easy to keep clean. Moderate price.
Polyester	Similar to wool in look, touch; good color and texture selection, and color retention; resists moths, mildew; nonallergenic.	Very durable, resilient; abrasion-resistant; sheds moisture; available in a wide range of colors.	Does not wear as well as wool or nylon; some pilling and shedding; susceptible to oil-based stains.	Good cleanability, enhanced by stain-resistant treatments; sheds moisture; static-resistant. Less expensive than nylon or wool carpet.
Olefin	Primarily loop and randomly sheared textures; nonabsorbent; resists abrasion, pilling, shedding.	Fibers can withstand moisture; use indoors or outdoors; very durable in level-loop styles.	Lower grades may crush and flatten.	Excellent cleanability, especially with stain-resistant treatments; resists static, acids, chemicals. Moderate price.

RESILIENT & HARD SURFACE

	Characteristics	Advantages	Disadvantages	Cleanability
Asphalt Tile	Porous; resists alkalis; low in cost.	OK on cement floor; can be below grade.	Noisy; dents easily; needs waxing.	Damaged by grease, harsh cleaners.
Cork Tile	Handsome, sealed surface.	Warm; comfortable and quiet underfoot.	Not for heavy traffic.	Easy upkeep; must be sealed for durability.
Rubber Tile	Handsome, clear colors.	Excellent resilience; quiet; durable.	Expensive; slippery when wet; must be above grade.	Resists dents, stains; damaged by strong detergents, grease.
Vinyl Composition	Resists alkalis; easy to install; low cost.	Durable; colorful.	Not very quiet and not a very resilient surface.	Embossing traps dirt; clean with heavy-duty detergents.
Cushioned Sheet Vinyl	Wide range of colors, patterns, surface finishes, and prices.	Superior resilience; quiet; comfortable; stain-resistant.	Expensive; lower-cost grades susceptible to nicks and dents.	Easy upkeep; some with no-wax or never-wax feature.
Sheet Vinyl	Wide range of colors, patterns, and surface finishes available.	Good resilience.	Less-expensive grades susceptible to nicks and dents.	Easily maintained; some with no-wax feature.
Solid Vinyl Tile	Often simulates natural materials.	Easy to install; durable.	Only fair resilience.	Stain-resistant; easy to clean and maintain.
Wood	Natural or painted; wide range of patterns possible.	Good resilience; hardwoods very durable.	Softwoods less durable than hardwood counterparts.	Should be sealed with a penetrating oil sealer (with wax protector) or waterproof polyurethane; manufactured floors usually are presealed.
Brick, Slate, Quarry Tile	Natural look; variety of exciting shapes.	Durable; beautiful.	No resilience.	Slate and quarry tile may need sealer; good stain resistance.
Stone (granite, limestone, etc.)	Offers a natural look.	Durable; beautiful.	No resilience.	Some types absorb stains easily.
Ceramic Tile	Colorful; many shapes and designs.	Beautiful; stain- and fade-resistant.	No resilience; cold underfoot; noisy under hard-soled shoes.	Clean with soap and water only.
Marble	Costly; formal.	Beautiful.	Hard underfoot; noisy under hard-soled shoes; stains easily.	Needs waxing; stains are difficult to remove.
Terrazzo	Smooth, shiny finish; variety of multicolored effects.	Durable; stain- and moisture-resistant.	Comes in limited designs; permanent installation.	Easily cleaned.

LIGHTING

THINK OF THEM AS BITS OF FIRELIGHT, AND YOU WILL UNDERSTAND why glowing pools of light not only serve our practical needs but comfort our psyches, too. In this chapter, you'll learn how easy it is to supplement your existing lighting to increase function and add drama to your home.

ONE: *An easy-to-create lighting mix makes this room a magnet for evening gatherings. In addition to table lamps, canister-style uplights (hidden on the floor behind the sofas) silhouette the tree trunks and cast leafy shadows on the ceiling.*

KNOW THE
BASICS

Good interior lighting is more than a single light fixture centered on the ceiling or a pair of lamps plopped on either side of a sofa. A well-balanced lighting plan contains three essential elements—general or ambient lighting, task or local lighting, and accent lighting. With the right mix, you bring "sunshine" to any room, create drama, and even visually alter a room's dimensions.

USE THREE BUILDING BLOCKS

• *General (or ambient) lighting* allows you to move safely through a room without running into the furniture or stepping on the kids' toys.

It's glare-free, indirect light that literally bounces off the walls and ceiling to provide comfortable background illumination. But an even distribution of light is key, so make sure you don't end up with areas that are overly bright or hidden in the shadows. What are some of the best general lighting sources? Recessed and track lighting are two good examples. Given their flexibility—with the help of a simple dimmer control—they can change the mood of a room in a matter of moments while maintaining their original objective.

• *Task (or local) lighting* provides necessary illumination for specific duties such as reading, cooking, and hobbies. Like general lighting, it should be shadow-free, but unlike its counterpart, task lighting should be localized according to the job at hand. Reading lamps and under-cabinet lighting fit into this category.

• *Accent lighting* is purely decorative in nature and can come from several sources. Including everything from floor-based uplights and torchères to sconces and direct spotlights, accent lighting draws attention to a room's most interesting aspects. Whether you want to accent a favorite work of art or enhance an architectural element, the right light is sure to set a dramatic stage.

TWO: *In this well-lighted kitchen, a grid of recessed ceiling cans provides general illumination; under-cabinet lights and a track-suspended pendant handle task lighting. For a decorative accent, a spotlight on the same track focuses on a wall display of collectibles.*

SPREAD
LIGHT AROUND

Well-balanced lighting is more than a matter of how much you have. The way you distribute it is just as important. Avoid glaring mistakes and create practical, beautiful pools that light your way around the room. Keep in mind, too, that different rooms need different kinds of illumination. Personalizing your lighting plan is imperative, but be sure that, overall, you cover the basics.

THE RIGHT LIGHTS

To create successful room-to-room lighting plans, match each fixture to the role it will play and provide enough light sources for pleasant, safe, comfortable spaces.

• *Mix sources for living and family rooms.* For television viewing or simply relaxing, general lighting from indirect sources is best—wall washers, uplights, and recessed fixtures. For homework, hobbies, and reading, you'll need task, or local, lighting—downlights, spotlights, and table or floor lamps. For accent, emphasize art over the fireplace or large plants with fixed spotlights. If you already have track lighting, consider adding one or more low-voltage spotlights; they produce especially dramatic accent beams, which vary from narrow to wide depending on the bulb you use.

• *Give dining rooms flexibility.* Tame that lovely but too-bright chandelier over the dining table with a dimmer control to soften the mood. Supplement general lighting with built-in recessed fixtures and portable accent lighting, including picture lights and plug-in shelf lights.

• *Light kitchens for efficiency.* Augment general illuminators—track lights or ceiling fixtures—with task lights beamed on counters and cooktops.

• *Add task lights to bedrooms and baths.* Put bedroom lighting on a dimmer switch for mood control. For young children, avoid halogen lamps, which produce scorching heat; ceiling or wall fixtures are safer than table lamps for young kids.

White-shaded lamps invite you to settle in for a little fireside reading. With light shades and three-way sockets and bulbs, you can turn up these lamps for reading or needlepoint and dim them for moodier party light. The beams from recessed ceiling cans accent artwork, and a lighted hutch offers a welcoming glow.

ONE: *Handsome strip lights—essentially large versions of picture lights—accent colorfully jacketed books in this den. Because fluorescents cause colors to fade quickly, choose incandescents for accenting artwork and books.*

TWO: *A new bulkhead and recessed can lights team with a new banquette and a trio of prints to transform*

a plain wall into a living room focal point. Spotlight bulbs shine clearly defined beams on the artwork; all three cans are wired to the same dimmer switch.

THREE: *Mini spotlights serve two functions in this entrance hall: They wash walls with radiance for a soft, indirect glow and silhouette a line-up of shapely pottery that introduces visitors to this collector's passion.*

You only need to attend the theater to see how lighting draws attention to certain stars. So why not set your home stage with creative accent lighting? Highlight your favorite work of art, focus on an important furniture grouping, or feature an intriguing piece of architecture. In essence, play up your room's best assets. However you use accent lighting, keep this formula in mind: Lighting that's meant to accent objects should be at least three times brighter than the room's general lighting.

SPOTLIGHT YOUR FAVORITES

• *Experiment first.* If you're unsure where to put accent lights, buy one or two inexpensive clamp-on lights fitted with spotlight bulbs. Try them in different locations. You'll soon see where you want to direct extra light, and,

DON'T FORGET THE ACCENTS

especially in contemporary settings, you may opt to keep the clean-lined clamp-ons instead of buying other lighting.

• *Limit your costs.* Strip lights cost less than $20 at most home centers. Attach one to a shelf and plug it into the nearest outlet to enhance books and collectibles. Try just one and you'll probably like the effect so well that you'll find yourself running back to the store for another.

• *Corral the cords.* For aesthetics and safety, run exposed cords along a baseboard or behind furniture.

• *Get your directions right.* To play up decorative belongings, light them from the front or above, emphasizing shape and texture. Picture lights are one of the easiest add-ons; angle the light toward the picture, not down on it, to minimize undesirable reflection and glare.

• *Be flexible.* A desk lamp with pivoting head can spotlight art when it's not needed for homework. Plug table lamps into a dimmer so you can dial down for mood light.

MAKE YOUR OWN LAMP

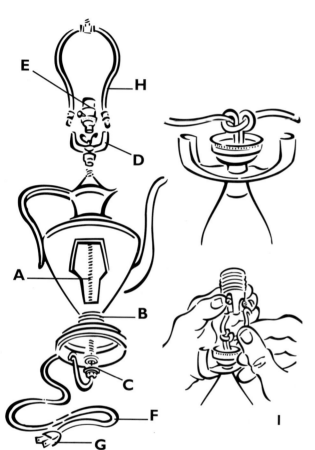

Consider the fixture as well as the effect when shopping for a light for a specific space. There are many innovative lamps on the market today, but why not make yours one of a kind? An antique vase, a canning jar, and even a sterling silver coffee pot are interesting bases for fun—and purely personal—table lamps. Almost any object works as a base as long as it's stable, hollow, and has center holes through both ends. However, if you drill holes in an antique to fit in lamp parts, you will reduce its value.

CHOOSE THE RIGHT SHADE

• *Consider function first.* If your lamp is intended for accent or task lighting, use an opaque shade that will cast light up and down. If your intent is general lighting, a translucent shade will bathe your space in a soft glow.

• *Pick a style suited to your room.* Pleated shades in fine fabrics such as silk fit traditional schemes. Checkerboard and stenciled patterns evoke a country mood. In contemporary or eclectic schemes, simple nonpleated shades are easy mixers. Select a texture that will complement the lamp base; for example, try a gathered silk shade on a crystal base.

• *Measure for size.* The visual weight of your lamp's base—not the actual dimensions—should be about two-thirds of the entire lamp with the shade making up the remaining third. Between the tabletop and the shade's bottom edge, the distance should be greater than the shade height so the lamp doesn't look top-heavy. The lampshade should extend at least 2 inches beyond the base on all sides.

ONE: *With a handful of hardware, it's relatively easy to make a lamp like this one. Slip a threaded rod (A) through the center of the lamp base (B), securing each end of the rod with a washer and locknut (C). Fit a harp retainer (D) onto the rod. Remove base from the socket (E) and screw it to rod. Push appliance cord (F) through rod. Split cord at top and tie with Underwriters knot (see top right diagram). If desired, secure* cord at bottom of base with another knot. *Strip insulation from split cords, attach leads to socket terminals (see bottom right diagram), and add plug (G). Reassemble socket, install lamp harp (H), and finish off your one-of-a-kind creation with a bulb and complementary shade.*

TWO: *A shapely silver coffee pot, newly wired and fitted with a traditional pleated shade, serves up vintage charm.*

DO LAMPS HAVE TO MATCH?

When matched suites were in style, there was an unwritten decorating rule: Lamps flanking a sofa or bed had to match. But in this age of personal style and eclectic tastes, lamps don't have to be mirror images. In fact, it's often more interesting if you do your own thing—as long as mismatched lamps share the same mood and visual weight.

SITING YOUR LIGHTING

These guidelines will help you place light in the right spot and not in your eyes: Space recessed fixtures with flood bulbs at least 4 to 6 feet apart for general light, 15 to 18 inches apart when used for tasks, such as lighting a kitchen work island. Site the lower edge of a hanging fixture 4 feet from the floor by a chair or bed, 15 inches above a desktop. Situate sconces above standing eye level and 65 inches from the floor. The bottom of a table lamp should be at seated eye level, 38 to 42 inches above the floor; for tasks, 10 to 12 inches below eye level. Line up short floor lamps with your shoulder when seated; tall floor lamps should rest about 15 inches to the side and 20 inches behind the center of anything you might be reading.

BULBS OF CHOICE

For best effect, mix and match bulbs as you work the three basic types of lighting into your home.

• *Incandescent lighting* is found in common lightbulbs (called "A bulbs") with their familiar yellowish light. A bulbs are inexpensive and readily available, but they aren't energy-efficient. In recessed cans and track fixtures, avoid A bulbs and opt, instead, for spotlight and floodlight bulbs; their silver coatings produce well-defined narrow rays for accents or wider beams for general lighting and wall washing.

• *Halogen bulbs* cast a crisp light that's whiter and more sunlike than incandescent bulbs, so they enhance a room's colors. Newer halogen bulbs can screw into existing fixtures. Halogen bulbs cost more than incandescents—and generate extreme heat. Always keep portable halogen lamps and torchères away from flammable objects.

• *Fluorescents* use the least amount of energy but can cause colors to fade. As you shop, consider spending a bit more for full-spectrum fluorescents, which more closely mimic natural sunlight.

ONE: *Lamps and fixtures have followed furniture as it has moved away from matched pieces to an eclectic look. In this living room, well-planned balance and proportion allow these lamps, finishes, and end tables—one's a primitive pine trunk—to work beautifully. Visual balance doesn't mean sameness here. Shorter than the painted table at the other end of the sofa, the trunk calls for a taller lamp.*

TWO: *More important than any other factor in achieving symmetry is the placement of light sources. You can have two completely different lamps, but to create a balanced setting on both ends of the sofa, they should have similar visual weight. This lamp is shorter in stature than its counterpart, but its bulbous base and generous shade make up for the difference in height.*

THREE: *Another trick that makes these eye-catching lamps amiable companions is making sure the bottoms of both shades are at about the same height. Both are at the right height for reading, which is at eye level when you're seated.*

DINING LIGHT

When you imagine the perfect dining light, does a chandelier come to mind? If so, it's no surprise. Chandeliers have been lighting dining tables for centuries. In colonial times, fixtures fitted with candles were hung high for practical purposes—to eliminate the danger of fire and of getting burned. Today beautiful chandeliers and their contemporary counterpart—pendant lamps—are both practical and beautiful. Not only do they provide task and general lighting, but they also contribute greatly to a dining room's style. No matter what you prefer for a primary dining fixture, the following tips will make the area all the more inviting.

• *What's the right height?* Suspend a pendant light or chandelier so the bottom is about 30 inches above the table. If your fixture has an open shade and bare lightbulb, hang it high enough to avoid harsh light in diners' eyes; a bulb with a silvered crown reduces glare considerably. A hanging light's diameter should be at least a foot shorter than the table beneath it. When a dining room's ceiling height is more than 8 feet, balance the space by raising the fixture 3 inches for each additional foot of ceiling height.

• *Consider light options.* Not all dining rooms call for a single hanging fixture. Above a long table, a trio of pendants or strip of track lights provides more even illumination.

• *Enhance the effect.* Technically, a chandelier is several light fixtures in one, so choose a fixture with light-catching crystal prisms or reflective shades.

• *Add missing links.* Too many chandeliers are sold with a short "leash." If yours hangs too high, add another length of chain. If old and new links don't match, add a new shirred fabric cover.

ONE: *Let a chandelier complement the size and shape of your table. Here a curvaceous chandelier beautifully echoes the lines of the bow-back Windsor bench. A good ambient light source, modern-day chandeliers such as this one with electrified candles should be controlled by a dimmer switch for quick mood swings.*

TWO: *There's no rule that a dining room has to have overhead light. Here a quartet of tall candles in antique holders sheds soft light on the table. A nearby table lamp and an uplight beneath the palm provide additional illumination.*

HELP FOR HIGH SPACES

The high spirits of rooms with vaulted ceilings often sink with the setting sun. With a little planning, however, it's easy to get any room glowing again.

LOWER LIGHT WHERE YOU NEED IT

In a room with a vaulted ceiling, light fixtures in or up against the ceiling are of little practical help to people below. Using torchères or spotlights mounted on open beams to bounce some light off the ceiling can provide a cheery general glow, but you'll need to supplement that light by bringing other fixtures down to your level. Here's how:

• *Hang 'em low.* In this dining room, *opposite*, a pair of contemporary pendant lamps drops from the high-rise ceiling to within 30 inches of the pine dining table. The twin fixtures are more than the ideal lighting solution. Their all-but-invisible silhouettes allow the eye to enjoy the colorful focal-point bookshelves. The same concept works in the living room, *above left*, where track fixtures suspended from the ceiling bring light down to a more intimate and useful level. Lights can be moved along the track and redirected to accent art or brighten the fireplace wall.

• *Use portable lighting as an anchor.* Think of lamps as heartwarming bonfires—reassuring gathering spots beneath the dark night sky of a vaulted ceiling. Intimate pools of task and accent fixtures will light your way after sunset; teamed with warm-hued rugs and low-hung artwork, they'll also comfort your psyche by lowering the room's visual focus.

ONE: *Suspended track lights in this living room do more than play an accent role. In their own way, they exude a sculptural quality.*

TWO: *Wall-mounted uplights draw the eye toward this bedroom's architectural assets— three treetop windows and a high-rise ceiling.*

THREE: *Beneath a vaulted ceiling, long cords of differing lengths put light where it's needed. Instead of boldly stating their presence, these pendants blend into the background, allowing the library wall to star.*

3

LIGHTEN UP WITH EASY ADD-ONS

Do you find yourself cursing the darkness in an underlit hallway or room? You're not alone. Despite the range of simple plug-in lighting solutions readily available, many home lighting plans end just where they should begin—with a couple of lamps flanking a bed or a sofa. To spread heartwarming points of light around your home, start small to build confidence and enthusiasm. Enjoy the effect of a plug-in shelf light or picture light today, and you'll be eager to add more special effects tomorrow. Check into these simple ideas:

• *Strip lights.* Available in varying lengths and finishes, many slim strip lights simply stick to the front edges of shelves to highlight displays.

• *Pinups and sconces.* Wall-mounted pinup lights are space-savers in small bedrooms and sitting rooms; sconces brighten halls, stairs, and entries.

• *Plug-in picture lights* give radiance to artwork after dark—and install in minutes. You'll find them at home centers and lighting shops and through catalogs.

• *Lamps.* If you've shopped recently, you know lamp choices have skyrocketed. Add a torchère to bounce a glow off the ceiling. Candlestick lamps are perfect for slim console tables and mantels. Small accent lamps brighten a sideboard, entry table, or kitchen pass-through, and even smaller miniature lamps turn dark shelves into glowing assets.

ONE: *Add a small or mini lamp to a dark shelf or hallway table. This rooster lamp turned a once-neglected side table into a reassuring nighttime beacon.*

TWO: *Replace a ceiling fixture with a strip of track lights. Here adjustable canisters with flood bulbs wash attic walls with light to visually expand the space.*

THREE: *A low-cost picture light lends a welcome glow of its own as it brings a painting to life. Candle-style pinup wall lamps heighten the fireside drama.*

FOUR/FIVE: *Sold in a range of styles and sizes, ready-made strip lights draw attention to favorite possessions and introduce a nighttime glow to any shelf. Some slim designs, often found at home centers, have self-adhesive backing. Just stick one to the front of a shelf and plug it into the nearest outlet.*

ACCESS

THINK OF ACCESSORIES AS JEWELRY FOR YOUR rooms. Just as a strand of pearls sets off a cashmere sweater and an antique brooch complements a lacy blouse, the things you love and display are part of your home's signature. Whether you choose art, heirlooms, or sentimental favorites like those gathered here, it's your chance to express yourself without necessarily making a major investment.

ORIES

FORMAL CASUAL

ECLECTIC SLICK

TASTY
SANDWICHES
HOT
DRINKS

New York, New York

DO YOU HAVE AN ATTITUDE?

Knowing what kinds of furnishings, accessories, and colors grab your eye—and heartstrings—is only part of the picture when accessorizing your home. By understanding your decorating attitude, you can pull your home together with beautiful arrangements of favorite things that consistently convey your decorating personality. Stop for a moment and ask yourself: "How formal or casual am I?" (For more help—and some fun—take our decorating attitude quiz starting on page 26 and our pillow pop quiz on page 87.)

FORMAL

A sense of order characterizes formal groupings. If that sounds like you, flank a gilded mirror with a pair of topiaries or hang paintings in perfect symmetry. Although a formal attitude can be expressed with contemporary accessories as well as classical ones, chances are you gravitate toward venerable objects with classic forms and flowing shapes. Accessories often include a mix of collected objects, antiques, or even contemporary art; personal photos and mementos convey a sense of heritage, too.

FORMAL: *In this entry hall, a pair of candlestick lamps and four Italian landscape prints mirror each other in classic symmetry.*

CASUAL: *A school of whimsical fish prints swims in this wall arrangement that features sunny hues and intriguing frame textures.*

ECLECTIC: *Juxtaposing formal ancestral portraits with gardening tools and a vintage diner sign gives this grouping visual punch.*

SLICK: *A plain painted wall gives an artistic edge to a sculptural lamp and black and white posters in classic museum frames.*

CASUAL

Accessorizing casually—with a fistful of fishing lures hung from a pegged rack, seashells scattered over a shelf; or vacation snapshots grouped in driftwood frames, for instance—conveys a put-your-feet-up decorating attitude. Balance and proportion remain important, but arrangements are more relaxed—and usually not symmetrical. A sense of nostalgia or whimsy often is more important than the pedigree of an object, and colors can be crayon bright or earthy as a desert landscape.

SLICK

Calm, cool, and composed summarize this sophisticated decorating attitude. Accessories—what few there are—tend to be chosen more for what they say about form and function than for what they convey about nostalgia and warmth. Collections are carefully edited and displayed in a way that gives each piece museum-like prominence. Color steps in mostly as an accent —but often in a bold way.

ECLECTIC

Far from anything goes, an eclectic approach to accessorizing involves planning and forethought. Keeping balance and proportion in mind, the idea is simple: Pick what you love. The secret is to find distinctly disparate objects that play off one another in an interesting and unexpected way with contrasting textures, shapes, and design origins.

FOR MORE ABOUT HOW TO DEFINE YOUR DECORATING ATTITUDE, REFER TO OUR DECORATING QUIZ STARTING ON PAGE 26.

HOW'S YOUR SENSE OF BALANCE?

ONE: *Asymmetrical balance is created in this contemporary living room by varying the visual weight and scale of objects. The painting, hung off-center, is balanced by a tall carved giraffe; mismatched shadow boxes at left balance the window at right.*

TWO: *If you could fold this elegant living room's mantel in half, you'd find that both sides match perfectly. For formal balance, the mantel arrangement makes art the focus and equally distributes objects of similar weight, shape, and size.*

The walls are painted. The furniture is arranged. The window treatments are hung. But until you start filling in the blanks with objects that express your personality, a room will never say enough about you. It may take years to properly accessorize a room. In fact, if you really love decorating and view it as a lifelong hobby, you don't intend for your home to ever be truly finished. You'll add items gradually, remove others, and let your accessories continually reflect your own changing interests. Even if your home is a work in progress, though, use your own sense of balance—the degree to which you lean toward formal or informal groupings—to help achieve and maintain harmony and consistency. Here's how you can get started:

• *Find your focal point.* A mantel often is the most obvious place to begin adding personal touches, although a built-in bookcase or empty wall also might serve as a starting point. In a formal room, a large painting or mirror centered over the fireplace can be flanked by identical objects such as porcelain vases. Casual settings call for asymmetrical groupings—perhaps a tall basket of willow branches or a painting placed off-center and then balanced by a trio of weighty beeswax candles.

• *Vary the pace.* A good story builds excitement then lets the reader relax for a moment, just as satisfying decorating schemes include quiet, uncluttered zones between high-drama areas.

• *Know when to stop.* Love what you display—but don't display everything you love. Whether your attitude is formal or casual, cluttered or minimal, remember that by paring and rotating your treasures you can give them greater impact.

TELL YOUR STORY

Decorating books and magazines are invaluable resources when you're collecting furnishings and design ideas. When it comes to choosing the accessories that will deliver your personal statement, however, you're on your own. Only you can write *your* story.

MAKE ACCENTS ELOQUENT

Your home should convey to visitors a sense of what and whom you love, where you've been, and where you're going. Even if you're just getting started, you may have some of what you need to accessorize your rooms. The trick is to view your possessions with a fresh eye.

• *Weave a story.* Grouped together, certain objects can create a narrative of your life. The story may be literal—perhaps told by photographs that show you and your parents over the years. Or, certain items or colors may cheer you, calm you, jog wonderful memories, and become conversation pieces as you recount their origins to friends.

• *Forage room to room.* Walk through your rooms, gathering things that speak to you—the seashells you collected on last summer's trip to the beach, the painting you bought at a gallery in Amsterdam, the apothecary jar full of marbles that your child collected. Shop your attic and albums for family photos; have some copied and enlarged for impact.

• *Edit for impact.* The best stories are to the point. Leave out extraneous objects that clutter your message.

ONE: *A grouping of colorful and useful bowls, dishes, and wood boxes reveals a practiced eye for form and function and a passion for collecting.*

TWO: *A serene display of earth-toned pottery and desert-hued accents conveys the collector's appreciation of craftsmanship, function, and artful expression.*

THREE: *A reverence for a family's past is evident in this arrangement of family photos. Sheer numbers make it a focal point; mat sizes, frame textures, and the photos rivet the eye.*

BIRDS O F A FEATHER

Even in decorating, the old maxim still applies: There's strength in numbers. When considering how best to display your collections, remember that grouping related things together will carry far greater impact than if you sprinkle lots of small items throughout a room, allowing them to get lost in space. (To learn more about the basics of arranging related accessories, turn to pages 276–277 in the "Elements" chapter.)

MULTIPLE CHOICES

Some types of accessories—smaller works or those with more detail—often look best when grouped together for impact. Beautifully detailed botanical prints, for example, can turn a dull wall into a virtual garden. Or, as shown *right*, small bird prints create drama—and humor—when allowed to flock together high on a wall. For fun, work flat and three-dimensional works into the same grouping. Small cat figurines on a shelf will be more interesting when you tuck a framed cat print or photo behind them.

ONE: *A series of related prints, such as these realistic antique-style drawings of birds, are most effective with identical matting and frames. Lined up between the windows, these prints draw the eye upward to the alcove's transoms and vaulted ceiling.*

TWO: Group objects that share the same colors. Here a symmetrical display of blue and white china helps convey this dining room's formal mood. In each grouping, a large platter anchors the middle ground; smaller plates and decorative pieces balance the top and sides. Hanging additional plates on the wall keeps the handsome cupboard from appearing too heavy against the light-colored backdrop.

THREE: A rare flag quilt forms the eye-catching background for this charming display of folk art. Contrasts give the arrangement punch. The busy, primary-hued flag motif is balanced by calming colors of the decoy quintet. The fruit basket on the floor anchors the display and repeats the rectangular shape of the quilt's grid; the fluid and varied shapes of the decoys' graceful necks create shapely contrast.

INCLUDE EASY
WARM-UPS

Accessorizing your home does more than impart personality; it conveys a sense of comfort and warmth. With a relatively small investment of money and time, you can turn a bland cold space into one that welcomes and enfolds you, your family, and guests.

TURNING UP THE HEAT

• *Warm the walls.* Blank walls benefit from even the simplest wall hangings. If you don't have the budget for expensive framing, hang a single large poster instead. Look for interesting old frames at flea markets and yard sales and mount them on the wall as is—without pictures—until you find just the right art to fill them. Suspend a favorite quilt or tapestry remnant from a wall-hung rod for instant warmth and color.

• *Add architectural interest.* In a white-box space, mount a window mullion above a mirror and sofa. Old columns and pediments instantly add a sense of history, plus texture and dimension, to rooms that lack character. Look at unused nooks and crannies—that black hole at the top of the stairs, for example—as spots for, perhaps, a tabletop gallery of family photos that beckons you.

• *Design quick warm-ups.* Cluster candles in an empty fireplace, a dreary corner, or on a tabletop. There's no need to invest money in fancy candlesticks; just rummage through cupboards for an array of pretty glasses, terra-cotta pots, or china saucers.

ONE: *By cozying up to the back of the sofa, this folding floor screen turns a blank corner into a colorful backdrop for the mix of seating in this oversize room. A trompe l'oeil wall covering on the screen creates an instant library.*

TWO: What if you don't have a real fireplace? You can create hearth-warming comfort—no remodeling necessary—with a vintage fireplace surround attached to the wall. Treat the mantel as a focal point and display spot. Filled with dried flowers and cut-to-fit mirror, this faux fireplace will radiate warmth year-round.

THREE: This warm-hued painting inspired a new wall color of deep, rich eggplant, creating an intimate setting that's especially dramatic for nighttime dinner parties. The golden tones of the oversize art also echo in the honeyed patina of the antique sideboard.

PICTURE ARRANGING

First attempts at picture hanging often result in walls that look like Swiss cheese. To avoid costly mistakes and frustration, carefully plan your wall arrangements before you hammer the first nail.

• **Get the picture.** The easiest way to get a feel for balance and spacing is to lay out on the floor all the pictures you plan to use. Or, cut paper templates of each picture, tape the templates to the wall, and move them around until you're happy with the results.

• **Create special effects.** Generally, walls wider than they are high call for horizontal groupings; narrow spaces welcome vertical arrangements. Arrange shapes within an imaginary framework with a strong horizontal anchor. Keep spaces between frames equal. To create intimacy, hang pictures low to visually link them with furniture.

• **Frame for personality.** Frames and mats should complement, not compete with, your pictures. Modern art often looks best in minimal frames such as metal; traditional paintings call for carved wood frames and multilayered mats. Let the framed image, not your room palette, guide mat color. Mats in dark hues are dramatic; white mats emphasize the art itself. As a rule, mats should be twice as wide as the frame for resting the eye, but tiny pictures with oversize mats are eye-catching.

ONE: *Often one big poster or painting can provide a focal point for an entire room. When this bedroom's budget didn't stretch for an expensive headboard, a large art poster—with a do-it-yourself metal frame—created drama and color inspiration.*

TWO: *Turn awkward spaces into artistic showcases. Here three prints, stacked one atop the other, nicely fill this narrow vertical space between two windows.*

THREE: *By wrapping around a corner, a series of like-size prints creates a sense of intimacy. To visually hug seating or dining pieces, hang prints low on the wall so that the artwork is at eye level when you're seated.*

FOUR: *This radial arrangement adds a sense of movement to what often is a static spot over the sofa. For color balance, the darker-hued plates are placed low and to the outside of the arch; all plates echo the painting's palette.*

FIVE: *One print hung at the bottom of the stairs would only accentuate the narrow floor and wall space. Instead, the spot gains visual width when three photos with wide white mats are grouped horizontally.*

BUILDING ON THE PAST

COLLECTORS TO THE CORE, THIS CALIFORNIA COUPLE MERRILY MINES THE PAST FOR RICHES—GEMS THAT BRING THEIR HOME TIMELESS ELEGANCE.

San Francisco designer Ann Jones describes her lifelong passion for collecting as a form of time travel. Even as a young girl, she recalls combing the beaches near her Florida home for shells and sea grass, sand-washed jewels that seemed to have floated ashore from another place and time. These days, she and her husband, Tim McDermott, are attracted to more sophisticated, if eclectic, treasures.

STORIES SIMPLY TOLD

Dolls and decoys, bracelets and silverware, metal cars and airplanes, cake stands and loving cups, animal portraits and postcards, old art and bottles—each object comes with a tale. "I'm interested in evocative things that give you a memory," Ann says. "I'm drawn to objects that have a history or may have been somewhere I would have liked to have gone." Ann and Tim have refurbished their late-Victorian townhouse to showcase ever-growing collections. Simple furnishings are timeworn in a warm palette of dusky browns with gallery-white walls. French doors bathe the living room in golden sunlight. This airy setting allows individual objects the space to breathe, giving them an almost modern sensibility. Ann also masses some of her collections, lending them more prominence and weight. She's always exploring new arrangements and combinations and moving things around. "There's definite power in numbers," she says. "Any collection, no matter how humble, takes on new importance and interest when clustered." Favorite haunts are flea markets, thrift shops, yard sales, and salvage yards. When her passions start to get too pricey, she says, "It just gets me excited about going out and finding the next greatest thing."

Ann Jones and Tim McDermott share a love of collecting and make a variety of vintage objects part of their own home's creative history. At the foot of an old campaign bed, a carved pediment serves as a tray table base.

Ann rotates her collections—adding new finds all along—to keep her striking vignettes from growing visually stale and predictable. Grouping objects by shape, color, or material is another way she ensures that a mix pleases the eye. Earthy clay colors and rounded shapes connect a group of pottery bowls and baskets on a bookshelf behind the sofa. The burnished metal of a classic French bistro table sets off an arrangement of tin boxes and a vintage alarm clock. To give collections much-needed breathing room and a sunny spotlight, Ann and Tim knocked down three walls in the living room and added a bank of 9-foot-tall French doors. A large mirror above the fireplace reflects light into the room and and visually expands the gracious space.

ONE: Ann and Tim's 1904 Victorian townhouse in San Francisco provides a perfect setting for their eclectic collections. The couple's treasure hunting takes them from architectural salvage shops to flea markets and garage sales.

TWO: Vintage tin boxes make a decorative statement but have a practical use as well. One holds a free-spirited bouquet of flowers and the other stows the remote control for the television.

THREE: In the dining room, a collection of silver loving cups is displayed en masse on a granite shelf that Ann designed. The shelf is large enough to double as a sideboard when the couple hosts dinner parties.

FOUR: Green wicker chairs lighten the look of an 11-foot-long harvest table, one of the many large pieces from an antiques store Tim co-owned. The painting is 1840s, an era when sportsmen commissioned artists to do portraits of trophy fish.

NEW DECORATING GLOSSARY

A - B

Adaptations: Furnishings that capture the flavor of the original but are not authentic.

Analogous colors: Any series of colors that are adjacent on the color wheel.

Antique: An object 100 or more years old.

Antiquing: A technique for applying paint, varnish, or glaze to a surface then blotting it off with a cloth to suggest age.

Armoire: A tall, freestanding wardrobe devised by the French in the 17th century; originally used to store armor.

Art Deco: A style of architecture and furnishings popular in the 1920s and 1930s; characteristics include streamlined, geometric motifs expressed in materials such as glass, plastic, and chrome.

Art Nouveau: The forerunner of Art Deco; a style of decoration between 1890 and 1910 characterized by flowing lines, sinuous curves, and stylized forms derived from nature.

Austrian shade: A shade shirred in scalloped panels; pulls up like a Roman shade.

Balance: A state of equilibrium; can be symmetrical or asymmetrical.

Balloon shade: A poufed fabric shade that forms soft, billowy folds when raised.

Banquette: A long benchlike seat, often upholstered, and generally built into a wall.

Barcelona chair: An armless leather chair with an X-shaped chrome base; designed by Ludwig Mies van der Rohe in 1929.

Bauhaus: An influential German school of art and design that operated from 1919 to 1932 and stressed functionalism; much of what we refer to as "classic contemporary" today can be traced to Bauhaus beginnings.

Bay window: A projecting roofed structure that includes windows set at an angle.

Bergère: An armchair with upholstered back, seat, and sides and an exposed wood frame.

Bow window: A curved bay window.

Breakfront: A large cabinet with a protruding center section.

C - E

Case goods or case pieces: Furniture industry terms for chests and cabinets.

Chair rail: A molding, usually of wood, running along a wall at the height of chair backs.

Chaise longue: Pronounced *shez long*; literally, a "long chair," designed for reclining.

Chinoiserie: Furnishings, fabrics, and objects inspired by Chinese design.

Chintz: Printed cotton, often glazed.

Chippendale: Name applied to Thomas Chippendale's 18th-century furniture designs, including the camelback sofa and wing chair.

Combing: A decorative paint technique for creating a striped or wavy pattern by pulling a special comb across wet paint.

Commode: French word for a low chest of drawers, often with a bowed front; in Victorian times, it referred to a nightstand that concealed a chamber pot.

Complementary colors: Colors that are opposite each other on the color wheel.

Console: A rectangular table usually set against a wall in a foyer or dining room; a bracketed shelf attached to a wall.

Cornice: Horizontal molding at the top of a wall, often used to conceal drapery fixtures.

Credenza: A sideboard or buffet.

Dado: The lower section of a wall, often paneled or decoratively treated to contrast with a wallpapered or painted top section.

Dhurrie: A traditional, colorful Indian woven carpet usually made of cotton or silk.

Documentary pattern: Copy or adaptation of a vintage wallpaper or fabric design.

Downlight: Recessed or attached to the ceiling, a spotlight that casts light downward.

Drop-leaf table: A table with hinged leaves that can be folded down.

Eclecticism: A style in which furnishings and accessories of various periods and styles are deftly and harmoniously combined.

Étagère: An open-shelved stand used for display of decorative objects.

F - J

Fauteuil: A French-style chair with open arms, upholstered back and seat, and small upholstered pads for resting the elbows.

Faux: Pronounced *foh*, French for "false"; describes something that is simulated.

Fiddleback: A chair with a center splat shaped like a fiddle.

French Provincial: A term describing countrified versions of formal French furnishings of the 17th and 18th centuries.

Futon: A Japanese-style mattress placed on the floor and used for sleeping or seating.

Gateleg table: A table with legs that swing out like gates to support raised leaves.

Gilding: A technique for applying gold to furniture and other surfaces.

Gimp: Decorative braid used to conceal tacks and nails on upholstered furniture.

Gold leaf: Wafer-thin sheets of gold used in gilding decorative objects.

Graining: A decorative paint technique to create the effect of wood graining.

Grandfather clock: A wood-encased pendulum clock that measures 6 ½ to 7 feet high;

shorter versions are called grandmother clocks.

Graphics: A broad term for reproductions of artwork such as lithographs, serigraphs, and engravings.

Halogen: A type of incandescent light that uses metal halides in compact, highly efficient bulbs, tubes, and reflectors.

Heading: The top part of a curtain or drape extending above the rod.

Highboy: A tall chest of drawers, sometimes mounted on legs.

High tech: A design style employing materials and objects from industrial settings.

Hitchcock chair: A black painted chair with a stenciled design on the backrest; named for its creator, an early American cabinetmaker.

Hutch: A two-part case piece that usually has a two-doored cabinet below and open shelves above.

Incandescent light: The kind of light that emanates from standard lightbulbs.

Indirect light: Light directed toward, then reflected from, a surface such as a wall or ceiling.

Jabot: Vertical fabric sections in swag drapery treatments.

Jardinière: An ornamental plant stand.

K-Q

Kilim: A reversible, woven rug made in Iran, Turkey, and other Middle Eastern countries.

Lacquer: A hard varnish that is applied in many layers then polished to a high sheen.

Ladder-back: A chair that has horizontal slats between its upright supports.

Marbling: A decorative paint technique used to create the look of real marble.

Modular furniture: Seating or storage units designed to fit many configurations.

Moiré: Fabric, usually silk, with a rippled, wavy pattern that gives a watered appearance.

Monochromatic scheme: A color scheme limited to one color in various tones.

Oriental rug: A handwoven or hand-knotted rug native to the Middle or Far East.

Palette: Term used by artists and decorators to describe a range of colors.

Parquet: Inlaid geometric patterns of wood; used primarily in flooring.

Patina: The natural finish on a wood surface that results from age and polishing.

Pedestal table: A table supported by one central base rather than four legs.

Pembroke table: A versatile table with hinged leaves at the sides; one of Thomas Sheraton's most famous designs.

Pickled finish: The result of rubbing white paint into previously stained and finished wood.

Picture light: A shaded metal light fixture that projects over a picture to illuminate it.

Picture rail: A molding placed high on a wall as a means for suspending artwork.

Plissé: Fabric with a puckered look.

Primary colors: Red, blue, and yellow, from which all other colors are derived.

R-S

Ragging: A textured effect produced by passing a crumpled rag over wet paint or glaze.

Refectory table: A long, narrow dining table; originally used in monasteries for community dining.

Reproduction: An exact, or nearly exact, copy of an original design.

Rococo: A highly elaborate form of decoration and architecture that dates from the early 18th century in France.

Roman shade: A flat fabric shade that folds into neat horizontal pleats when raised.

Scale: A term referring to the size of objects in relation to one another.

Secondary colors: Colors produced by mixing two primary colors, such as yellow and blue to form green.

Shaker design: Furniture made by the Shaker religious sect; noted for its functional simplicity and austere beauty.

Shoji screens: Japanese-style room partitions or screens made of translucent rice paper.

Spattering: A decorative paint effect produced by tapping or flicking a loaded paintbrush onto a plain background.

Sponging: A paint technique involving dabbing on colors with a sponge.

T-Z

Ticking: A striped cotton or linen fabric used for mattress covers, slipcovers, and curtains.

Tieback: A fastener attached to the sides of a window to hold back curtains.

Tint: The lighter values of a particular color obtained by mixing the color with white.

Tone: The darkness or lightness of a color; different colors may be of the same tone.

Trompe l'oeil: Pronounced *tromp loy*, French for "fool the eye"; a two-dimensional painting designed to look three-dimensional.

Uplight: A light fixture that directs light toward the ceiling.

Valance: A drapery treatment made of fabric or wood used as a heading.

Veneer: A thin layer of wood, usually of fine quality, that is bonded to a heavier surface of lesser quality wood. Most new furniture is made of veneer construction.

Wainscoting: Wood paneling applied to walls from baseboards to the desired height.

U.S. UNITS TO METRIC EQUIVALENTS

To Convert From	Multiply By	To Get
Inches	25.4	Millimeters (mm)
Inches	2.54	Centimeters (cm)
Feet	30.48	Centimeters (cm)
Feet	0.3048	Meters (m)

METRIC UNITS TO U.S. EQUIVALENTS

To Convert From	Multiply By	To Get
Millimeters	0.0394	Inches
Centimeters	0.3937	Inches
Centimeters	0.0328	Feet
Meters	3.2808	Feet

NEW DECORATING INDEX

DECORATING THAT DOES IT ALL

I magination, style, practicality. Yes, it's possible, thanks to the library of *Better Homes and Gardens* decorating books. Millions of readers like you depend on *Better Homes and Gardens The New Decorating Book* to transform conventional spaces into havens of personal expression. Now, five more books—subject specific and information packed—show you how to decorate with panache while sticking to a budget. Hundreds of rich photographs in each book give clues to artful arrangements, fabrics, furniture, accessories, windows, walls, floors, and more. "How to" has never been as beautiful, affordable, or doable.

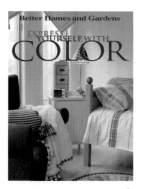

Cottage Style
Flourishes of fabric, furniture, color, and accents turn everyday space into a dreamy retreat exclusively yours.

Decorating Kids' Rooms
From nursery to teen hideout, our room schemes "grow up" with your children.

Easy Style: 300 Decorating Shortcuts
Fun strategies let you design rooms on a reasonable schedule and smart budget.

Express Yourself With Color
Do-it-yourself projects reach high aesthetic levels with the power of color: fresh schemes, popular and classic palettes, and fabulous projects.

Window Treatments
Dress your windows, casually or formally–and affordably–with the flair of leading designers.